£16.95

CH00923576

Praise for *International Brigade Against Apartheid*

'This wonderful book is a treasure trove of insights into the historic national solidarity effort that was mounted by the liberation movements of South Africa. The youth of today will appreciate the value of global solidarity in pursuing freedom struggles by reading this book.'

NALEDI PANDOR, MINISTER INTERNATIONAL RELATIONS, SOUTH AFRICA

'This inspiring, exhilarating, stirring narrative of human solidarity tells the hitherto virtually unknown story of how fiercely dedicated individuals risked everything, including sometimes their lives, to assist the ANC wage armed struggle against apartheid South Africa. This storytelling tapestry is imaginatively orchestrated by Kasrils, their brave white South African leader, woven together by the recollections and heroic deeds of these militant internationalists. Reading this book will make you believe that global solidarity can work wonders when individuals of conscience and courage act together.'

RICHARD FALK, PROFESSOR OF LAW EMERITUS, PRINCETON UNIVERSITY AND AUTHOR, FORMER UN RAPPORTEUR ON PALESTINE

'This moving, humane and heroic chronicle of solidarity in the face of brutal oppression is both an impressive commemorative project as well as an inspirational guide for the future. It records through short and moving and at times painful recollections the story of the anti-apartheid solidarity movement. Read together these accounts present a lucid and poignant articulation of what solidarity was all about and what a price it demanded from those involved in it. It is a testimony to people's courage and determination that can only rise to such high levels of humanity because they are fueled by a struggle for one of the most just causes of the 20th century.'

'Alongside the individual stories, the book offers an incisive and accessible analysis of the historical and ideological contexts in which these acts of solidarity were performed. For those of us still struggling against apartheid elsewhere, especially in Palestine, this is the inspirational guide that would help to sustain the international solidarity until freedom comes to Palestine and to every corner of the world still oppressed by colonialism and neo-capitalism.'

ILAN PAPPÉ, PROFESSOR, EXETER UNIVERSITY ENGLAND, AUTHOR, ISRAELI ADVOCATE FOR PALESTINIAN RIGHTS

'Not infrequently, I find myself reflecting on the role international solidarity played in the achievement of our hard-won freedom. Invariably, I arrive at the conclusion that it is universally invaluable, which this inspiring book grippingly illustrates. 'Progressive humanity stood as one, not just behind us as is usually said, but with us, as we fought an evil regime in a brutal, protracted struggle. It is international solidarity that gave us the requisite tools of the trade; that provided financial, technical and diplomatic backstopping; and, not least, that afforded us rear bases. From the frontline states, heroic internationalists assisted the transit of freedom fighters and weapons to the epicentre of the struggle – brave people who populate this book. 'This monumental contribution, public and secret, is brilliantly articulated in this collective effort which I strongly recommend as a must-read for humankind who need to be constantly aware of the power and morality of international solidarity in action.'

MAVUSO MSIMANG, ANC AND UMKHONTO WE SIZWE VETERAN

'This book is a timely reminder of the strength of international solidarity. It reminds us of the international volunteers who fought fascism in Spain and those who went to Nicaragua to support the Sandinista Revolution and defy the US Contra terrorists. The stories here will tell of ingenuity, commitment and courage, qualities apparent today in all those who fight for human rights and against present day apartheid. Ronnie Kasrils is one of the great figures of the age, his reputation established in the struggle in South Africa and now ensured by his trenchant analysis and powerful words on international issues, including not only developments in South Africa, but also in Palestine and the UK. This new book is essential reading.'

KEN LOACH, FILM MAKER

'Apartheid shocked the conscience of all humankind, and people from all humankind risked their lives and freedom to support the struggle to bring it down. How diverse in every way the women and men who took part. And how beautiful their stories of idealism, ingenuity and courage, related with evocative detail and unusual modesty in this wondrous and heart-warming book.'

ALBIE SACHS, RETIRED JUDGE, HUMAN RIGHTS ACTIVIST AND AUTHOR

'This is an inspirational book edited by the South African freedom fighter, Ronnie Kasrils. It's about courage and determination - the true enemies of apartheid, whose demise, writes Ronnie with the raw truth of experience, "was a turning point in history, not an end in itself. It opened the way for the next stage of struggle." This book is a rallying cry. Today, we need the likes of Ronnie Kasrils and his comrades more than ever.'

JOHN PILGER, AWARD-WINNING JOURNALIST, FILMMAKER, AND AUTHOR.

'Unlike most national liberation struggle leaders we meet or read about, Ronnie Kasrils's first noticeable distinction is his reassuring, contagious smile. Ronnie is almost unique in being a leading freedom fighter turned government minister who organically and seamlessly blends in with progressive activists, generously sharing his experience and inquiring about theirs with his sharp analytical mind, and always with his lovely smiles.

'A walking school in struggle, dignity and humility, Ronnie has taught many activists, including Palestinian human rights defenders like me, how to fervently and strategically struggle for justice and emancipation while always nourishing our humanity – never forgetting why we struggle, ultimately.

'Ronnie stands tall with leaders from the Global South who have truly practiced and deeply appreciated the crucial value of internationalism as a moral compass for any struggle against oppression. He teaches us to never forget to celebrate our successes and to smile whenever possible. Reading Ronnie's new book will prove to anyone all the above.'

OMAR BARGHOUTI, CO-FOUNDER BDS MOVEMENT FOR PALESTINIAN RIGHTS AND CO-RECIPIENT OF THE 2017 GANDHI PEACE AWARD

'Ronnie Kasrils writes that "the internationalists in this book provide a wealth of understanding about what leads a human being to sacrifice for the cause of another". Absolutely true. But perhaps the most important take-away is Kasrils's own deep understanding that internationalism means that no struggle, no cause, is really that of "another". The internationals documented in these remarkable stories carried out some of the anti-apartheid movement's most critical tasks – to mobilise world-wide opposition to apartheid. They were not supporting someone else's cause, they were part of a global movement for liberation and equality that would reach far beyond South Africa. Kasrils quotes his comrade Nelson Mandela, speaking to international ANC activists in 1993, "You are the friends from five continents who kept hope alive. You took the plight of our people, our hopes, our dreams and our struggle to your hearts, and made it your own." From Palestine to Haiti and beyond, those lessons of internationalism and solidarity continue to resonate across global movements today.'

PHYLLIS BENNIS, DIRECTOR, INSTITUTE POLICY STUDIES, WASHINGTON DC AND AUTHOR

'Supporting the struggle against apartheid was one of the formative experiences of my youth. I learned the power of international solidarity and the importance of taking sides when we see oppression and abuse of human rights. These accounts of people far braver than me create a powerful addition to the archive of that revolutionary change in South Africa. It did not come from nowhere; it involved activism on many fronts. New generations need to know that all of us have roles to play in creating a just world.'

BARONESS HELENA KENNEDY, QC INTERNATIONAL HUMAN RIGHTS LAWYER AND MEMBER OF THE HOUSE OF LORDS, UK

'Ronnie Kasrils has edited a vital archive for our collective memory about what it took to build a global anti-apartheid movement, part of the massive upsurge that went from the Durban Strikes of 1973 to the Soweto Uprising of 1976 to the Battle of Cuito Cuanavale in 1987–88, that drew in university students in the United Kingdom and trade unionists in India. To read this book is both to remember the past and to recognise what needs to be built in the present.'

VIJAY PRASHAD, DIRECTOR, TRICONTINENTAL: INSTITUTE FOR SOCIAL RESEARCH; INDIAN HISTORIAN, EDITOR, AUTHOR AND JOURNALIST

'International Brigade Against Apartheid is a collection of profoundly moving accounts and entertaining anecdotes from those many thousands of activists from other countries who participated in the South African liberation struggle. From the Basque country to Palestine, from the giants of the USSR and the USA, from tiny Lesotho to beleaguered Swaziland and Mozambique, the stories that Ronnie Kasrils has put together remind us of the debt of gratitude we owe to the "good people" of the world. One contributor, Canadian trade unionist Domenic Bellissimo, writes that "those who were in the trenches against apartheid are written out of history". This collection is one contribution to ensuring that they are re-inserted in their proper place.'

PROF JANET CHERRY, NELSON MANDELA UNIVERSITY, AUTHOR AND ACTIVIST

'A rare and gripping compilation of stories about what inspired internationalists to commit themselves to waging the secret war waged against the apartheid state. The pivotal role of foreigners in special ops, gun running, secret reconnaissance missions, dead letter boxes, disguises and cross border infiltration has never been so vividly recorded. Recognition of the selfless and often dangerous work undertaken by activists who comprised the international brigades is long overdue. Ronnie Kasrils has managed to bring together an impressive array of activists from around the world to share their accounts from those perilous times. We salute them for their invaluable contribution to our struggle for freedom.'

SHANNON EBRAHIM, GROUP FOREIGN EDITOR, INDEPENDENT MEDIA

'This is an incredible collection of narratives by internationalists who committed their lives to South Africa's freedom struggle. From working undercover in direct support of the ANC/MK's armed effort, to campaigning for sanctions and boycotts internationally, these stories form a complex and dynamic mosaic of the international solidarity movement, where each and every one played a necessary part. In today's world where capitalism appears to have won and individualism and self-interest have become the norm, they remind us of the collective power of doing things with and for others – not for personal gain or individual glory, but for a common ideal and good.'

ARIANNA LISSONI, HISTORIAN, WITS HISTORY WORKSHOP, UNIVERSITY WITWATERSRAND

'I thought I had a pretty good understanding of the global anti-apartheid movement, until I read this extraordinary collection of essays. This book blew my mind! The overthrow of apartheid was not accomplished merely by corporate divestment, economic and cultural boycotts, stay-at-homes and millions of youth toyi-toyiing in the streets. It took decades of total war – within the country and without, involving genuine internationalists who understood what was at stake. Now that the "secret" is out, the story of South Africa's liberation struggle can never be the same.'

ROBIN D. G. KELLEY, AUTHOR AFRICA SPEAKS, AMERICA ANSWERS: MODERN JAZZ IN REVOLUTIONARY TIMES; CHAIR IN U.S. HISTORY, UCLA

'This book is a fitting tribute to millions of people around the world and our comrades in the frontline states who made it possible for us to liberate our country and establish a free non-racial, non-sexist democratic state. I witnessed the important role played by our foreign comrades and committed internationalists who both in the frontline areas and in the country made a valuable contribution at personal risk and sacrifice.'

EBRAHIM EBRAHIM, STRUGGLE VETERAN, FORMER POLITICAL PRISONER, DEPUTY MINISTER FOREIGN AFFAIRS, PRESIDENTIAL ADVISER, RETIRED

'Revealing this phenomenon of comradeship that is deep rooted in the development of contemporary political consciousness, the book International Brigade Against Apartheid, offers a rare encyclopaedic insight into the personal accounts that delivered the triumphant victory of freedom and democracy to South Africa and humankind. 'What lessons for today's world are found in the history of individual struggle icons, each of their own incredible stature in this book, is a question that exposes our need to approach our past as a spherical narrative. The higher interests of humanity are never linear nor isolated and nor should our approach be to progress, for it is only together that we may achieve any ideals of collective cooperation and it is only in unity that we may watch over the global neighbourhood with equitable, inclusive and liberating eyes.'

KGALEMA MOTLANTHE, FORMER SOUTH AFRICAN PRESIDENT

'This fine collection is of great value to historians, especially those working in the fields of Global and African History, but also scholars and students working on resistance movements, transnational networks and solidarity practices. Anyone with an interest in auto/biographies will greatly enjoy reading these personal accounts which complement scholarly work on South African liberation in important ways.

'The moving accounts give much inspiration to young people to get involved in solidarity work which in many contexts is as much needed today as it was then.'
BIRGIT ENGLERT, ASSOCIATE PROFESSOR, DEPARTMENT OF AFRICAN STUDIES, UNIVERSITY OF VIENNA, AUSTRIA

'As early as 1940, the African peoples were requisitioned, with their wealth, to contribute to the defeat of Nazism and the dictatorships that polluted Europe until 1975, the year Franco died.
'As soon as World War II ended, these peoples demanded emancipation from colonialism and apartheid and were forced, in the face of brutal repression by the white colonial powers, to resort to armed struggle and mass mobilisation.
'This book by my friend Ronnie Kasrils provides an exemplary account of part of the history of these struggles and how they led, in Africa, Europe and around the world, to the mobilisation of anti-colonial and anti-apartheid solidarity movements which emerged from anti-fascist and anti-imperialist resistance.
'Still today, the heirs of the great causes such as the wars in Vietnam, Algeria, the Portuguese colonies and the struggle against apartheid in South Africa and Namibia, these heirs, bearers of the ideals of their elders, are resolutely on the side of the legitimate demands of the peoples of Palestine and Western Sahara.
'Today too, animated by the same ideals, they are fighting racism and xenophobia which pollute and weaken our democracies. They denounce the capitalist system of concentrating wealth for the benefit of a minority. They campaign for a fair distribution of humanity's common goods and the protection of all living beings.
'The struggle against neo-colonialism and apartheid is far from over. The Russell Tribunal on Palestine, the Monsanto Tribunal, the Peoples' Tribunal on Migration are all examples of the vitality of solidarity movements alongside grassroots movements in Africa and Europe.'
PIERRE GALAND, EX-SENATOR BELGIAN PARLIAMENT, SOCIALIST ACTIVIST, CONVENOR RUSSELL TRIBUNAL ON PALESTINE

'The struggle for freedom and self-determination by the people of South Africa continues to be an inspiration to those many millions of oppressed people who live under the yoke of imperialism and repression.

'The courage, vision and determination of countless South African activists at home and in exile made a free South Africa possible.

'So too did international solidarity. The support of peoples and governments for the Anti-Apartheid Movement, the African National Congress and the people of South Africa were decisive elements in the decades-long campaign to end apartheid and establish a democratic South Africa.

'International Brigade Against Apartheid: Secrets of the People's War that Liberated South Africa tells this significant part of the struggle.

'Ronnie Kasrils has produced a wonderful book. An insightful, thoughtful, perceptive account of the role of international solidarity in supporting the struggle for democratic change in South Africa.

'It is also a deeply moving account of the challenges and hardships faced by some of the many individuals and groups, from all corners of the world, who were part of this solidarity movement.

'Some engaged in peaceful protest as part of their active solidarity. They helped raise public awareness about the horrendous conditions that millions of South African citizens lived in. They exposed the absence of human rights and the widespread poverty and brutality of the South African white supremacist regime. This active solidarity also helped expose the exploitative role played by multi-national companies and western governments who had investments in South Africa and a vested interest in opposing change.

'And then, when peaceful means of effecting democratic change were blocked, uMkhonto we Sizwe (Spear of the Nation – MK) was established to engage in armed struggle. International solidarity for some meant not just supporting but become part of this aspect of struggle.

'Irish republicans proudly played our part in supporting the freedom struggle in South Africa.

'In a world where slavery, exploitation, inequality, the denial of human rights and imperialism in all its cruel forms still exists this book informs and educates and provides hope for those struggling for freedom and democracy.

'In his introduction Ronnie Kasrils refers to the concept of ubuntu. It is a recognition that we are all connected together in our humanity. This is the essence of international solidarity. Where we see injustice either in our own place or in another we have a responsibility to help end it.

'International Brigade Against Apartheid is an important contribution to our understanding of the anti-apartheid struggle, the importance of international solidarity and of the role it can still play in the future.

'Well done Ronnie.'

GERRY ADAMS, IRISH REPUBLICAN POLITICIAN, FORMER PRESIDENT OF SINN FÉIN

'In this compelling and moving book Ronnie Kasrils has reanimated two networks of the brave volunteers who helped constitute the "international brigade" that fought against Apartheid between 1960 and 1990, a brigade that attracted its followers from across four continents. Both with the women and men engaged in open active solidarity and those whose contribution was clandestine and linked to the ANC's armed struggle, their experiences are essential chapters in the narrative of South Africa's liberation. Ronnie Kasrils was one of the planners engaged in coordinating these solidarity undertakings. As was the case then and now in this volume he has chosen his collaborators shrewdly and carefully. For many of the people who tell their stories in this volume so vividly were people he recruited and helped to train. Here his efforts have been richly rewarded. From this collection we learn about the beliefs, traditions and genealogies that helped to constitute this fraternal band and we gain fresh insights into a history that has remained partly hidden. The evocation in the title of an earlier assembly of anti-fascist combatants is deliberate: this was a movement formed by a particular understanding of political obligation and inspired by an optimistic faith that still manages to survive today.'

TOM LODGE

INTERNATIONAL BRIGADE AGAINST APARTHEID

EDITED *by* RONNIE KASRILS

With Muff Andersson & Oscar Marleyn

SECRETS OF THE PEOPLE'S WAR THAT LIBERATED SOUTH AFRICA

First published by Jacana Media (Pty) Ltd in 2021

10 Orange Street
Sunnyside
Auckland Park 2092
South Africa
+2711 628 3200
www.jacana.co.za

© Individual contributors, 2021

All rights reserved.

Royalties from sales of books will be donated to The Liliesleaf Trust, Rivonia, to assist in ensuring the rich history and legacy of our liberation struggle is preserved and protected (www.liliesleaf.co.za).

The financial assistance of the National Institute for the Humanities and Social Sciences (NIHSS) towards this publication is hereby acknowledged. Opinions expressed and those arrived at are those of the author and are not necessarily to be attributed to the NIHSS.

ISBN 978-1-4314-3202-8
Also available as an ebook.

Cover design by publicide
Text editing by Muff Andersson and Oscar Marleyn of RawContent.org
Editing by Lara Jacob
Proofreading by Megan Mance
Indexing by Oscar Marleyn and Megan Mance
Set in PSFournier Std 10/15pt
Printed by ABC Press, Cape Town
Job no. 003856

See a complete list of Jacana titles at www.jacana.co.za

Solidarity is the tenderness we owe to others. Never to forget or overlook those who made freedom happen.

'International solidarity is not an act of charity: It is an act of unity between allies fighting on different terrains toward the same objective. The foremost of these objectives is to aid the development of humanity to the highest level possible.' – Samora Machel

'Our bedrock is unshakeable; it is international solidarity that so firmly rejects apartheid and race oppression.' – Oliver Tambo

'There exists no they and we, only us. Solidarity is and has to be indivisible.' – Olof Palme

'If any part of the human body feels pain, even a fingertip, the entire body feels the discomfort, and so with humanity. If one member, no matter how distant, is suffering, the whole human race is in torment.' – Sadi of Shiraz, 13th-century Persian poet and sage, whose words are inscribed on a wall of the UN, New York

'Those who are confronting apartheid should know they are not alone.' – Jean-Paul Sartre

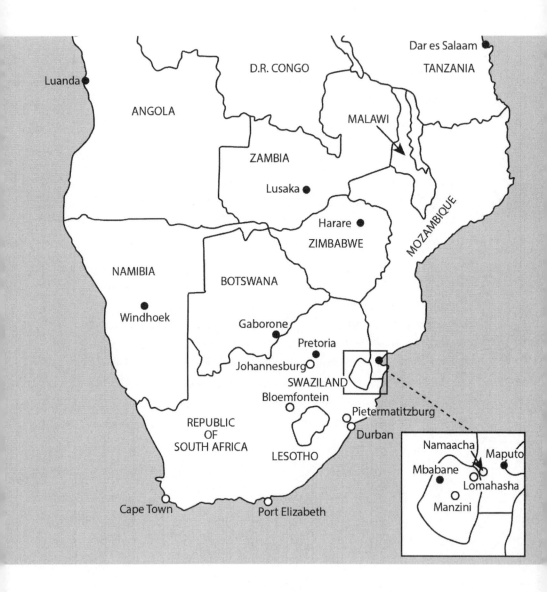

Contents

Acknowledgements

I NEED TO PAY TRIBUTE to my close assistants Muff Andersson and Oscar Marleyn: for their multiple tasks, including editing support, research and written work, preparatory indexing and general dogsbody chores. They shared with me the task of contacting and delicately hassling contributors, and above all, significantly reducing the time of handing the manuscript to the publishers (and thereby hangs a tale). This entailed loads of energy expended and juggling of time to meet my demands. It was like being back in the trenches and a reminder of solidarity in action. All tasks performed with exquisite charm and professional aplomb – as well as friendship.

Thanks to the contributors – heroes of this book – who displayed the same dedication they demonstrated during their line of duty during the struggle. In responding to a frantic request from this editor to provide their contributions well ahead of the original deadline (we will come to the tale that hangs by).

To my publishers, Jacana, for the professional work I have grown accustomed to and their willingness to respond to my request to advance the publication date by several months. My original idea was a sedate work plan. I visualised this book in June 2021, and that's when I first contacted Muff and Oscar and bounced the idea off my fellow Southpaws (lefties), Jacana's dynamic managing duo Bridget Impey and Maggie Davey. The original aim was a publication date of April 2022.

I was coming down with a serious bout of Covid-19 which gripped me for four weeks, mid-June to mid-July. Fortunately, most of the contributors-to-be had been contacted – albeit with an easy deadline of 1 October 2021. Lying semi-comatose with the dreaded virus, I was suddenly jogged into the realisation that 16 December was the sixtieth anniversary of MK. What if Jacana could advance the date of publication to coincide with that date? From 1 April 2022 to 1 December 2021. Was Covid turning me mad?

I summoned up the energy and courage to broach the idea with the publishing duo. They consulted the team of Olympians led by production leader Megan Mance, Lara Jacob and Aimèe Armstrong, and got back the next day. Yes, it was doable – if we could present them with a clean manuscript on 1 September for them to polish, design and publish. This is no mean feat in the publishing business. They agreed to pull out all the stops, understanding the reason I provided. If contributors, editorial team and publishers were up to the request, the book would be ready on the sixtieth anniversary of Umkhonto we Sizwe's formation.

Now was the time to bowl a googly at the contributors. That meant informing them that their deadline had advanced by two months. Only three protested; and then soon agreed. What dedication. Thanks again, one and all.

Last but not least, my appreciation to my wife Amina for her support and especially the way she looked after my needs during my suffering from the Covid-19 beast. Her tender, loving care and the litres of ginger tea, endless supply of Lucozade, chicken noodle broth, my favourite comfort food of mince and mush (thanks to friends too) helped me through the ordeal and the editing demands.

A luta continua! We live another day.

ANC-MK Timeline

1912	African National Congress (ANC) formed
1921	Communist Party of South Africa (CPSA) established
1942	ANC Youth League formed
1948	National Party comes to power
1950	CPSA banned
1952	ANC launches Defiance Campaign
1953	Underground SACP formed
1955	Congress of the People adopts the Freedom Charter at Kliptown
1956	Treason Trial of 156 leaders of Congress Alliance
1958	ANC calls for international boycott
1960	Sharpeville massacre; Tambo goes into exile; Anti-Apartheid Movement (AAM) mobilises to isolate SA
1961	Formation of Umkhonto we Sizwe (MK); ANC and Pan Africanist Congress (PAC) banned
1961–63	Sabotage Campaign; training of MK cadres abroad; Tanzania becomes independent
1962	Mandela slips abroad, arrested 5 August, sentenced to five years' imprisonment; Algeria becomes independent
1963	Organisation of African Unity (OAU) established; Rivonia Raid, top leadership captured
1964	Rivonia Trial; Mandela and others sentenced to life imprisonment; huge international condemnation;

	Zambia becomes independent
1965	Remaining MK and SACP leadership, including Bram Fischer, captured
1967–68	MK-ZIPRA incursions into Rhodesia
1969	July – Morogoro conference, Tanzania; July – Radio Freedom inaugural broadcast from Tanzania; establishment of Revolutionary Council (RC) to develop military and political work inside SA
1973	UN declares apartheid a Crime Against Humanity
1974	Collapse of Portuguese colonialism
1975	Angola and Mozambique become independent; SA invades Angola; repulsed by Angolan-Cuban forces
1976	Soweto uprising
1979	Delegation to Vietnam; emphasis on political work as prerequisite for armed struggle
1980	SASOL bombed by MK; increase in operations
1980	Zimbabwe becomes independent
1981	Matola massacre, Mozambique
1982	First Masseru massacre
1983	Politico-Military Council (PMC) replaces Revolutionary Council
1984	Nkomati Accord between SA and Mozambique
1984–89	Township uprisings underway; MK operations and mass struggles increase; SA rendered ungovernable; apartheid unworkable
1985	June – Gaborone massacre; Kabwe conference, Zambia; struggle intensified; December – Maseru Massacre
1986	Operation Laaitie/Hinterland begins
1987	Battle of Cuito Cuanavale in Angola
1988	SADF effectively defeated in Angola
1987–91	Operation Vula commences with aims to install senior underground leadership inside South Africa
1988–89	Harare Declaration by ANC adopts negotiation strategy; secret talks between regime and Mandela, and ANC externally; negotiated settlement achieved in Angola: Walter Sisulu and other ANC leaders released

1989	Berlin Wall demolished: symbolic of changes in socialist camp
1990	Namibian independence
1990	F.W. de Klerk announces lifting of ban on ANC, SACP, PAC; Mandela released; Groote Schuur Talks commence; ANC suspends armed struggle
1991	ANC conference, Durban, elects new National Executive Committee
1992	Soviet Union dissolved
1990 –94	Violence between ANC and forces of reaction – Buthelezi's IFP, and 'third force' – escalates; MK creates township self-defence units (SDUs)
1993	Chris Hani assassinated
1994	First democratic national election votes ANC into power; Mandela becomes president
1994	Formation of new SA National Defence Force (SANDF) composed of former SADF and MK, along with other former statutory and non-statutory forces.

Foreword – Z. Pallo Jordan

IN A LETTER ADDRESSED to the US Secretary of State in 1890, documenting the atrocities being perpetrated against the Congolese people during King Leopold's personal dominion over that African territory, George Washington Williams, the first African American member of the Ohio state legislature, employed the concept 'crime against humanity'. He used the term to convey the essentially criminal character of the regime amounting to more than a thousand atrocities and individual acts of brutality. It is estimated that some ten million Congolese were killed during the 23 years of King Leopold's possession of the Congo!

The international outcry that followed this exposé forced the Belgian government to intervene and take over governing the colony in 1908.

Since the second quarter of the 19th century, black South Africans had been keenly aware that our country was enmeshed in a developing international order in which the influence of the world community could be marshalled to attain one's objectives.

In 1835, Dr John Phillip initiated a deputation of blacks from the Eastern Cape, led by Jan Tshatshu and Andries Stoffels, to petition against colonial expansion and to reinforce the struggle for political equality in Britain's Cape Colony.

Prior to the opening of the Suez Canal, because South Africa occupied a strategic geo-political position, communities from the Caribbean, West Africa, St Helena and even the Philippines had settled in Cape Town.

Durban's population too had a rich admixture of peoples from Africa's east coast and the Indian Ocean. As a result of the Ethiopian Movement among African Christians in the 1880s, there was also an African American influence on South African affairs, reinforced by the first black graduates who received their training in Britain and the USA.

When a group of intellectuals in the African diaspora convened the first Pan-African conference in 1900, its principal organiser was Sylvester Williams, a Trinidadian barrister who practised law in Cape Town and helped found the African People's Organisation (APO) in 1903, before returning to Britain.

The founding of the African National Congress (ANC) in 1912, followed by the appearance of the first black labour movement, the Industrial and Commercial Workers Union (ICU) in 1919, both broadened and deepened the level and quality of support. Thenceforth, the Pan-African freedom movement and the international labour movement became the most consistent supporters of our freedom struggle.

In 1919, at Versailles, the Pan-African movement, in cooperation with the ANC delegation, thwarted attempts to distribute Germany's African colonies, including Namibia, among the victorious Entente Powers. The mandate system was the one meagre concession the movement managed to extract from the victors at Versailles, imposing obligations of trusteeship on them that implied that these territories would temporarily be governed by a mandated power that assumed the obligation to prepare the territory for self-government.

All the colonial delegations, save one, came away from Versailles empty-handed. Barry Hertzog's Afrikaner Nationalist delegation returned to South Africa with firm promises of greater autonomy, later confirmed in the Statutes of Westminster, for South Africa's white government.

The most ambitious attempt to mobilise the international working-class movement in support of the liberation movements, South Africa included, was the League Against Imperialism led by Willi Münzenberg. Its programme of action inspired the communist-led Red International of Labour Unions (RILU), to establish the International Trade Union Committee of Negro Workers (ITUCNW), headed by an African American, James W. Ford, in 1928.[1] Its publication *The Negro Worker*, launched in

---

1   Seventeen delegates from the USA, British Guiana, Trinidad, Jamaica, several west

1931, covered the US, the Caribbean and colonial Africa. As the most industrialised part of the continent, South Africa featured regularly. Southern Africa came to occupy an important place on the Pan-African movement's agenda, with both positive and negative consequences.

By the end of the Second World War, large portions of the world community were aware of a special system of settler colonialism in South Africa. The most significant breakthrough came on the eve of India's independence in 1946.

During the course of the Second World War, banking on his status as an imperial statesman, General Smuts attempted to have Namibia formally annexed to South Africa with the support in the newly founded United Nations Organisation (UN). Dr A.B. Xuma, then president of the ANC, was able to mobilise the support of the Council on African Affairs, led by Dr W.E.B. Du Bois in the USA. Mrs Pandit, representing India, the Reverend Michael Scott and the two African states, Ethiopia and Liberia, who had been members of the League of Nations alongside South Africa, cited the racist policies of the Pretoria regime, and compelled Smuts to abandon his plans.

Before 1945, the only government that supported the liberation movement, either morally or materially, was the Union of Soviet Socialist Republics (USSR). After 1946, the issue of South Africa's racist policies regularly featured on the UN's agenda. India initiated the establishment of an increasingly powerful bloc of Asian and African states, capable of intervening in world affairs as the tide of anti-colonialism post-1945 radically altered the international environment. Though three of the victorious allies were colonial powers, within those very countries there were significant pockets of opposition to colonialism, imperialism and its corollary, racism. The coming decades would witness growing mutual support among these players and close coordination of their actions.

The solidarity movement in Europe and the US was anti-establishment and tended to attract the support of persons on the left of the political spectrum. The overwhelming majority of them were in non-governmental

African countries and South Africa were at the founding of the ITUCNW in Hamburg. Albert Nzula, the first African general-secretary of the CPSA, was in attendance as was a delegate from Kenya who signed the attendance register as Johnstone. 'Johnstone' was Jomo Kenyatta, Kenya's future president, using a pseudonym to conceal his activities from the British authorities.

bodies. With the passage of time, a few governments in which left-wing politics had a decisive sway began to support liberation movements.

Ghana's independence in 1957 created the opportunity for the Pan-African freedom movement to hold its conference on African soil for the very first time. Pursuant of the resolutions of the Manchester conference of 1945, the Accra conference was dedicated to the complete emancipation of the continent from colonial and white domination. Led by Ghana, the newly independent African states were able to join India in supporting the liberation movement on the international arena.

When the regime attempted its most aggressive act of repression, arresting and indicting 156 political activists with charges of treason in December 1956, Bishop Ambrose Reeves of Johannesburg sent an appeal to Canon John Collins of St Paul's Cathedral, London to raise funds for the defence of the Treason Trialists. As repression increased, it grew into the International Defence and Aid Fund (IDAF), assisting South African political prisoners and their families.

The Sharpeville massacre on 21 March 1960 laid bare the real character of the apartheid regime. A 'boycott apartheid goods' campaign, launched in 1959, was quickly transformed into the Anti-Apartheid Movement (AAM), the first of many such bodies that sprang up all over Europe in the decades that followed.

The AAM in Britain was led by a Labour Party MP, Barbara Castle, and attracted the support of Liberals like Jo Grimond and Jeremy Thorpe. It also drew the support of a number of religious leaders from all faith communities as well as leading trade union figures.

The challenge facing the AAM was to persuade the government of Britain, a country deeply implicated not only in the political evolution of our country but also in the economy, to change its policies towards South Africa and the region.

Solidarity extended beyond effective lobbying of government and political parties. For political impact it required motivating the average citizen to take an active interest in the politics of another country and the struggle of another people. To achieve that, the movement placed attainable goals before activists and citizens.

The primary objective of the solidarity movement was to isolate the racist regime and mobilise support for the struggle. The shape and form these assumed could evolve and develop over time.

The front ranks of the solidarity movement were the fraternal links among the liberation movements of southern Africa and other parts of the world, ranging from the governments of the frontline states to other members of the Organization of African Unity (OAU). After Tanganyika attained independence, Dar es Salaam, followed by Lusaka and later Luanda and Maputo, became operational centres for the ANC and other liberation movements. These states offered the movement land on which to build training camps, settlements, schools and other facilities, including a clinic in Lusaka.

The foot soldiers of the movement outside the African continent were non-governmental organisations, ranging from the secular to faith and multi-faith organisations. Solidarity activity invariably included lobbying but, as the movement gained momentum, came dis-investment campaigns and effective boycotts targeting corporations engaged in business in South Africa.

The strength of the international solidarity campaign was that it spoke directly to the ordinary citizen and challenged each one singly, and communities collectively, to take action. The campaigns offered the citizen numerous points of intervention. The consumer who refused to buy Outspan oranges, knowing their quality, exercised the small measure of power he/she had as a consumer. But multiplied a thousand-fold, in hundreds of markets, in scores of countries, that tiny consumer action had an impact.

The African American churches were at the forefront of the freedom struggle in the USA and that influence had radiated through the religious communities of the USA. Their collective impact extended also to the World Council of Churches where the issue of racism could no longer be ignored. During the 1970s, the World Council of Churches established its own Programme to Combat Racism. The liberation movements of southern Africa were direct beneficiaries of that programme. Moral support was later complimented with material support.

The organised pressure of such bodies began to shift and change the attitudes of political parties as growing constituencies of opponents of apartheid could affect elections. By the mid-1970s a number of governments, besides those of socialist countries, established links and offered moral and material support.

The re-emergence of a democratic non-racial trade union movement after the 1972 Durban strikes created new opportunities to directly assist the struggle. Monies raised by solidarity funds attached to a number of individual unions and union federations assisted in building effective unions. In the 1940s and early '50s, the Council on African Affairs had raised funds for poverty relief and to support the 1952 Defiance Campaign. Such direct intervention and participation once more became possible during the 1970s and '80s as the drive to freedom gathered momentum.

In 1973 the UN General Assembly declared apartheid a Crime Against Humanity, invoking the concept first employed by George Washington Williams, giving the armed struggle moral justification.

At various times between 1967 to 1976, the ANC succeeded in smuggling propaganda and war material into the country with the assistance of white supporters from Europe and the US. Many more were willing to offer their skills in communications, the media, engineering and research after 1976. From the mid-1970s the ANC benefited from an international network that included supporters from Britain, Belgium, Netherlands, France, Italy, Greece, USA and Canada offering assistance with intelligence, reconnaissance and military engineering. Dutch communications workers set up 'Omroep voor Radio Freedom' to train the ANC's broadcasters and build secret transmitters to be smuggled into South Africa.

From 1977 MK camps in Angola were sustained by muesli, canned goods and high calorie biscuits from the Netherlands.

After 1978 an Italian 'Ship of Solidarity' delivered cargoes to Luanda, Maputo and Dar es Salaam twice a year. Solomon Mahlangu Freedom College could expect both educational materials and teaching personnel from volunteers in Anglophone countries.

International solidarity assumed an important dimension of the ANC's overall strategy during the 1980s when, by its own actions, the racist regime had destroyed what credibility it still enjoyed. The veil of legitimacy the regime had was thanks to the policy options of the UK and the US, both of whom insisted on treating it as a possible agent of change.

After 1960, in the parliaments of Western Europe, the social democratic and communist parties could usually be relied upon, while the liberal parties in Sweden, Norway and Finland were equally unstinting in their support. On the other hand, while a liberal–conservative coalition government in Sweden had no difficulty giving the ANC direct material support, the German Social Democratic Party hesitated even offering moral support.

When a group of MPs in the European Parliament decided to establish an organised body, AWEPAA, to coordinate their activities in that parliament, it was clear the liberation movement had won the moral high ground. When the Botha government shot down the Commonwealth's Eminent Persons Group in 1987, its action opened the floodgates for international sanctions. All that was needed to compel the Pretoria regime to capitulate was a nudge from the banks who refused to renew credit. On 2 February 1990, when De Klerk unbanned the ANC and other prescribed organisations, the ANC had more functioning foreign missions than the Pretoria regime.

By slow and sometimes unsteady steps, the ANC had established a credible international profile and was regarded as the authentic voice of liberation by millions in South Africa.

The support the ANC had won among the peoples of the world contributed in no small measure to that outcome.

ZWELEDINGA PALLO JORDAN is a struggle veteran, author, historian and scholar, who served the ANC in senior positions and government in various ministerial portfolios.

A Concept of Internationalism:
The Ubuntu Brigade – Ronnie Kasrils

THERE IS A SAYING THAT 'solidarity is the tenderness among people.' It will be recalled that Che Guevara referred to revolution as an act of love.

South Africans have a word 'ubuntu', which encompasses that meaning. It derives from the phrase, 'umuntu ngumuntu ngabantu', which means 'a person is a person because of other people'.[2]

The aphorism represents a universal bond of communal sharing that connects all humanity in a relationship of positive solidarity.

When Swedish leader Olof Palme stated that 'There exists no *they* and *we*, only *us*. Solidarity is and has to be indivisible', he captured the essence of ubuntu.

When internationalists from many countries rallied to Republican Spain's defence in an International Brigade of volunteers to stave off General Franco's fascist coup in the 1930s, that was the spirit of ubuntu.

Whether the values of a social democrat, a communist, a revolutionary nationalist, someone of liberal persuasion, or a believer in the power of faith – serving the yearnings of humanity for a better life – solidarity is at the core. The spirit of ubuntu shines through.

The International Brigade of this book's title consisted of two independent entities: open advocacy entailing peaceful active solidarity;

---

2   Nguni proverb.

the other clandestine and linked to the armed struggle.

The Anti-Apartheid Movement in its various forms mobilised millions of people and governments globally to isolate the South African white supremacist regime. In parallel were many activists from diverse countries who directly assisted the military wing of the African National Congress (ANC) in furthering its armed struggle. Some had preferred nonviolent forms of resistance but came to accept that apartheid brutality left the ANC no alternative but to resort to armed action, following years of nonviolent struggle, with the prospect of change obstructed. What was important was the ANC's stance of seeing the enemy as a system and not a people. This meant that the organisation was primarily political in its objectives and eschewed terrorism – the indiscriminate killing of people. It occupied the moral high ground.

These two formations, independent of one another, combined as an International Brigade. They served a just cause for freedom against tyranny, and were composed of volunteers motivated by the spirit of international solidarity. Whether on street demonstrations in far-flung towns and cities across the world or in clandestine activities across South African borders, they interlinked in serving the universal cause of freedom, equality and internationalism. Samora Machel explained that international solidarity was an act of unity between allies fighting on different terrains toward the same objective.

The South African Congress of Trade Unions (SACTU)[3] had on its masthead that simple of all mottoes: an injury to one is an injury to all. 'Our bedrock is unshakeable,' stated Oliver Tambo from exile in 1971, 'it is international solidarity that so firmly rejects apartheid and race oppression.'

This quality of international solidarity for a just cause against oppression – in contrast to the reactionary pacts of oppressors and exploiters – does not simply descend from the blue. The inspirational spirit of support and cooperation across borders invariably begins with local experience.

SACTU's motto applied to solidarity with farm labourers and the persecution they were subject to under the exploitative regime in the then

---

3   A non-racial, political national South African trade union federation established in 1955, banned in 1962, linked to the broader ANC liberation movement.

Eastern Transvaal potato fields – part of today's Mpumalanga. A national boycott of potato products was launched and soon incorporated in a comprehensive list of agricultural products from wine to tobacco. From local roots this campaign was globalised.

In 1958 the ANC, with Ghana's support, called for an international boycott. At a 1959 public event in London – Britain being South Africa's chief trading partner – Julius Nyerere, later president of Tanzania, led the call on behalf of Africa. In March 1960, the Sharpeville massacre occurred and prompted international condemnation of the apartheid regime. The British Anti-Apartheid Movement (AAM) emerged. The initiative was followed by various groupings on all continents. The process was spurred on by the internationalism of African leaders alongside Nyerere, such as Nkrumah, Sekou Touré, Nasser and Kaunda, and the newly formed Organization of African Unity (OAU), along with an increasingly active United Nations (UN).

The balance of forces was swinging in favour of the demands of the newly independent African states.

The mobilisation of millions of people around the world in protest actions against apartheid South Africa occurred in that remarkable upswing of armed liberation struggles after the Second World War in Africa, Asia and Latin America, followed by former Portuguese colonies, along with white supremacist Rhodesia, occupied Namibia, Palestine and South Africa. In all of these territories, it was evident that peaceful change alone was not possible. From a world where popular protest was in the ascendancy – from the civil rights movement in the USA, the liberation of Cuba and Algeria, France's 1968 wave of protests which spread through Europe, and support for the Vietnamese people in their resistance to US imperialism – the AAM grew to become one of the most successful movements of the 20th century. This inspired many highly committed supporters to seek more direct involvement with the ANC and the other liberation movements in Africa and elsewhere.

From the early years of apartheid repression in the 1950s and 1960s, internationalists from abroad funnelled funds for the legal defence of those on trial, and smuggled literature for the underground for distribution inside the country.[4] Such activists were what the French called *porteurs de*

---

4   The London Recruits played a key role in distributing leaflets at a time when the ANC

valises – suitcase carriers. The term emanated from the use of couriers during the resistance against Nazi occupation, and assistance provided to the Algerian FLN (National Liberation Front) during its liberation war against French colonialism.

Following the 1976 Soweto student uprising, the ANC was boosted by hundreds of youngsters joining the ANC's armed wing, Umkhonto we Sizwe (MK), which led to a marked increase in its armed activities. Its clandestine structures benefited from the support of African nationals from across its borders, and foreigners from abroad.

Although these volunteers operated in isolation from one another, were never physically connected as a single body (except in small units), and could not emerge as a military formation, they indeed composed an Ubuntu Brigade.

Shortcomings in developing the armed struggle became evident in the failure to focus on political preparation. Much soul searching led to a high-level delegation to Vietnam, in 1979, to study the concept of People's War, in which the USA and its surrogate forces were defeated. They were told by General Vo Nguyen Giap, the genius of guerrilla warfare, that the ANC 'had to walk on two legs – political and armed struggle' if it were to succeed. This advice was incorporated into what the ANC came to refer to as 'the four pillars of struggle'. The primary element was the mass political struggle of the people; reinforced by armed operations; an underground network capable of facilitating all aspects of resistance; and international solidarity.

The latter pillar was regarded as hugely significant as seen in the role it played in mobilising global opposition to USA's war in Vietnam.

By the time of an ANC consultative conference in Zambia (June 1985), and the call for increased military and political work inside the country, to match the growing insurrectionary mood of the masses, there was a need for increased assistance from internationalists. One cannot exaggerate the significant contribution of this force. Invariably modest about their achievements, they kept their actions secret for decades, not caring to divulge what they had done. To this day many are reluctant to even consider publicising their activities. Others have been encouraged to

---

and SACP underground structures had been eliminated. See Ken Keable, ed. *London Recruits: The secret war against apartheid*, Merlin Press, 2012.

do so and have agreed, not out of self-promotion but because they have either come to be persuaded of the necessity to bring to public knowledge the importance of international solidarity in assisting oppressed people everywhere in the world or came to that conclusion themselves.

These volunteers asked for nothing in compensation. They did not receive salaries; and were in most cases dependent on finding jobs to make ends meet and provide the necessary cover they required, to disguise their undercover activities from inquisitive neighbours and associates or the suspicious eyes of the police.

Some were able to give a few years of their time to the movement, while others did so for a prolonged period.

Those who served the Ubuntu Brigade were convinced of its just cause. Whether as a result of family background, often through relatives who had opposed fascism and colonial repression in a previous era, or independent experiences which shaped their own lives, the spirit of the 1960s certainly played a significant role in developing their international consciousness. They were attracted to movements struggling for freedom and independence in Africa, Latin America, Asia, the Middle East and elsewhere. They saw in these movements the justice of the cause, a democratic objective, that there was no other reasonable way of securing change without recourse to armed struggle, that the policy and principles for freedom and independence were anti-racist, anti-colonialist.

Encountering ANC members in protest demonstrations, or in South Africa's neighbouring states, they found that the non-racism was visible in its membership, encompassing black, brown, mixed race and white comrades. They found they could readily support the principles of the ANC's policy even if some felt that details of the economic objectives were rather sketchy. As three of the North American contributors write on meeting their fellow Canadian unit members for the first time: 'We had an immediate bond of a shared history and references, and our shared commitment to internationalism – united in doing our utmost to support the liberation of South Africa and our MK comrades.'[5]

Training followed recruitment. This consisted of creating a legend (cover story) to screen their movements and behaviour; disguises; reconnaissance; detecting enemy surveillance, and the use of countermeasures (counter-

---

5   See Gordon, Godt & Craig's contribution in this volume.

surveillance) for protection; use of codes and passwords; running a safe house; constructing DLBs (dead letter boxes) to secretly pass information; and creating arms caches. They were instructed on how to behave if captured. In other words, the craft and skill required to outwit the enemy.

Those involved performed their duties and tasks admirably. Given the number who were involved at one time or another, only a handful was captured. The areas in which they operated were closely monitored by apartheid security and rife with their spies. It was often less risky being in South Africa than in neighbouring states, where massacres and assassinations occurred such as Matola (1981), Gaborone (1985), Maseru (1982 and 1985), and the parcel bombs or car bombs that killed and injured so many more, including local nationals.

The accounts of the internationalists in this book provide a wealth of understanding about what leads a human being to sacrifice for the cause of another. They speak from their own experience. Whatever the differences of background and circumstance, what emerges is the values and spirit of ubuntu. While there exists a world-view of crass individuality, and self-gratification, encouraging a person to be concerned only with their own happiness and achievement – claimed to be man's natural state – a different world-view exists. History has shown in so many different ways, from ancient times to the present day, that people do care for one another, and are prepared to make sacrifices for the common good. The very existence of the international solidarity of those who supported, among so many causes, the liberation of South Africa, and were prepared to risk so much, is one such illustration. As Gordon et al. point out,

> We also realised that our work with MK was very different from international solidarity work (which could be energising, dynamic, out in the open) compared to secret lives, false identities and all that goes with that. Both were needed. But moving from solidarity to MK ... brought a profound internal change and devotion to the cause and to our international and South African comrades – whom we would die for.

These moving experiences are encountered in Part One of this book.

Part Two features the accounts of those involved in the Anti-Apartheid Movement, mobilising popular support and pressure in countries around the globe. This Movement on all five continents, where governments were either supportive or opposed to the apartheid regime to varying degrees, involved institutions from the United Nations to the Organisation of African Unity, formations such as the Non-Aligned Movement and the Organisation of Latin America, Africa, and Asian Solidarity (OLAS). Included in the ranks was the International Defence and Aid Fund (IDAF), the international trade union movement, the World Council of Churches and other faith groups. Whether clandestine or public, those involved are all part of the International Ubuntu Brigade.

'You are the friends from five continents who kept hope alive,' Nelson Mandela told representatives from around the world at a conference in Tanzania in 1993. 'You took the plight of our people, our hopes, our dreams and our struggle to your hearts, and made it your own. You refused to let the world ignore the tragedy wreaked by apartheid.'[6]

The solidarity in action we speak of contributed to the downfall of the apartheid regime, and the establishment of a democratic South Africa, needing to face new challenges in today's world. That struggle, and the international support it received, was a phase in the centuries-long global struggle against slavery, racism and colonialism – an integral part of Africa's struggle for independence and economic development, and a process of liberation in every continent where humanity yearns for justice, freedom, equality and a safe, eco-friendly world. Our mother planet requires the powerful weapon of a united international solidarity if we are to succeed in making it a brighter, better, safer, healthier, equitable habitat for our children, grandchildren and all future generations – caring for one another in the spirit of ubuntu.

RONNIE KASRILS, a retired struggle veteran and former government minister, is active in international solidarity and writes books and articles. He was recently appointed Research Associate at History Workshop, School of Social Sciences, University of Witwatersrand, after dropping out of three universities including Wits Law School in 1958.

---

6   Address by Nelson Mandela to International Solidarity Conference, Tanzania, 19 February 1993. www.nelsonmandela.org. Retrieved 28 September 2021.

Declaration – Oliver Tambo's Call on MK's Tenth Anniversary, 16 December 1971

NOW LET US TALK OF FREEDOM. Everywhere in the world today, the oppressed and exploited masses of people are up in arms. They are fighting against the forces of colonialism and imperialism. They are making great sacrifices to redeem their human dignity and fundamental liberties from the shackles of bondage. They are revolting against oppression, against foreign aggression, against the usurpation of their land, against human degradation. They stand for peace and justice: they clamour for an end to imperialist wars; they yearn for the birth of a new order. And to uphold their convictions they are prepared to pay with their own lives.

These men, women and children whose lives are massacred in the struggle for liberation are in Vietnam, in Laos, in Khmer, in Thailand; they are in Palestine, in the Sinai peninsula and other Arab lands under Zionist occupation. There are fierce struggles being waged in Angola, Mozambique, Guinea-Bissau; there are battles in Zimbabwe and Namibia; in Comoro and other islands in the Indian Ocean.

Yes, there is a life and death struggle against United States imperialism and its lackeys throughout the Latin American continent. And in our fatherland – South Africa – the fascist monster of apartheid is resorting to more and more draconian tortures and murders in a vain attempt to extinguish the fires of struggle that are also aflame there.

We call upon all the oppressed and exploited black masses of the people of South Africa to unite and close against the apartheid monster.

We call upon the miners deep down in the bowels of the earth; we call upon the labourers in the Boer farms and on farm jails; we call upon the workers in the factories, in the shops, in domestic employ. We call upon the men who keep the railways going, and on those who bear heavy loads at the ports and harbours; we call upon the men who keep the towns and cities clean; we call upon teachers, nurses, doctors, sportsmen; we call upon all working people and peasants throughout the length and breadth of our country to rise and demand the freedom of the black majority.

Ten years ago on 16 December, the first salvos of our demand shook the enemy. On that day we spoke to the white oppressor in a new way. We blew up the hated symbols of oppression with our homemade bombs. In 1967 we made our voice quite clear in the battlefields of Zimbabwe. There the white oppressor learnt the lesson which we must teach him again and again – that a bullet kills a white man too. And out of the barrels of guns and homemade bombs, let us go on showing Vorster and his Gestapo that we are determined to smash apartheid, to end racism and to liberate the oppressed black people of our country. We are many and the white oppressors are few; our cause is just, and white domination is condemned everywhere. The hour to talk freedom has come. And freedom means struggle against every form of injustice, against every instrument of oppression, against low wages and high taxes, high rentals, high bus fares, high hospital fees, high school fees; it means struggle against the police, against the army, against police informers; it means getting yourself armed to resist the apartheid regime.

Resist the apartheid regime in the towns and cities; in the villages and farms; in the factories and mines; in the townships and slums; in the detention camps and jails. Resist the apartheid regime in the Urban Bantu Councils, in the 'Bantu', Indian and Coloured Advisory Boards; yes, even in the Bantustans resist the apartheid regime, for freedom is indivisible. There can be no freedom in those Bantustans unless it extends to all black people wherever they live in South Africa.

Freedom cannot be confined in Bantustans: just as Hitler could not provide freedom in the ghettos; just as United States imperialism cannot provide freedom nor peace in the hamlets of Vietnam. Refuse to be hoodwinked by empty promises. Fight for freedom, throughout our country; smash apartheid and the vile system of racist oppression of the blacks.

The African National Congress of South Africa has remained faithful to the cause of freedom. It leads the national struggle for the emancipation of all oppressed and exploited black people. It stands for a new order in South Africa where racism shall be a thing of the past and human dignity and equality shall prevail in the life of our country.

But before that new order shall be born, many lives will be lost. We are ready to meet the challenge. The ANC and its military wing Umkhonto we Sizwe and all revolutionary opponents of the political system represent the unbreakable will and determination of the African people of South Africa to spare no effort or life in order to attain our goal – the total liberation of South Africa from white racist domination and imperialist exploitation. To achieve such a noble goal; to fight for the realisation of such a lofty ideal no sacrifice could be too great.

It will not be easy to accomplish this task. Initially the white oppressor enjoys land, air and naval power. He is backed by a mighty industrial-military machine whose bedrock is international imperialism. But the same white oppressor has a very soft underbelly. He depends on cheap black labour to keep the wheels of the economy turning. Let us now mobilise our black power to liberate ourselves from alien bondage. It is our power that sustains the life in South Africa. Let us fight for freedom.

Let us arm ourselves with the willpower and fearlessness of Shaka; the endurance and vision of Moshoeshoe; the courage and resourcefulness of Sekhukhune; the tenacity and valour of Hintsa; the military initiative and guerrilla tactics of Maqoma; the farsightedness and dedication of S.P. Makgatho, Sol Plaatje, Langalibalele Dube, Pixley ka Isaka Seme, W.B. Rubusana, Meshach Pelem, Alfred Mangena, Paramount Chief Letsie II of Lesotho and all founding fathers of the African National Congress. Let the dream of Moshoeshoe who cherished a great alliance of African people to resist their separate conquest come true in our lifetime. Let us fight for freedom. The white enemy in South Africa can and must be defeated.

Our bedrock is the support of our own black masses; it is the support of all national liberation movements in Africa, Asia, Latin America; it is the support of democratic forces in Europe, Scandinavia, North America; it is the stirring conscience of humanity that is at last echoing from worldwide religious organisations; it is the consistent anti-imperialist support that the entire socialist camp renders to our liberation struggle.

Our bedrock is unshakeable; it is international solidarity that so firmly rejects apartheid and race oppression. Today, 16 December 1971, we celebrate the tenth anniversary of the formation of Umkhonto we Sizwe. This is not a day of festivity. It is a solemn day of rededication to the struggle to liberate our fatherland – South Africa.

This is the day when we pause and re-examine ourselves and our organisation. Are we living up to what is expected of members of a revolutionary and fighting organisation? Is the OATH we took of any meaning and substance to those who swore to fight until freedom is won? We must unite and follow in the footsteps of our martyrs – in the footsteps of the men who fell in the frontline in South Africa and Zimbabwe and in other countries – men such as Molefe, Mini, Khayinga, Mkaba, Bongco, Solwandle, Saloojee, Imam Haroun, Paul Petersen, Patrick Molaoa, and yesterday, Ahmed Timol. What hope do their children have? What hope do all oppressed black children have? Let us think of all the patriots languishing in Vorster's dungeons – Mandela, Mbeki, Motsoaledi, Bram Fischer, Ahmed Kathrada, Goldberg. Others like Mrs Florence Matomela, Alpheus Madiba and Caleb Mayekiso were killed in prison. And many more have been killed and continue to die in jail. They go unheralded but confident that we will avenge their death.

Let us rededicate ourselves to the struggle to liberate South Africa and smash the apartheid monster. Let our courage and inspiration spring from those fallen heroes who have already set us a good example on the battlefield.

Eternal glory to the martyrs of freedom!
To battle, Comrades, to battle!

Mayibuye! Mayibuye! Afrika!!
Tokoloho ka nako ya rona!!
Freedom Now!!

16 December 1971

Nelson Mandela – MK and People of the World 1991

University of Venda, Thohoyandou, 9 August 1991 [Extract]

I WANT TO USE THIS OCCASION to salute and address – special words of thanks to all those friends and allies, from every part of the world who assisted us in building, training and maintaining our people's army. We must mention in the first instance, the countries of Africa, through the OAU Liberation Committee and Fund, who have been a source of moral and material support to all the liberation wars waged in southern Africa. In this regard special mention must be made of the Democratic Republic of Algeria, which trained many of our earliest fighters and combatants and has over the years provided very generously towards the liberation army.

We recall with especial warmth the sterling contribution made by the frontline states, chief among them Angola and Tanzania, who have housed the combatants of Umkhonto we Sizwe (MK) within their borders and been compelled to fend off numerous acts of aggression as a result.

Amongst African countries we must count also Uganda, Ethiopia, Somalia and Egypt, all of whom at one time or another made their own unique contribution to the growth and the development of our people's army.

The socialist countries made and continue to make an outstanding contribution to the training and upgrading of our army. It is no secret that without this assistance we, and all the liberation movements of our region received from this quarter, colonialism and apartheid would still be dominant. We single out for special mention in this regard the USSR, Cuba, the GDR and the People's Republic of China. There are few struggles in the world that have attracted as wide ranging and ecumenical support as ours. Despite the attitude adopted by the majority of governments in the west, large numbers of people in Europe and North America, disgusted by the policies of their own governments, found ways and means to lend practical assistance to the liberation movement in this respect as well. The committed anti-apartheid fighters from countries such as Britain, the Netherlands, France, Greece, Canada, the USA, Belgium, Germany, Sweden, etc., acting in the best traditions of democratic internationalism, who have risked life and limb to contribute directly to our struggle are too numerous to mention. There will come a time, and it is not too distant, when we will be in a position to give these extremely courageous comrades in arms the recognition that is due to them. The spirit of selfless assistance to the cause of human liberation, which moved many others to lend their full support to the national liberation struggle in our country, also animates the average MK combatant. MK cadres were to be found in the trenches, together with their comrades from other movements in the region. At the height of South African aggression against Angola, numerous of our comrades laid down their lives in defence of Angolan independence. MK combatants were among those who helped defeat Portuguese colonialism in Mozambique. MK comrades fought alongside the patriots of Zimbabwe who brought down the illegal regime of Ian Smith. These are the traditions we cherish and shall uphold for all South African democrats to emulate.

PART ONE

Clandestine Solidarity inside the Belly of the Beast

1

Fish Keitseng – The Underground Route

FISH KEITSENG WAS THE first born of six in a peasant family living in Kanye, southern Bechuanaland (Botswana). He left his home at 23 to work in the South African mines.

Lacking formal education, he taught himself to read and write by reading newspapers. He was recruited into the African Mineworkers Union by the then Transvaal African National Congress and South African Communist party leader J.B. Marks, who was a leader in the Defiance Campaign. In 1948 Keitseng joined the ANC. In 1949 he shifted his residence to Newclare[7] where he worked in a factory and became a leader in the local ANC structures. Keitseng became volunteer-in-chief during the 1952 Defiance Campaign. That year, he was arrested and charged for high treason along with Chief Albert Luthuli, Nelson Mandela, Walter Sisulu and other activists in the infamous Treason Trial.

In 1956 Keitseng was jailed for one year, following an incident of popular retaliation against police who were arresting pass offenders. Keitseng took the lead in a crowd of angry onlookers, and ordered the police to release their victims, to which they complied. Uprisings continued

---

7   An area of Johannesburg close to Coronationville.

in Newclare for two days. The violence only ebbed after Keitseng turned himself over to the police at the request of his lawyer Nelson Mandela.

Following this incident, he earned the nickname 'the Robin Hood of Newclare'. While in jail for the Newclare riots, and on Treason Trial charges, Keitseng lost an appeal to the Supreme Court in mid-1957. Keitseng was brought daily from his cell to attend the Treason Trial. He was released in 1958 although the Treason Trial continued until 1961. Following the trial he was deported to Bechuanaland in 1959 before the Sharpeville massacre.

Keitseng, along with Joe Modise, MK commander, was instrumental in establishing underground routes across South Africa's borders into Botswana and further north into independent Africa for ANC members going for training, and then returning home, from 1960. He arranged transport at the border crossings: safe houses for those in secret transit; transport for the arduous drives north to Zambia and Tanzania and at times rented aircraft for urgent flights – all under the noses of racist agents intent to kill.

Former presidents Nelson Mandela and Thabo Mbeki stayed with Keitseng in Lobatse in 1962. Fish Keitseng safely secured Mandela's return journey from Tanzania to Kanye in July 1962. By the morning of 24 July 1962 Mandela had safely reached Lilliesleaf, two weeks before his subsequent arrest (5 August 1962) outside Durban.

Fish Keitseng, along with 39 comrades including Thabo Mbeki, were detained in Southern Rhodesia, now Zimbabwe, in October 1962 in a massive joint operation by the apartheid regime and the Rhodesians. However, Keitseng and others managed to escape. The freedom fighters had been put on a Rhodesian Railways train bound from Plumtree to the waiting apartheid regime authorities in Mahikeng via the Bechuanaland Protectorate. Fortunately Fish was able to smuggle information of their intended fate to the late Motsamai Mpho and Klaas Motshidisi in Palapye, who organised protests to prevent the train from proceeding with its detainees.[8]

In Botswana, Keitseng founded the Bechuanaland Trade Union Congress (BTUC).

---

8   Motsamai Keyecwe Mpho (1921–2012) and Kebotse Klaas Motshidisi (1932–2015) were two of the four founding members of the Bechuanaland People's Party in 1960 of which Keitseng was an early executive member. It is the forerunner of the Botswana People's Party.

The BTUC was the forerunner of the current Botswana Federation of Trade Unions (BFTU). He was active in the organisation of farm workers in the Lobatse region.

In 1963, Keitseng represented BTUC at an international conference in Moscow, where he met Kenneth Koma.[9] Keitseng was an executive member of the Bechuanaland People's Party (BPP) and later Bechuanaland Independence Party (BIP), after the BPP split in 1962.

Keitseng was also one of the early leaders of the Botswana National Front (BNF), which was launched in 1965. With his experience of working in the ANC, Keitseng defended the BNF from infiltration by agents of the South African Bureau of State Security (BOSS) in the 1970s.

He passed away on 28 March 2005 in Gaborone. Fish Keitseng's residence in Botswana is a national monument.

Like his comrade-in-arms, Michael Dingake, Fish Keitseng's internationalism enabled him to be equally at home in the South African and Botswana struggles. He considered the territorial division between Botswana and South Africa as a creation of colonialism; and could naturally cross those borders in the physical as well as the mental sense, as his life demonstrated.

NTWAESELE THATAYAONE 'FISH' Keitseng (1919–2005), a Motswana political activist and trade unionist, invested years in South Africa's liberation struggle. He was also a prominent leader of the opposition inside Botswana.

REFERENCES

Edited and expanded with permission from an article in SA History Online. https://www.sahistory.org.za/people/ntwaesele-fish-keitseng. Retrieved 9 August 2021.

MA

---

9   Gaobamong Kenneth Shololo Koma (1924–2007) founded the Botswana National Front party in 1965.

2
Michael Dingake – A True Internationalist

DINGAKE, BORN IN BOTSWANA, saw himself first and foremost as an African duty-bound to fight for the liberation of Africa. That he was a Botswana national did not prevent him from engaging in the struggle to liberate South Africa. He was born in 1928 in the village of Bobonong, Bechuanaland where he attended primary school, before higher education in South Africa.

He joined the ANC in 1952 and was active in many capacities.[10]

In 1960, he was recruited into the SACP during the state of emergency and in 1961 joined MK. After Wilton Mkwayi's arrest in 1964 he assumed all responsibility for MK operations, including the infiltration of trained MK cadres.

In 1963 he narrowly avoided being arrested by the Security Police when he went to a hideout to warn Mac Maharaj to escape because people they knew were being arrested. He disguised himself as a municipal policeman. Just as he got to the entrance of the house, the security guard who was at the gate saw him and signalled that he should go back, as the police were

---

10 Parts of this article have been edited with permission from an article in SA History Online. https://www.sahistory.org.za/people/michael-kitso-dingake. Retrieved 7 August 2021.

inside. The guard whispered that the police had arrested Maharaj. In this way Dingake was able to escape.

After Maharaj was arrested Dingake had to leave the country. In a letter to the editor of this book, 16 August 2021, he takes up his story:

1. The episode of my close shave with possible arrest was to alert Mac Maharaj of the vulnerability of his hideout. I had read in the *Sunday Times* of Piet Byleveld's detention and suspected he might have cracked. Piet and I were the only comrades who knew Mac's hideout.

2. I was sent on a secret mission to the ANC's Dar-es-Salaam offices after the Rivonia arrests, which development had disrupted the communication link with the ANC London office; the disruption had in particular affected our financial resources.

3. Returning to Johannesburg beginning of October 1964, I found that the rest of the National Secretariat, except comrade Josiah Jele, had been rounded up.

4. I had a secret contact arrangement with Bram Fischer (who had gone underground shortly) and comrade Albertina Sisulu, who I had entrusted some of the underground business with.

5. Back in Lusaka, after reporting the dire situation, I was instructed to open a new front in Botswana. The infiltration routes from Zambia into Botswana and South Africa were my major assignment. Needless to say, apartheid sleuths and their political agents watched me from all angles; nonetheless I was determined to give all of them a run for their money. I hardly suspected that the weak link in my new post would emerge on the Zambian side! Shockingly this was the side that caved in. Tennyson Makiwane suddenly cracked under enemy pressure. Through information he gave the Boers I was intercepted by the BSAP in a train and sent to South Africa after a month detention in Khami Prison, Bulawayo. While in prison I was to learn that the smuggled letter to Makiwane was received and dismissed with unconcern by this man who had lured me into the trap. Later we learnt he was among the eight expelled from the ANC. He surfaced in Matanzima's Transkei and was eliminated, apparently by those who had had a bellyful of his nonsense.

6. In Pretoria where I was eventually transferred, I was subjected to a cocktail of torture methods. For over 60 hours I was stood with my back against the wall, fired with interrogative questions to disclose comrades

and agenda of the ANC inside and outside the country; without sleep, without food, with many taunts and petty abuse of spitting in my face and jeered at and told to bid farewell to my 'white' girlfriends, I was pummelled without stop.

From sheer exhaustion and mental disorientation I made some innocuous statement ... This didn't satisfy the brutes, who resorted to dangling irresistible rewards before my tortured eyes, to turn state witness against Bram Fischer. When nothing worked for them, I was charged for belonging to banned organisations and statutory sabotage. Piet Byleveld and Bartholomew Hlapane, both members of the central committee of the SACP, gave evidence for the state. Fifteen years was the verdict and Robben Island Prison the destination.

7. Subsequent to the joint ZIPRA and Umkhonto Wankie assault, Colonel Swanepoel, of the Compol Building torture squad, sent for me for further interrogation. Comrade Phokanoka, one of those arrested in the Wankie operation and another comrade who had allegedly worked under me in Botswana had ostensibly revealed more of my activities outside the country to the Swanepoel squad. It was 1967 with one year chipped off from my 15-year sentence. When I refused to confirm allegations against me from the duo, I was handcuffed and hung in a cell obviously designed for the purpose. It was the ultimate of physical pains.

8. I was sent back to Robben Island Prison to complete my sentence. During my incarceration, my wife was never allowed to visit me. It was alleged she was continuing where I left off. In the long 15 years, I had only three visits from my mother-in-law, sister-in-law and Mac's wife, Tim! No visit from my wife.

9. 1981 arrived. South African authorities had lied that I wasn't Motswana but a South African citizen, to nullify the allegation of illegal arrest. Had my wife not made representation through a Member of Parliament, I'd have been released to my in-laws in Soweto. My release document, which I still have, shows my initial release document pointed to 898 Diepkloof Soweto but later the address was crossed and substituted by Gaborone Botswana.

10. On the morning of 5 May 1981 I was picked up by two Special Branch officers from Leeuwkop Prison, Johannesburg to escort me to Tlokweng border, Gaborone.

11. Shortly after my release I applied for a passport to enable me to report to Lusaka on the battles we fought, lost and won on the Robben Island battlefield and the morale that continued to suffuse and bubble along the prison corridors. Moreover I had Walter Sisulu's manuscript, *In our Lifetime* to deliver to O.R. for future publication, Mac Maharaj had smuggled out Nelson Mandela's manuscript safely and here I was carrying Walter's. The liberation movement was winning in spite of appearances.

12. Not very long after my taste of 'freedom' I accepted instruction to serve in the RPMC (Regional Political/Military Command) with comrades Wally Serote, Barry Gilder and Lambert Lehlohonolo aka Comrade A. Chris Hani was an ex-officio member. The body among other duties serviced and coordinated cadres in passage and was responsible for ordnance in transit, besides counterintelligence work. I served in the RPMC until the CODESA era.

I wish to add that though born in Bechuanaland Protectorate, outside the so-called Union of South Africa, personally I never pictured myself as an outsider.

Having schooled, lived and worked in South Africa, I became part of the liberation struggle like all those born and bred in South Africa. My impetuous plunge into the fray during the Defiance Campaign marked me as a national reacting to wrong national policies. Moreover when one views the fact that the South African Native National Congress (SANNC) later the ANC, was originally composed of people of the so-called High Commission territories, present-day Botswana, Lesotho and Eswatini were full members of the ANC, so nationals of these territories were virtually one with their South African counterparts! The motion that the SANNC be formed in Bloemfontein on 8 January 1912 was seconded by one of the Bechuanaland chiefs, Chief Mokgalagadi and the House of Chiefs which was one of the components of the ANC, first president was Chief Letsie, of Basutoland!

When I was awarded the Grand Companion of O.R. Tambo, Comrade Msimang, who was one of the members of the awards committee, told me that there was debate in the committee whether Michael Kitso Dingake did not deserve two awards – one that recognised him as a foreigner and another that recognised him as South African! It was tricky! My involvement in the struggle of course expanded my fellowship with humans everywhere. What with slogan of 'workers of the world, unite, you have nothing to lose but your chains' perpetually ringing in my ears.

Some Batswana still don't appreciate why I got involved in the South African liberation struggle to an extent of being imprisoned on Robben Island. Yet there are many more who appreciate my involvement, because we are essentially one people with close relatives across the border.

My father traces our clan's origins in Phalaborwa, on the border of the North West Province and Mozambique. Fish Keitseng, Theo Mmusi, Motsamai Mpho and Jonas Matlou were in the Treason Trial of 1956 although born in Botswana. Many more Batswana were members of the ANC while they lived and worked in South Africa. During the armed struggle, Batswana in numbers participated in the freedom struggle. The chief of the Bakgatla tribe (in Botswana) is also chief of the Bakgatla tribe in South Africa! Territorial borders are artificial. However once one gets the hang of human rights, one becomes a Thomas Paine who was a citizen of England, France and the United States of America, bound by the cord of humanity and human rights.

MICHAEL DINGAKE helped to found the Botswana Congress Party (BCP) and became its president from that year until 2001. He retired from politics in 2004. In April 2007, the South African government conferred Dingake with the Grand Companion of the Order of the Companions of O.R. Tambo in Gold in recognition of his services to South Africa.

SA History Online lists the following achievements for Dingake: He obtained his BA (Political Science and Economics), B.Admin (Public Administration and Local Government Accounting) and B.Com (Business Economics and Accounting) while serving his jail term on Robben Island.

FURTHER READING

Padraig O'Malley, Michael Dingake, 16 April 2003. Available at www. nelsonmandela.org.

Michael Dingake, *My Fight Against Apartheid*, Kliptown Books, 2016

RK and MA

3
Fidelis Hove – Zimbabweans as Comrades-in-Arms

FROM PRE-COLONIAL TIMES, Zimbabwe and South Africa have had unbreakable cultural, political and economic ties. For example:

- Today, of Zimbabwe's 16 official languages, nine of them are also included in South Africa's 11 official languages.
- Before Jan van Riebeeck's 1652 arrival on the Cape shores and before Cecil John Rhodes expanded the British empire across southern Africa, the Bantu-speaking people of modern-day Zimbabwe and South Africa lived and traded with each other, unfettered by boundaries.
- Temporary labour migration to South Africa from then Rhodesia was a prominent feature of both societies, facilitating the enmeshment of political and cultural norms and ideas.
- Africa's oldest liberation movement, the ANC, helped birth the Southern Rhodesia African National Congress (SRANC) circa 1957.

Many of Zimbabwe's leading nationalists, including Robert Mugabe (ZANU), Joseph Msika (ZAPU), Joshua Nkomo (ZAPU) and Herbert Chitepo (ZANU), attained their tertiary education in South Africa. While there, they formed long-lasting relationships with ANC leaders such as O.R. Tambo, Albert Luthuli and Nelson Mandela.

From 1947, Nelson Mandela, J.B. Marks and Robert Resha were among some of the outstanding speakers who captured the imagination of young activists through their fiery speeches delivered at Sunday rallies at Freedom Square in Newclare Western Native Township.[11] There, urban South African youth like Joe Modise and Andrew Mlangeni interacted with contemporaries from the then Rhodesia[12] (e.g., Thomas Nkobi) and Botswana (e.g., Michael Dingake and Fish Keitseng).

What's less known is the role that the ANC, and Joe Modise in particular, played in the formation of African liberation armies, including the formation of the Zimbabwe People's Liberation Army (ZIPRA). Joe Modise nurtured relationships with senior Zimbabwean and Batswana nationalists as far back as 1961–62. Literally, thousands of MK cadres left South Africa through the 'pipeline' and infrastructure that Joe Modise set up, working with the likes of Fish Keitseng and ZAPU's Dumiso Dabengwa (Rhodesia). Joe Modise personally arranged for and oversaw Mandela's transportation into exile in 1962 and later on that of Raymond Mhlaba, Joe Gqabi, Thabo Mbeki and Chris Hani.

In 2018 I teamed up with former South African diplomat and MK guerrilla fighter Nat Serache to interview prominent ZIPRA commanders in Zimbabwe. The project allowed us to record remarkable insights on the solidarity between MK and ZIPRA. Guerrilla fighters (retired or otherwise) are fiercely secretive, and our mission wouldn't have been possible if it weren't for the close relationship between the Dabengwa and Modise families. Dumiso Dabengwa personally arranged for all interviews and ensured we had access to the material we needed.

According to the late Zimbabwean liberation icon Dumiso Dabengwa, he first met Joe Modise while playing a pivotal role in receiving recruits from South Africa, housing them in Bulawayo and seeing them off further north. As Dr Dabengwa explained, in 1963, he and other ZAPU comrades sought out Modise's assistance as they began the process of establishing ZAPU's military wing.[13] They witnessed Modise's knowledge

---

11 Joe Modise, 'A 70th birthday tribute to Nelson Mandela by Joe Modise, the Army Commander of Umkhonto we Sizwe', *Dawn*, Vol.1, No.1, 1988.

12 Interview with Michael Dingake, conducted by Nat Serache, 2018

13 Interview with Dumiso Dabengwa, conducted by Nat Serache and Fidelis Hove, 2018.

and experience as a founding member of MK High Command[14] and his involvement in establishing MK regional commands across South Africa and leading the 1961–63 Sabotage Campaign.

Joe Modise and other senior ZAPU and ANC leaders further cemented their personal relationships when the ANC and ZAPU set up station in Tanzania. By 1964, Tanzania hosted the ANC, People's Armed Forces for Liberation of Angola (FAPLA), Mozambique Liberation Front (FRELIMO) and the African Party for the Independence of Guinea and Cape Verde (PAIGC). While in Tanzania, Joe Modise lived and worked with Abraham Nkiwane (former ZIPRA chief of logistics who also held ANC membership).

Joe Modise was one of a few people Nkiwane credits for ZIPRA's successful acquisition of their first set of conventional weapons. Nkiwane described their collaboration in Tanzania as 'a start of a life-long friendship which grew from strength to strength through the sharing of everything from living quarters, family events to core military businesses of strategy and tactics'.[15]

In 1965, a year after Zambia became independent, the ANC and other liberation movements opened official offices in Lusaka. Zambia 'offered a practical manifestation of the Pan-Africanist cause'. According to Dumiso Dabengwa, diplomatic negotiations to create a military alliance between ZIPRA and MK began in 1966 (at various locations in Tanzania and Zambia). The ANC assigned Joe Modise, Chris Hani and Zola Zembe to undertake a feasibility investigation on the possibilities of military cooperation between ZIPRA and MK – and Dabengwa and Modise held several discussions before they made recommendations to the political leadership of the ANC and ZAPU.[16] The leaders agreed that the ZAPU-ANC alliance would aid the use of Rhodesia as a route for MK forces to enter and execute military activity in South Africa. ZAPU and ANC's cultural and political stars lined up sufficiently to make the launching of MK and ZIPRA joint missions into Rhodesia sensible, if not inevitable.

---

14   For his role as a member of the High Command and involvement in the organisation of MK activities and the execution of acts of sabotage, Joe Modise was officially named as co-conspirator during the Rivonia Trial. See, Joel Joffe and Nelson Mandela, *The State vs. Nelson Mandela: The trial that changed South Africa*. Richmond, Oneworld Publications, 2009, p. 61.

15   Interview with Abraham Nkiwane, conducted by Nat Serache and Fidelis Hove, 2018.

16   Interview with Dumiso Dabengwa, conducted by Nat Serache and Fidelis Hove, 2018.

The 1966 agreement was put to the test during the Wankie (1967) and Sipolilo (1968) MK–ZIPRA joint campaigns. The leaders of the two political parties, O.R. Tambo and James Chikerema, directed the campaigns at the political level. Joe Modise (MK commander-in-chief), Akim Ndlovu (ZIPRA commander), Archie Sibeko (Zola Zembe, MK chief of operations), Dumiso Dabengwa (ZAPU chief of intelligence), Mjojo (General Tshali, MK chief of staff), Walter Mavuso (Mavuso Msimang, MK chief of communications) and Chris Hani (MK commissar) assumed responsibility at the military level – including personnel, reconnaissance, intelligence and logistics.

In the ZAPU report of the Central Committee to the Congress of 12–15 October 1984, Joshua Nkomo said: 'One of the most important experiences of the armed struggle was contained in the Wankie/Sipolilo campaigns of 1967 and 1968. Using the experiences of the 1960s, these became the first large-scale operations ever launched in Zimbabwe, which involved several men. These campaigns were planned and jointly led by ZIPRA and MK commanders. Their full history is yet to be told, like so much of our rich history of the liberation struggle. But we would like to mention two important aspects of these campaigns. In the first place, because of the scale of the fighting and the outstanding courage of our fighters, these battles had a profound effect on the people of Zimbabwe. They showed that it was possible to tackle the enemy on our own soil with modern weapons and inflict serious damage on the regime. They showed that the racists were not as invincible as they claimed. In the second place, these military campaigns provided invaluable lessons for the future conduct of the armed struggle and gave us concrete experience of battle conditions in our country.'[17]

Similarly, O.R. Tambo acknowledged the outstanding display of courage at Wankie and Sipolilo and how the enemy was rendered panic-stricken by the relentless courage of the MK–ZIPRA combined forces. As ZIPRA commander Moffat Hadebe explained to us, 'We as the Sipolilo veterans know Joe Modise as a great commander and our hero, and the only army commander who crossed into the interior and to where the soldiers were, and he was with them all the way into the interior. He treated ZIPRA

---

17   Dumiso Dabengwa, 'The impeccable ZAPU and ANC alliance in retrospect: The 1967 Wankie and 1968 Sipolilo campaigns', *The Thinker* , Vol. 80, 2019.

troops with the same care as he did his own.'[18] Essentially, MK and ZIPRA fighters fought as true brothers in arms.

Building on the epic battles fought during the Wankie and Sipolilo campaigns, MK–ZIPRA cooperation continued to the extent that by 1974, John Vorster, South Africa's prime minister, announced that South Africa would maintain a permanent security force in Rhodesia to mitigate the threat of ANC attacks being launched from Rhodesia.[19] As ZANLA and ZIPRA forces were on the verge of forcing Ian Smith to call for a negotiated settlement, in 1979 O.R. Tambo made a case to the ANC's National Executive Committee (NEC) to continue sending more MK troops to fight alongside ZIPRA forces with a view to eventually operate independently and launch attacks from the new Zimbabwe.[20] Some MK fighters embedded within ZIPRA included Kenneth Phiri, Buti Barks (aka Thomas Victor Hlabane), Madimetsa Ranoto and Raymond Zulu.[21]

When the Rhodesian government, ZAPU and ZANU eventually agreed to a ceasefire, assembly points were set up across Zimbabwe to receive and house ZANLA and ZIPRA guerrillas. Dumiso Dabengwa estimated that in February 1980, Juliet and Kilo assembly points in Matabeleland South had at least 200 MK fighters embedded within ZIPRA. After Zimbabwe attained its independence in 1980, several MK fighters who had started families in Zimbabwe stayed on – with a few remaining in the country even after 1994.

Post-1980, the bond between Zimbabwean and South African liberation movements grew. The new government in Zimbabwe made significant sacrifices to support the ANC's aims to topple the apartheid regime. According to former South African president Thabo Mbeki, on the day Zimbabwe achieved its independence in 1980, O.R. Tambo met then Prime Minister Robert Mugabe to discuss the possibility of the ANC opening an office in Harare and using Zimbabwe as a base for political and military operations in South Africa. Prime Minister Mugabe pointed out that the

---

18   Interview with Moffat Hadebe, conducted by Nat Serache and Fidelis Hove, 2018.

19   Thula Simpson, *Umkhonto we Sizwe: The ANC's Armed Struggle*, Penguin Random House South Africa, 1996, p. 190.

20   Simpson, *Umkhonto we Sizwe*, p. 249.

21   In 1978, '79 and '80, several Rhodesian intelligence reports confirm this after several ZIPRA fighters reveal that they are working with MK fighters. See Simpson, *Umkhonto we Sizwe*, pp. 190–270.

ANC should consider the fact that the new Zimbabwe administration would include many people it would inherit from the Smith regime (i.e., former Rhodesian security forces). The ANC decided to proceed and put Chris Hani in charge of the ANC's 'underground' operations in Zimbabwe, while Joe Gqabi served as the public chief representative.

The apartheid regime saw the cooperation between the ANC and the Zimbabwean government as a significant threat and they launched several covert missions to flush out ANC operatives – with the 1981 assassination of Joe Gqabi in Harare being one such operation. In the 1980s, O.R. Tambo ceaselessly called for the ANC to intensify the 'four pillars of struggle' and ANC operatives working from and through Zimbabwe were instrumental in heeding the call. Chris Hani, Joe Modise, Joe Slovo, Jackie Sedibe, Garth Strachan, Derek Hanekom and many others directed several operations and activities from Zimbabwe, efforts which undoubtedly reinforced South Africa's internal mass democratic movement's successful efforts to make South Africa ungovernable.

According to former president Mbeki, in 1990, after negotiations with the apartheid regime had started, the then secretary-general of the Commonwealth, Chief Emeka Anyaoku, requested President Mugabe to halt their programme of radical land reform despite the expiration of the Lancaster House Constitutional 10-year prohibition on the matter. The request was driven by the concern that any radical land redistribution in Zimbabwe at that time would scare white South Africa and imperil the ANC's negotiation processes. In often unheralded acts of sacrifice and solidarity, the Zimbabwean government acceded to the request despite the political and economic costs that were certain to follow. The Zimbabwean government delayed their agrarian reform programme for almost a decade even though 'the reforms had been a central objective of the political and armed struggle for the liberation of Zimbabwe'.[22]

Another instance of solidarity between former liberation parties of Zimbabwe and South Africa is the former's role in building the South African National Defence Force. 'If it wasn't for the assistance of the Zimbabwe National Army and the training former MK commanders and soldiers received in Zimbabwe between 1993–1995, the process of

---

22   https://www.sahistory.org.za/archive/south-africas-policy-towards-zimbabwe-synopsis-thabo-mbeki-22-february-2016.

integration would have been even more challenging.'[23] Such is the view of General Gilbert Ramano (Rtd), the first black chief of the army of the South African National Defence Force (SANDF). In support of General Ramano's view, Colonel Tshinga Dube (Rtd)[24] attributes the success of the collaboration between the Zimbabwean National Army and SANDF to the strong personal and professional relationships that Joe Modise (South Africa's defence minister at the time) had with Dumiso Dabengwa (then Zimbabwe's minister of home affairs), Joshua Nkomo (then vice-president of Zimbabwe) and Movan Mahachi (Zimbabwe's defence minister).

The above examples show only a few dimensions of the collaboration between Zimbabwe and South Africa's liberation movements. Akin to a relationship between siblings, it wasn't always smooth sailing. What is undeniable is that the historical, cultural and political backgrounds of freedom fighters from these liberation movements blossomed into personal friendships and comradely affection that endured decades of strife and sacrifice and ultimately aided the attainment of freedom in both Zimbabwe and South Africa.

FIDELIS HOVE was born in Zimbabwe and currently works as a senior technical advisor in a South African government department. He writes and speaks on African liberation history and has published in the *Mail & Guardian* and *The Thinker,* among others.

---

23 Interview with General Gilbert Ramano, conducted by Nat Serache and Fidelis Hove, 2018.

24 Tshinga Dube is a former ZIPRA commander and former Zimbabwean cabinet minister.

4

Jeremy Brickhill – The Secret History of Zimbabwean Support for Umkhonto we Sizwe

WHILST HISTORY DOES RECORD the close cooperation, military alliance and joint military actions of ZAPU and ANC in the 1960s and 1970s, the post-1980 support provided to Umkhonto we Sizwe (MK) and the ANC underground structures in Zimbabwe has remained secret for almost four decades.

It was only in March 2019 at the Umkhonto we Sizwe (MK) Liliesleaf Conference that the late ZPRA Commander, Dumiso Dabengwa, finally revealed for the first time some details of the hitherto secret history of support provided by former ZPRA (Zimbabwe People's Revolutionary Army) and NSO (National Security Organisation – the intelligence and security arm of ZPRA) operatives to the ANC and MK after Zimbabwe's independence in 1980.

Addressing the Conference, Dabengwa noted that following independence in April 1980 'ZANU were openly hostile towards the ANC and they were assisted in their efforts to block ANC/MK presence in Zimbabwe by former Rhodesians and the many South African agents operating in the Zimbabwean security services... During this period and whilst we of ZAPU and ZPRA were under direct threat and facing a wave of terror unleashed against us by the ZANU government, we continued to provide support and assistance to MK and to underground ANC operatives in Zimbabwe.'

Dabengwa went on to reveal details of some of these secret operations, including hiding MK fighters clandestinely in ZPRA Assembly Points, providing safe passage, weapons, intelligence information, and the continuation of longstanding joint military cooperation.

At the time of the ceasefire in Zimbabwe in late December 1979 there were a number of MK fighters already secretly integrated into ZPRA units inside the country and they joined ZPRA forces in the Assembly Points. When the apartheid regime discovered this information and disclosed it to the ZANU government the ZPRA Commander, the late Lt General Lookout Masuku, and Dumiso Dabengwa were ordered to immediately remove these MK fighters to Zambia. However, as Dabengwa revealed at Liliesleaf: 'We made a show to ZANU of removing some of them, but others were hidden and provided with assistance by ZPRA to establish themselves in our towns and villages. So the first MK presence was established secretly in Zimbabwe with support from ZPRA.' This secret operation was carried out by the ZPRA Commander of Zezani Assembly Point, Irvine Sibhona.

MK fighters who remained undetected in other Assembly Points and some MK fighters who had been captured in the Wankie and Sipolilo operations were released following amnesty and were similarly assisted by ZAPU and ZPRA and also provided with false Zimbabwean identity documents and hidden by ZAPU members.

Weapons were also secretly cached by ZPRA and NSO operatives for use by MK. Some of these weapons were later 'discovered' by the ZANU government with the direct involvement of apartheid agents and provided the basis for launching the treason trial against Dabengwa and several other senior leaders of ZAPU and ZPRA and unleashing the 'Gukurahundi' massacres. Dabengwa and his comrades were acquitted of all charges but subsequently detained. Ironically the only person convicted of caching weapons was the late Misheck Velaphi Ncube who was in charge of the operation to establish secret weapons caches for MK. He never revealed this information and instead went to prison with his secret.

I served in ZPRA as one of the four directorate heads in the National

Security Organisation (NSO), and following independence when we were given instructions to disband our units by commander Dabengwa he also gave me secret instructions which involved establishing clandestine capacity to continue support for ANC and MK. Apart from myself and Misheck Velaphi Ncube a number of other comrades were no doubt given similar instructions by Dabengwa, but I leave it to them to reveal their identities.

On this basis I was also involved in providing weapons and other assistance to MK and underground ANC operatives during this period, acting under the direct orders of Comrade Dabengwa. I established arms caches for ANC and MK comrades in Salisbury and Bulawayo and these were distributed on instructions from MK Commander Joe Modise relayed through the late Krish Ragadoo, a fellow NSO operative.

My late brother, Paul Brickhill, was also recruited by Dabengwa to carry out various intelligence and communications functions in support of the ANC and MK during this time. My wife, Joan Brickhill, was herself an ANC member based in Zimbabwe and had her own links with ANC and MK. We all operated on the 'need to know' principle and so we avoided sharing information which could endanger each other. However one secret operation we did share information on concerned the attack on the Koeberg nuclear power plant in December 1982.

Shortly after independence in Zimbabwe one of my NSO underground intelligence officers reported the presence of two young South Africans who were trying to secretly make contact with the ANC in Zimbabwe. At that time there was no reliable ANC presence available and acting on Dabengwa's instructions I made personal contact with Rodney Wilkinson and Heather Gray. Having carried out an initial assessment, which convinced me that they were genuine and having discovered that Rodney was in possession of highly secret planning documents of the Koeberg nuclear power plant I reported to comrade Dabengwa.

I was concerned that in their impatience and haste to find an ANC contact they would inadvertently reveal themselves to hostile agencies, including both Rhodesian and apartheid agents operating in Zimbabwe. I proposed that I should conduct a direct recruitment myself in order to contain this threat until we could establish safe contact with an appropriate senior ANC/MK comrade. This was authorised by Dabengwa.

We also sent a secret communication to MK requesting an urgent visit to Zimbabwe of a senior ANC/MK operative. Unfortunately it took some time before this could be arranged and in the interim Joan Brickhill and I undertook a preliminary training and orientation process with the young comrades to keep them contained and safe. My brother Paul arranged a safe house for this purpose. I eventually handed over the comrades to Mac Maharaj who proceeded with the process of MK recruitment. My wife Joan and I did, however, maintain a rear base secret communication with Rodney and Heather throughout the operation and assisted in the safe exit of the comrades at the conclusion of the successful operation.

This particular collaboration with ANC/MK was kept secret, along with our other secret support for ANC/MK, until it was finally publically revealed following Comrade Dabengwa's revelations at the Liliesleaf Conference in March 2019. However, some aspects of our role obviously did become known to the apartheid security system, leading to the assassination attempt carried out against me in October 1987 by a CCB hit squad. I was seriously injured in the resulting car bomb attack and spent several years receiving medical treatment.

We have kept these secrets for many years, having understood that the ANC needed to develop and maintain relations with ZANU and this required us to conceal the post-independence ZAPU and ZPRA role in supporting the armed struggle in South Africa. As Dabengwa told the Liliesleaf Conference: 'We understood that the ANC was trying to build bridges with ZANU and the role of ZAPU and ZPRA in supporting MK operations had to be kept secret. As a result this history has never been told, but today I would like to appeal to our comrades from the ANC and MK to acknowledge this history.' I hope that the ANC and MK comrades will now respond to this appeal by Comrade Dabengwa. This revolutionary bond between comrades-in-arms, sustained during a period of great difficulty, should be acknowledged and celebrated today as part of our common history of struggle.

JEREMY BRICKHILL lives in Zimbabwe and works as an international advisor and mediator on conflict mitigation, ceasefires and security sector transformation.

5
Ronnie Kasrils – Landing Guerrillas by Sea: The Aventura Episode

ONE OF THE MOST astonishing episodes in MK's history, utilising internationalists as a ship's crew, and as a reception party on a remote Transkei beach, where a group of 25 MK combatants would come ashore, was the 1971 *Aventura* episode.

The *Aventura* was a second-hand ship, originally bought by the United States government for use by President Franklin D. Roosevelt back in the 1930s, and later sold into private hands. We obtained it through a private deal in 1971 at a Mediterranean port and, although old, it was confirmed as seaworthy after machinery and equipment was upgraded as recommended by a Lloyds survey. A crew of Greek exiles living in Poland was recruited and the ship headed for Somalia to take on board the MK cadres.

Somalia, at the time under the leadership of President Said Barre, was a stable, left-orientated, anti-imperialist country, fully committed to assisting the ANC, and other African liberation movements struggling against colonialism. There the MK cadres were met by Oliver Tambo, Moses Mabhida and Joe Slovo, who would brief them for their mission. This attempt to infiltrate MK combatants, fully laden with weapons, resulted from the 1969 Morogoro conference decision to step up the armed struggle.

In South Africa, waiting to receive them on the Transkei beach was a reception party composed of a Greek citizen, Alex Moumbaris, a couple of Londoners, Daniel Ahearn and Bob Newlands, and a former seafarer from Liverpool, Bill McCaig. The first three had already participated in clandestine leaflet distributions in South Africa in the late 1960s. McCaig had been smuggling leaflets into South Africa from Union Castle lines on which he was a crewman, before settling in South Africa and taking a job at a Durban refinery on our instructions. Moumbaris and Ahearn had spent most of 1970 reconnoitring the South African coastline in search of the best possible landing places.

They had reported to me in London, providing countless photographs and video films of possible landing sites on the Indian Ocean coast. These had been presented to Tambo and Slovo, and the best possible landing point on a remote beach near Port St John's was selected. The four waited there in keen anticipation of receiving the MK contingent and spiriting them off in vehicles to various parts of the country where they would begin their work of establishing units among the people.

From London I handled incoming communications from Somalia and from Moumbaris to synchronise the landing. This was done very simply by telephone using coded language. Expectations of success was very high among us all.

Unfortunately, after the ship departed from Somalia it ran into engine problems off the Kenya coast and had to turn back. Suspicion fell on the crew who it was thought might have sabotaged the boat out of fear of possible consequences off the South African coast. A dedicated British comrade, Laurence Harris, who had played a key role in purchasing the ship and managing it for us, rapidly assembled a replacement crew of British seamen who travelled to Somalia. Their speedy recruitment was aided by our very good contacts with British seamen prepared to take on the challenge in the spirit of international solidarity. They were soon in Somalia, took charge of the boat and set sail. Disaster again struck, for within a day out at sea the engines again packed in, and the boat limped back to the Somalia base.

If anything, the ANC leadership were extremely quick thinking and resolute. I soon received a coded message from Slovo to ask whether I could organise foreign assistance to receive the MK comrades in batches, as a decision had been taken to fly them from Somalia via Kenya to Swaziland and Botswana. I had cabled Moumbaris that 'mother has died' which aborted the mission. When he was back in London I asked if he would be prepared to fly out to Swaziland and then Botswana and rendezvous with the MK comrades.

He had recently married a French woman, Marie-José, and asked if she could accompany him. She was a very calm, witty and brave person, who I felt would give him assistance and in fact the added cover of a couple touring the area. The leadership agreed and soon they were flying off to Swaziland.

They infiltrated several MK comrades across the Swazi border, and then met up with others in Botswana. They began dropping cadres off at the border and then meeting them on the South African side. Disaster, however, struck with their arrest, as one of the comrades they had earlier infiltrated proved to be a traitor who had gone straight to the police to report the ongoing operation. Moumbaris stood trial with the guerrilla infiltrators Justice Mpanza, Theophilus Cholo, Petrus Mthembu and Sandi Sijake. Sean Hosey, an Irishman, was the sixth accused, sentenced to five years. He was arrested near Durban in a trap attempting to pass money and documents to a man he thought was Mthembu. The South Africans were jailed for 15 years each and Moumbaris 12 years. He escaped from Pretoria prison in 1979 after serving seven years. His wife, Marie-José, was deported after a few months of her arrest owing to pressure from the French authorities.

The episode illustrates the extraordinary range of internationalist support and solidarity in action the ANC received. This included the British and Greek seamen, the Soviet training, which Alex Moumbaris also received, the reception party on the Transkei coast, and crucially the enormous assistance provided by the Somalia government of the time, headed by Said Barre.

6

Alex Moumbaris – Arrest at the Border

IT WAS ONE OF THE worst experiences of my life. My young pregnant wife and I were arrested on the South African border in 1972. We were manhandled and taken off to a nightmarish detention in Pretoria by the security police. It was the last time I saw her free for many years.

I had met Marie-José on a flight to a holiday resort in Kalogria in Greece in August 1970. We married on 3 April 1971.

She was born in Clichy la Garenne, a municipality near Paris on 5 July 1949. Her maiden name was Smoothy. Her paternal great-grandfather came from Scotland as a lad and became a jockey. He fought in the First World War. Her maternal grandfather's name was Kasal. He came from Bohemia in Czechoslovakia and was a blacksmith. Both Oliver Smoothy and Frantisek Kasal were married to French women.

I was born in Alexandria, Egypt, in 1938 of Greek parentage. My parents divorced in 1945. At the time Alexandria had a multiethnic, multilingual and multireligious population. In 1952, after King Farouk was overthrown, my family felt there was no future in Egypt anymore and dispersed to Greece, France and, in my case, Australia, with my grandmother, where I acquired Australian nationality.

When I was 23, I joined my mother in France hoping to study at university. When this fell through, I left for the UK with just £100 in my pocket. It was early 1964.

I obtained a job with the American markets section of Reuter-Comtel. Three or four years later, in 1966–67 when data processing was introduced, I was selected to become a programmer. We were promised an increase after six months. At the end of that period, I got a raise of about two shillings and sixpence. I was furious. It was a turning point for me. This was when I 'declared war' on the bourgeoisie, becoming active in trade union activities, eventually joining the Communist Party of Great Britain. It was the time of the colonel's putsch in Greece, the Vietnam War and South Africa. All this along with the distressing background of living in bed-sitters with a salary I could just subsist on.

I did not join Umkhonto we Sizwe (MK), and later the SACP, for specifically anti-racist or pro-South African reasons. Not that I was not anti-racist or that I had no interest in South Africa. Anti-imperialism englobed anti-racism and other forms of discrimination. The central object of my struggle being anti-imperialist, the theatre could have been Vietnam or Greece. I happened to be involved in South Africa, where it took an anti-racist form.

All of us foreigners involved in the South African struggle were in essence expressing international indignation against the apartheid regime, even though the approach of each one could have been different.

My first contact with the movement was David King, Young Communist League (YCL), Communist Party of Great Britain (CPGB). We met at the League for Democracy in Greece. We saw more and more of each other. At one point he said to me that he would be leaving for a couple of weeks, but that I should not worry nor make a fuss 'if something happened'. I found that strange, but suspected a mission of some sort, and did not ask any questions.

A few days later he asked me if I would be prepared to go to South Africa on a mission as a courier. I accepted. A few days later he introduced me to Ronnie Kasrils. We met at an A1 Café in Fleet Street, near where I worked, and it was raining. My mission-to-be consisted of taking two suitcases with false bottoms containing letters to be posted at the Durban Central Post Office. The next time we met was inside St Paul's Cathedral. There Ronnie gave me £500 or so, for my fare and stay in South Africa. My big problem surged when I later saw the size and weight of the suitcases. I had to leave with two empty suitcases, filled with scanty clothing, that weighed a lot. I just hoped that the Customs would not want to inspect the contents. It was scary.

A second mission in Durban followed in June 1968. I had some letters to post and a banner of about 7–8m long to unfurl. On it vertically was written 'The ANC fights' followed by the colours of the ANC flag. The rolled-up banner contained about 500 leaflets referring to the MK's Wankie campaign, where their combatants had fought the then Rhodesian colonial forces. They dispersed into the busy streets below as the banner unrolled from the top of the multi-storeyed garage next to the Indian market. The unrolling was activated by a time device based on acid that ate through wire.

David King and his then partner Deirdre Drury carried out a similar operation in Johannesburg, involving a loudspeaker broadcasting a tape-recorded message from the ANC. In August 1969 I went to Moscow and then to Baku for a three-month course.

On my return from the Soviet Union, I worked fulltime under Ronnie's command.

I received further training in driving from Stephanie Kemp, and filming from Ivan Strasburg on Hampstead Heath. I was provided with an 8mm cinecamera and a second-hand Pentax. I struggled to learn to drive and after failing several tests I lied to obtain an international driving licence from the Automobile Association.

My mission was to reconnoitre landing points for MK cadres along the East coast of South Africa, from Kosi Bay – on the border with Mozambique – to East London. I had maps drawn with secret ink on a pad, which I developed as I went along and destroyed when I had finished.

On my arrival in Durban, I bought myself a fishing rod and materials, etc., hired a Ford Escort and started my safari. I went to the nearest game reserve but could not go any further as access was difficult and restricted – because, according to a game warden, of 'terrorists'. I carried on with St Lucia, Richards Bay... All of the landing points involved staying mostly in game reserves or holiday resorts.

Beyond Durban in the south I visited Port Grosvenor, Lusikisiki, Ntafufu and Agatha Beach north of St Johns, among others. If the place was remote and deserted, I went alone, otherwise I took a 'gilly' (a black fishing assistant) with me. He did all the work, and I just held the fishing rod. I played and lived like a 'master', which, I am ashamed to say, was not all that painful. If you were white, you were almost part of the family – everybody was nice to me, except of course the Hertz manager whose car I wrecked.

Having finished, I flew back to London. I spent the next two months of 1970 preparing a report with slides and film. Ronnie found me a room with his friends, Thelma and Stephen Nel and their children, in Muswell Hill and it was there that I did all my homework. I was there 'incognito', as a Greek communist, surrounded by many South Africans opposed to the apartheid regime.

By that time, I had been meeting Ronnie quite often in Golders Green and had been a few times to his house where I met Eleanor. In her cheerful, casual manner she gave the appearance of just being Ronnie's wife and the mother of Christopher and Andrew, both of whom at the time were very young.

But it is only in 2009, after her painfully untimely death, that I found that she was a cadre in MK and the SACP, and that she had been active in clandestine operations such as logistics, communications, liaison, recruiting as well having acted as the driver for the secretary-general of the SACP, Moses Kotane in Dar es Salaam. I knew about her escape from custody, but then in South Africa you did not need much to get arrested.

We talked about Brigid, her young daughter from a previous marriage attending school in Durban and with whom she had lost touch. I proposed to contact her in Durban on my next mission. My suggestion was, of course, turned down. (Much later, in 1996, when Ronnie was a government minister, he and Eleanor befriended Marie-José and Chloé, my daughter, and organised our stay when we visited South Africa on the official invitation of the ANC.)

Just before the next mission I met Daniel Ahearn who was to participate in the landing reception team. We received special training in Baku related to seafaring and landing from a ship.

The mission took place in 1971. The object was to check some of the landing points by night with Daniel. Four possible landing points were checked, and we returned to London for further orders.

The landing at a point on the Transkei coast involved a score of MK combatants, heavily laden with arms and ammunition, that were to come in on two dinghies from a mother ship, which I later discovered was the *Aventura*.

I was to be in command of the landing and Bob Newland, a London YCL recruit, was with me on the main beach. There was an alternative beach where London YCL member Daniel Ahearn and Bill McCaig, a Liverpool seaman, were to be held in reserve. The signalling had been arranged and we also had walkie-talkies, brought in by Bob Newland.

At one point Ronnie cabled me a message 'mother has died' (mission aborted). Back in London we learnt that the *Aventura* had broken down. A while later Ronnie approached me about assisting comrades infiltrating from Swaziland and Botswana across the borders into South Africa. I later discovered this was the group that had meant to land on the coast. I was to rendezvous with them in those ostensibly independent states, under close observation by South African security, and guide them to the crossing points and then pick them up on the South African side.

When I announced to Marie-José that I would be leaving on a mission, she rebelled: 'No way, unless I come with you.' (By then she had realised, and I had admitted, that I was not working for the Greek resistance but for the South Africans.)

I informed Ronnie who was not averse to the idea but said he would take it up with higher authority. I later learnt he was referring to SACP leaders Dr Yusuf Dadoo and Joe Slovo. A few days later he informed me it was agreed, since a couple would make a good cover.

Marie-José and I decided not to tell Ronnie that she was three-months pregnant at the time. We arrived in Swaziland through Portugal and Mozambique. Marie José had been sick all the time. The groups were code named 'Anthony', 'Bertrand', 'Charlie'. We decided to transfer the first two groups simultaneously, from two different crossing points.

When the second group, Bertrand, arrived, inevitably in such a small place, the two groups recognised each other. The transfer on the Swazi side was carried out successfully, except for minor mishaps, such as wrecking the carburettor of the Mercedes on a huge piece of coal while travelling at night along the road. Problems though arose on the South African side. After having left the Bertrand group on the Swaziland border; we could not locate them at the rendezvous point, and we were stopped on the highway by the police on what was supposed to be a routine check. One of the Bertrand group gave himself up to the South African police the next day. He knew who the other five were and became a state witness in the subsequent trial.

Next, we went to Botswana. We stayed at the President Hotel in Gaborone, Botswana, and there we met the Charlie group. We drove the four to the border, dropped them off, arranging to meet them the other side.

That was when things went so dreadfully wrong. As we filled in the immigration forms at the border post, the policemen swooped.

They grabbed Marie-José by the hair and one of them put a strangle hold on me and another put handcuffs on my right arm. I yelled at them that Marie-José was pregnant. They started interrogating us separately and transferred us in separate cars to Pretoria.

I sat in the front seat between two policemen. They were driving at 80 mph. I seriously thought of grabbing the wheel and bringing the car crashing against something, but the thought of Marie-José in the second police car behind us made me abandon the idea. Marie-José was taken to the women's prison in Pretoria Central where she was interrogated by Captain Trevor Baker.

At one point, when she was being examined by a doctor, she saw him getting ready to put his weight on her belly to make her abort. She had the reflex to stop his hands. We both started a hunger strike that lasted seven to eight days.

It was evident that Marie-José was an embarrassment to them. She was French and pregnant, and whereas I could be considered an international terrorist with apparently no real national attachment, this was not the case with her. The relations between France and South Africa were very important and the political pressure that started to mount in France forced them to release her four months later.

We met on two occasions: the first one, eight days after our arrest, when I asked her to stop her hunger strike; the second just before she left. I remember the enormity of her belly and the thinness of her legs. Prison experience had taken its toll. She was courageous and irreproachable in prison.

Marie-José, on her return to France, was extremely active politically. Her youth and spontaneity were inspirational. She gave evidence at the

United Nations, along with Sean Hosey's father. Sean, of Irish descent, a British YCL member, was put on trial with me [his account follows]. Marie-José also went on a solidarity trip to Canada. During the trial she participated in the demonstrations in front of South Africa House, together with Sean's family, who were politically very staunch and whom I hold in great affection and esteem.

Marie-José pursued anti-apartheid work in France in very difficult conditions, together with members of our families, friends and comrades, to have me released.

There were six of us on trial: Theophilus Cholo, Justice Mpanza, Petrus Mtembu, Sandi Sejake, Sean Hosey and myself. I first met Sean in the van that took us to court.

I got 12 years (plus one year awaiting trial), the South African comrades got 15 years each and Sean Hosey five years (the minimum; some comrades called that a parking ticket). The reason for my slightly reduced sentence was that I was not South African and consequently not guilty of treason.

A special mention ought to be made about those in our families, particularly my mother, who supported us but suffered because of the situation we put them in. The reactions within the families were complicated: some agreed with us and helped us, others helped us even if they did not approve of what we did, some felt betrayed, some neither approved nor helped us and others made life very difficult for us on our return.

Also, I am thankful to all the South African friends and comrades who befriended my mother and son, when they visited me: Esther Barsel, Sheila Weinberg, Ilse Wilson.

I escaped from prison after seven and a half years. It takes time, months, to return to mental normality. There is also the question of earning a living and other accidents of life, not the least the impact on the children. I say this to pay homage to those who unexpectedly and even reluctantly contributed to the struggle.

I cannot pay a high enough tribute to my late comrade, companion and wife Marie José, whose courage, devotion and love accompanied me and gave me strength all these years in and out of prison and whose recent untimely death leaves me with so much emptiness.

I would also like to express my appreciation to our comrades who trained me in the Soviet Union. I cannot ignore the contribution to the struggle of countries such as Algeria, Angola, Mozambique, the DPRK, the GDR, the People's Republic of China, the Republic of Cuba and the USSR.

ALEX MOUMBARIS publishes a political journal *Les Dossiers du BIP*, translates articles from English and Greek into French and lives in Normandy, France.

This contribution is based on his article in London Recruits: *The Secret War Against Apartheid*. Edited by Ken Keable, Merlin Press, 2012.

7

Sean Hosey – When My Irish Luck Ran Out

WHAT WAS TO PROVE MY last day of freedom for nearly six years began with a short sedate train trip from South Africa's port city of Durban to Tongaat.

As the train trundled along on a minor branch line through miles and miles of Natal sugar cane fields, my mind lurched forward and backwards, about my presence on this journey. Forwards, to an anticipated rendezvous with an underground ANC member, to whom I simply had to hand much needed funds and identity documents. Backwards, to a meeting in London where I had met a South African exile who briefed me on the mission. This was not the first time I had undertaken such work.

As a young man of 22, originally from Ireland, I had been living in London for 18 months. I had a room in the house of an Irish family in the Islington area, just around the corner from Arsenal's ground at Highbury, where I used to meet the football-mad South African comrade.

My family and I had immigrated to England in 1960. I had come with a head full of catechism and an acute sense of Irish repression which, on reflection, was partly historical and partly romanticised.

My parents were staunch socialists and were active in the British Communist Party in the English Midlands. I followed in their footsteps and joined the Young Communist League (YCL) when I was 15. I also supported the Anti-Apartheid Movement (AAM). It's important to remember how strong feelings were against apartheid at that time. It was not just the political left, deeply engrossed in the anti-Vietnam War campaign, who were involved in AAM. Campaigns against South African produce and the whites-only South African sporting teams were widely supported.

Church clerics criticised apartheid from the pulpit regularly and middle-class housewives shunned South African fruit in the supermarkets. Several ministers in Labour governments over the previous ten years were prominent in the campaigns – Peter Hain, Jack Straw and Charles Clarke to name but three. Everyone had heard of Nelson Mandela.

I had made some good friends in London. One of those was Steve Marsling, a slightly cheeky chap and fellow YCL member, who asked me in strict confidence if I would be prepared to go to South Africa to disseminate anti-apartheid material for the African National Congress (ANC). It didn't take me long to agree. Of course, part of me saw the adventure of it, although by far the predominant reason was the moral one. Anything I could do to dent the apartheid regime, however small, had to be the right thing to do.

I recall a conversation I had with Steve about the dangers that faced us if we were caught. We knew that it would not be a holiday camp because our 'handler' and Arsenal fan, Ronnie Kasrils, had explained in some detail the sort of treatment we could expect.

Our training was quite surreal, taking measures to ensure we were not followed, understanding the extent of police and security networks in South Africa, planning how to act the part of carefree tourists. Our mission was to distribute leaflets by a method using non-lethal 'bucket bombs', set with timing devices, to launch the literature into the air at strategic points where black people gathered.

The explosives were little more than firework strength, enough to lift a small platform of leaflets from a bucket 30 feet or so into the ether. The ANC avoided indiscriminate anti-civilian tactics. What we took in could do no damage to people. What we wanted to do, and spectacularly succeeded in doing, was to dent the arrogance of the South African police state and encourage the oppressed Africans within the country.

If I ever had any doubts about what we were doing, that quickly disappeared when I saw the 'whites only' signs, even on park benches, all over our destination, Cape Town.

Another episode reinforced the apartheid reality check. Steve and I befriended a couple of young women and took them for dinner.

In the middle of our meal a uniformed policeman entered the restaurant. Both the girls froze. They later told us they were classified 'coloureds' (mixed race) and since that was a whites-only restaurant they could have been in serious trouble.

We had six devices to place in the city, near the railway station and taxi ranks. They were timed for 17:00 to coincide with the trains taking black workers home.

We carried the bucket contraptions in shopping bags. We set the timers, moved well away from the area and awaited developments which were pretty spectacular, as the black workers scurried to pick up the leaflets and quickly departed the scene.

Every South African newspaper had screaming headlines about the leaflet bombs. These had been synchronised for distributions in all the major cities. I well remember the satisfaction of that trip.

Just over a year later I met up with Ronnie near the Arsenal ground, and he outlined a new one-person mission which appeared simple and straightforward. On the face of it, taking some passbooks and money to a comrade not far from Durban seemed a far simpler mission than the previous trip.

All I had was a description of the man: small and stocky, wearing a hat and glasses. A successful exchange of passwords would mean I would hand over the passbooks and money to him.

As the train drew into Tongaat station I thought of the meeting ahead, expecting it to last no more than a minute, and away I would go.

Tongaat revolved around the sugar industry. Mainly an Indian town, it was near the aptly named crocodile creek. Other sorts of manhunters were waiting for me.

The walk from the train station to the place of exchange, the post office, was hot and sultry. I carefully approached the post office and there was my contact, wearing a hat and glasses. We quickly exchanged passwords and I gave him the parcel. I felt completely relaxed and started to walk away. Then came the words that would stay with me for a very long time:

'Hold it boss.' I turned around and was faced by four men displaying a considerable amount of firepower, aimed at me.

I was whipped off to police headquarters in Durban. I tried desperately to keep my wits about me and not to crumble. What followed was eight months of solitary confinement and interrogation. Ronnie had given me some indication of what to expect if I was caught. Suffice to say that all his warnings, plus some, did happen. Many other comrades have described that process and many never got to tell their tales. A peculiar element was an obsession that a couple of the senior security police had with Britain's Prime Minister Harold Wilson. They seemed to believe that I knew something of Wilson's visit to Moscow and were convinced that he was an agent of international communism. Now this was both laughable and frightening.

After my arrest and throughout my imprisonment, there was a magnificent campaign of support and calls for my release in the UK and Ireland. This was led by my parents, Kay and John, and my sister Noreen, as well as the Trade Union movement, the ANC and the AAM. My folks spoke at the United Nations and several other countries, as well as at countless meetings in Britain to rally support for South African political prisoners and the release of Nelson Mandela.

Early in my prison term I was visited by Vic Feather, head of the Trade Union Congress at the time, and Jack Jones, then general secretary of the Transport and General Union.

My family, together with a French comrade, Marie-José Moumbaris, wife of a fellow trialist with me, protested outside the South African Embassy in London. Her husband was Alex Moumbaris, of Greek background. She had been arrested with him whilst infiltrating some fellow trialists, across the borders. Pregnant at that time, and owing to French government protest, she had been released and deported.

The knowledge of this campaign and support for us was very important for our mental state and helped cope with incarceration.

Throughout that time my only objective was to get through to the next day. I was in limbo land and had no idea what they were going to do to me. At best I hoped they would just deport me. But eventually, in May 1972, I was brought out of my cell to an interview room where I met George Bizos, a well-known lawyer who had represented many comrades over the years and had been on Nelson Mandela's defence team.

He showed me a lengthy charge sheet and I realised it could be some time before I left South Africa. George was very supportive during the trial period, which lasted more than three months.

A number of interviews were held in the adjacent 'awaiting hanging' wing where at any one time there were up to a hundred condemned men awaiting execution. Hanging day was Thursday, when usually eight people were hanged at the same time. I learnt much later on that our prison doctor would occasionally administer a fatal injection on the occasion the hanging rope had not completed its task. I asked him how he squared that with his Hippocratic Oath, and I got a couple of days without food for my impertinence.

George and I had a meeting one Wednesday before a hanging day. It was practice to notify the unfortunate eight of their fate the day before with a decree from the State President, introduced with the preposterously inappropriate word 'greetings'. The practice then was for the other prisoners to start singing to help the condemned through their last day and night. I have never heard such soulful and moving singing in my life – a harmony of the hopeless in support of the lost.

I only met my fellow accused on the first day of the trial in Pretoria. They had also been through hell and the black comrades had taken more of a physical battering than I had. It felt slightly weird seeing the real Petrus Mthembu. He had been caught and tortured. With the information they had obtained, the trap was set for me.

Shortly afterwards I had a great surprise when my dad visited the prison and told me he was going to stay for the trial. At that time we did not know if it was going to last for three months. With great support from all my family, as well as financial help for my defence from International Defence and Aid, the finance to do this was found.

Early on in the trial there was a surprise celebrity attendee, the actor David Tomlinson, who was interested in jurisprudence and attended trials around the world. I was able to have a brief conversation with him.

The Terrorism Act was an effective catchall for anything that threatened apartheid supremacy. Any breach carried a mandatory minimum sentence of five years. Eventually I was found guilty and sentenced to five years in prison. This brought me into contact with a number of inspirational and supportive comrades such as Bram Fischer, Dennis Goldberg, Dave Kitson and John Matthews, all serving very long sentences or life terms. Even in prison, whites were segregated from black prisoners. History certainly vindicated them all, thanks to the mass struggle of South Africa's people, led by the ANC, and international solidarity.

SEAN HOSEY was born in 1949 in Dublin, Ireland. Married with three daughters, he was previously assistant director of housing in Sheffield, and is now retired.

This contribution is based on his article in London Recruits: *The Secret War Against Apartheid*. Edited by Ken Keable, Merlin Press, 2012.

8

Fatima do Rosário Cordeiro –
Tribute to a Gallant Mozambican

ANTÓNIO DA SILVA GOMES Cordeiro was fondly known as Toni or Papa to MK fighters.

Toni was born on 15 January 1942 in Lourenço Marques, as Maputo was formerly called. He died on 23 December 2006 of natural causes.

He lived with his beloved wife Inácia and children in a large house in Malhangalene, Maputo. We all have happy memories of those times.

Toni was slight in statute, and was known for his calm, assertive words and a frank smile. Son of a black Mozambican mother and a white Portuguese father, he had five siblings who left Mozambique, leaving Toni involved in the struggle for his country's liberation from Portuguese colonialism, and later the struggle against apartheid South Africa.

At an early age, Toni underwent military service with the Portuguese. At the beginning of FRELIMO's armed struggle, he started to support the fighters for liberation, transporting them from Cabo Delgado and other provinces in his vehicle to the capital.

Toni had a degree in accounting and worked as a bookkeeper. He had a highly developed sense of justice and believed in the liberation of people so much that – soon after Mozambique's independence when ANC guerrillas were introduced to him by a family member – he did not hesitate to show solidarity with them.

He had safe hideouts in Mozambique providing military and logistical support for MK comrades. He stored weapons and built special hidden storage spaces in their vehicles.

His farm (*machamba*) in Michafutene, 18 kilometres from the city, was remote and safe for this purpose. Toni instructed us young children never to reveal his MK connections to our friends. In Malhangalene there was a basement and a huge warehouse where the weapons were stored. The weaponry, arms and explosives were hidden in specially prepared vehicles and ferried by Toni to ANC bases in Swaziland.

Toni's sons, Celestino and Victor, helped pack the weapons during the entire period that the struggle lasted from the early ages of 12 and 15. Toni had the loyal support of our mother and all the children, including me and my sisters.

Our father was a warm, generous and hospitable human being, who, together with our mother, welcomed ANC leaders, like Joe Modise and Joe Slovo, and MK commanders like Job Tabane (Cassius Make), Siphiwe Nyanda (Gebuza), Muzi Ngwenya (Thami Zulu) and others, to family weddings and celebrations. We thought of them as our uncles.

The MK guerrillas appeared and disappeared, according to their missions.

They were our big family. They joked with us, talked, played like any free men. They were, however, discreet and always tried to remain unnoticed.

Toni watched two of his stepdaughters marry MK guerrillas: Sello Motau (MK name Paul Dikaledi) to sister Carla and Lungile Pepani (Sbali) to sister Suzanna. Despite the joy and celebration that marriage creates, Toni gave them away, knowing the risk of grief and pain, a fatal legacy of the struggle. He was well aware that his work for the ANC put his family at risk, but he was careful and responsible. He was grateful that nobody in the ANC ever betrayed him.

In 1987, the year before Albie Sachs was struck by a bomb in Maputo, our brother-in-law Sello Motau was assassinated by Boers in Swaziland, along with Job Tabane, known to us as Uncle Cassius.

Shaken by the news of his death, disoriented, suffering and in mourning, Toni saw Sello, who was like a son to him, buried in the ground he sought to free (the funeral was in Soweto). There was inconsolable grief in our family.

Toni intensified his contribution for South Africa's liberation by continuing with his mission by going on periodic trips to Swaziland to assist the MK there. Of the various memories I have, one is recalling him arriving home from Swaziland, lucky to be alive, his car riddled with bullets.

Toni's involvement lasted until 1990 when the apartheid regime finally surrendered, freeing Nelson Mandela, which led to the first democratic elections in 1994.

Our father enjoyed life and had a large circle of friends and many hobbies, among which were chess and hunting. He enjoyed his glass of beer and loved football to such an extent that, when he died, he was laid to rest in the colours of his favourite club. He was greatly loved by family and friends and is deeply missed. He was a patriot of his country and an internationalist who worked so that South Africa could be free.

FÁTIMA DO ROSÁRIO CORDEIRO, daughter of the late António Cordeiro, holds several higher degrees in law, finance and public policy, including a doctorate gained in Portugal, and works for the Mozambique Reserve Bank.

9

Siphiwe Nyanda – Mozambique Panel Beaters & a Swazi Farmer

IN DEVELOPING OUR ARMED struggle, we owed so much to the courage, skill and devotion to African freedom by nationals of the frontline states. Here are just three examples to illustrate that magnificent international commitment.

BERNARDO

In 1979 I was introduced to a Mozambican panel beater by the name of Bernardo, with whom I discussed several options for reconfiguring vehicles for the purpose of infiltrating weapons into South Africa from Swaziland. He suggested that we purchase a Ford F250 van. We bought the vehicle through a Swazi contact and transported it to Maputo for Bernardo to work on. It was a masterful design in adaptation and camouflage. The carrying capacity of the vehicle was huge – it could carry two RPGs and eight rockets, ten AK47 rifles and their magazines and ammunition as well as huge amounts of explosives in a single haul without sagging from the weight.

Four steel compartments were soldered onto the undercarriage of the vehicle from the bottom, two at the front towards the cab, behind the driver and passenger seats, and the other two at the rear a little distance from the ones on either side of the axle, for balance and symmetry. The two at the front were about a metre square each with a width of about 18cm. They had a trapdoor which opened downwards for loading and offloading. The rear compartments open from the back were about one and a half metre long and a metre wide. They were painted black to blend with the rest of the undercarriage. You had to go right underneath to notice the compartments built onto it. Even from this viewpoint you had to have a thorough knowledge of the original and tempered undercarriage to know that there had been any interference with the vehicle.

Those who drove the vehicle never encountered problems on the numerous trips into the country. They would cross legally through the borders of Swaziland and South Africa using Swazi documents prepared for us in Luanda. Later we organised our own contacts at the Home Affairs offices in Mbabane to issue genuine passports for use by our operatives, including the couple infiltrating the limpet mines that blew up the Sasol oil refinery in June 1980.

We organised another car, a Toyota panel van. The vehicle was what I called a natural. Behind the bottom back of the seats of the panel van was a deep hollow into the body of the van which ran from the driver to the passenger door. This long deep hollow originally housed the fire extinguisher, jack, wheel spanner and other accessories. All we had to do was enclose the hollow from door to door behind the seats in order to conceal anything hidden inside. Bernardo chose a hardboard of sufficient thickness which he fastened perpendicularly onto the metal body of the vehicle that screws to conceal the hollow and whatever was to be hidden inside. He riveted a number of clamps onto the board which he glued on a carpet matching the interior to hold the spanners, jacks and other accessories. The handiwork looked more professional than the original. It was so impressive it looked innocent even to those who were in the know. If Toyota had seen the design, they would have adapted it for the later models, the handy plastic toolkit to keep the screwdrivers and screws to remove the board and replace it was elegantly attached on a clamp alongside the other impressively arrayed accessories.

António da Silva Gomes Cordeiro

Before the Nkomati Accord [March 1984 between South Africa and Mozambique which saw MK cadres having to leave the latter country in return for South Africa ceasing to support RENAMO's insurgency], we accessed our weaponry from the depot which the father-in-law of Sello Motau [MK Paul Dikaledi] kept in his massive garage in Maputo. He also had a farm which Logistics used to store a large arsenal which we drew from after the Nkomati Accord. His name was António da Silva Gomes Cordeiro. He was a soft-spoken affable businessman whose daughter Carla was married to Paul.

... [António] would drive to Swaziland on agreed days and hand over the weaponry we had sent requests for.

Max Plimenteira

We obtained a Peugeot 404. The compartment in this vehicle was built by Max Plimenteira, a Mozambican based in Swaziland. It was a simple concealing device built in the boot of the car. He created an optical illusion by building a metal plate behind the original one to which the boot carpet was extended. The carpet was shortened and neatly glued onto the new plate behind which was a hollow running from left to right. This reduced the capacity of the boot, but the boot seemed normal because the original size was very large. There were several other vehicles we employed in the constant search to remain ahead of the enemy and outwit him.

Swazi farmer Paris Twala

One of the preparations we had to make before the signature of the Nkomati Accord was the creation of depot facilities in Swaziland. We preferred to create depots in the terrain. By far the biggest such depot we created was at Motjane in Swaziland south of the Oshoek border post, on a small farm of one of our contacts, Paris Twala, who we called Peasant. It was a veritable room in the ground. This was made possible because it was his private property, and he could work without the concerns and the risks we undertook while digging in open terrain. He also did not have neighbours in close proximity snooping, but he still had to be careful in case people driving walked in and discovered him digging; so he worked at night and carefully dispersed the massive soil excavated around the farm. When the depot was finished a six-foot-tall person could walk erect inside it; it was about 5–6 metres in length and about 1.5 metres wide with three 2-metre-deep shelves on which we stored rifles, rockets and launchers, mines, explosives and all manner of weapons which we received from Mozambique.

Paul's father-in-law drove to Swaziland on agreed days and handed over the weaponry we had sent requests for. We would then drive to the farm and give the supplies to Paris to store.

General Siphiwe Nyanda was the chief of staff of MK before its disbandment in 1993 and integration with the SANDF in 1994. He served as Chief of the SANDF from 1988–2005 and Minister of Communications from 2009–2010. He is presently South Africa's High Commissioner in Mozambique.

References

Edited and abridged extracts from his article 'Weapons infiltration by the Transvaal Urban Machinery', *The Thinker*, Vol. 58, 2013. https://docplayer.net/89950803-December-2013-volume-58-the-thinker-lest-we-forget.html.

10

Aboobaker Ismail (Rashid) – Internationalists who Joined the People's War

THIS BRIEF PIECE ON a subject that could entail volumes focuses on aspects of the role of internationalists not only in South Africa's neighbouring states but further afield. They participated as volunteers in various activities directly related to MK activities.

My involvement relates to my role as commissar and later commander of special operations from 1979, and from 1987 as chief of ordnance and member of the Military Headquarters of MK until April 1994, when we integrated into the new SANDF.

My engagement with these internationalists started with the initial support I enjoyed from the anti-apartheid organisation the Action Committee on Southern Africa (AKZA) in Belgium where I applied for political asylum after avoiding arrest for opposing the regime in South Africa.

To understand the critical role played by internationalists in the armed struggle one needs to appreciate the difficult conditions that pertained in southern Africa and especially South Africa. Ours is a country not blessed with the ideal conditions for guerrilla struggle. It is highly developed with all of the rural areas having a good road network and does not have huge areas of forests or rugged mountains from which large groups of guerrillas can operate.

The apartheid government and security forces pursued a so-called 'total war' strategy of coercing neighbouring countries into fulfilling the role of buffer states and acting against the ANC and MK. It invaded Angola, supporting UNITA, fought alongside the racist regime of then Rhodesia, and supported RENAMO against the FRELIMO government in Mozambique. The Mozambican government, under President Machel had taken a decision not to allow direct guerrilla operations across the Mozambique–South Africa border into South Africa, due to the heavy burden they already carried in directly supporting ZANU in the struggle to free Zimbabwe. Due to the threats of retaliatory attacks by the apartheid regime, the ANC and MK was forced to operate clandestinely or semi-clandestinely through all of the neighbouring countries.

In classical struggles, guerrilla forces are highly dependent on the local population to support and feed them, to act as couriers and assist in the transportation of armaments and logistics. The ANC/MK forces did not enjoy conditions that allowed the easy mobilisation of the rural people and therefore did not have much direct support in such areas. We had greater support in the townships within the cities in South Africa. The challenge for us in waging the armed struggle was to be able to develop clandestine routes for personnel and material, from the countries where we had base camps, such as Angola and Tanzania, into the neighbouring states which allowed only a clandestine or semi-clandestine presence, such as in Mozambique, Zambia, Botswana, Swaziland and Lesotho. From Mozambique we were only allowed to cross into Swaziland, from where we could then access South Africa.

During all those years we developed networks of supporters, contacts and operatives among the local populace in all of the neighbouring countries and encountered genuine support, kindness and solidarity of countless people to be able to get across the borders into South Africa.

This ranged from ordinary people who offered us a mug of 'mageu' (a nourishing maize drink) in addition to a glass of water after a hard night's march across the mountains from Mozambique into Swaziland, people pointing out where enemy soldiers were deployed, to contacts willing to provide passports to some of our comrades whom we would infiltrate into South Africa as Swazis. Many of the people in these neighbouring countries opened their homes to house combatants on route to South Africa. Some of these supporters stored ordnance in their homes or farms and helped transport explosives and weapons across borders.

In 1979, President Tambo, working closely with Joe Slovo, obtained a mandate from the NEC of the ANC to establish a Special Operations unit to carry out attacks against oil refineries which were identified as a strategic economic target. The objective was to carry out attacks that would win the imagination of our people, to show that the ANC and MK was a credible and legitimate movement that could engage the enemy with the support and active participation of the people, and to galvanise them into action against the apartheid regime. These attacks were seen as armed propaganda actions that the regime would not be able to cover up, as it was wont to do, and to show that the enemy was not invincible.

The establishment of Special Operations had come about after the visit of a high-level delegation to Vietnam to study the concept of the People's War. In order to root the struggle among the population, we needed to show that the enemy was not invincible, and this was achieved through armed propaganda. There is a very close nexus between carrying out operations and winning the support of the people.

In the latter part of 1979, while I was in Angola, I was given the mandate to train a specially selected group of comrades to prepare for the attacks against the oil refineries. After training this unit, I was deployed to Mozambique by Joe Slovo, who was appointed commander of Special Operations.

I entered the country on a reconnaissance mission of the Mobil Refinery in Durban. After my return to Mozambique, a decision was taken not to carry out that attack as I thought it posed a serious risk to the populace that lived in proximity in the event of a vapour cloud explosion. I was appointed commissar in the Special Operations unit, working alongside Joe Slovo and Motso Mokgabudi, who was tragically killed in the 1981 Matola raid. The June 1980 attacks on the oil refineries at Sasol I and Sasol II were successful and won the imagination of the people. The enemy was surprised at the scale and audacity of the operations. The key elements to the success of this operation depended on leadership given by ANC

President Oliver Tambo and Joe Slovo, detailed planning by the Special Operations Command, the indomitable will of the cadres in fulfilling the mission, and the role of the foreign internationalists who carried out the initial reconnaissance as well as the support of African internationalists in neighbouring states. It was they who supported, assisted and housed cadres en route to the target.

Given the spectacular success of these initial operations, Special Operations was given the mandate to continue with attacks against strategic targets, such as power stations and road networks, as well as enemy personnel.

In the following years, Special Operations carried out attacks against power stations, against the Voortrekkerhoogte military base, the Koeberg nuclear plant, the Air Force headquarters in Pretoria, and numerous other operations. All these operations contained the key elements of trust between the cadres and the leaders in the Command along with the ongoing support of the internationalists.

These operations had the effect of mobilising people within the country into political and armed action. While the enemy applied increasing measures to prevent some of the cross-border operations, the ANC and MK understood the need to embed the struggle within the country. The number of operations significantly escalated year upon year and by 1985/1986, the enemy declared a state of emergency because they were unable to quell the rising tide of internal resistance and demand for change.

From 1987 to 1988, Operation Vula, under Tambo and Slovo's leadership and under direct command of Mac Maharaj, infiltrated senior cadres within the country to embed the struggle amongst the people, and link directly with the emergent political movement – including a secret communications link with the imprisoned Mandela.

As the struggle grew inside the country, the demand for material increased. MK was able to get increasing numbers of cadres into the country, who, in turn, trained operatives and recruits. Despite the Nkomati Accord and a secret agreement with the Swazis in 1984, Special Operations was also instructed to carry out 'smaller pot-boiling operations' and assist with supplying material to other frontline states, including Lesotho.

White internationalists from Europe and North America were especially successful in getting material into the country with the application of the 'reverse apartheid' thinking where whites were generally not suspect and had freedom of movement denied to black people.

These internationalists carried out initial reconnaissance against strategic targets, smuggled material in vehicles specially prepared for the purpose, created arms caches in the terrain or passed the contents onto other operatives' storage and later distribution. In one of the more successful large-scale operations the Ordnance department of MK ran a truck of tourists from Kenya through Africa into South Africa, with weapons and explosives expertly hidden in specially prepared compartments. This was directed by MK in Zambia, while the tour group, with the commercial title 'Africa Hinterland' was busy with other activities. The drivers were internationalists carefully selected to fit the profile for this arduous mission. The internationalists worked extremely hard: digging DLBs (dead letter boxes) is a difficult task. Many often worked alone or in pairs having to cover their tracks continuously. This demanded many sacrifices on their part, often being away from family for long periods.

Other internationalists such as Hélène Passtoors and Klaas de Jonge served time in prison for their activities. Some volunteered to carry out operations themselves, but we dissuaded them from doing so as we did not want the enemy to be able to claim that operations were being carried out by foreigners should they be arrested.

In 1987, after the killing of Cde Cassius Make (Job Tabane) by the enemy in Swaziland, I was appointed chief of Ordnance in his place, and a member of Military Headquarters.

The mandate of Ordnance was to meet the immediate short-term operational needs for material by units inside the country and to build up a large stockpile for future needs. At the outset we had to significantly increase the efficiency and effectiveness of operations, including that of the African Hinterland operation which was able to get large volumes of ordnance into the country. Some of the Special Operations units inside the country were transferred to Ordnance to create additional storage and distribution facilities.

As the initial negotiations processes got underway between the ANC and the regime, it became increasingly clear that the People's War strategy of MK actions reinforcing the mass political struggle had succeeded, and that the regime had no alternative but to negotiate. The unbanning of the ANC, the SACP and others in 1990 led to a new terrain of struggle. Shadowy elements within the regime attempted to derail the negotiations process, pitting 'black on black' by provocations. The ANC and MK thus faced a new challenge of defending the people from the vicious attacks by these so-called Third Force elements.

The ANC and MK, under the leadership of Mandela, Slovo, Hani and Kasrils (despite being underground) instructed Ordnance to arm the people's emergent self-defence units (SDUs) as well as the security units of the ANC who protected its headquarters and leadership. The arming of the SDUs played a crucial role in defeating these sinister attempts which had taken a heavy toll in life between 1990 and 1994. Many internationalists continued to play an important role during this time.

After liberation in April 1994, some of the internationalists chose to take up South African nationality. The people of South Africa are indebted to the Internationalists, from within Africa, from Europe, the Americas, the Soviet Union, the GDR and elsewhere who played such a critical role in our liberation struggle under some of the most difficult conditions. They indeed form part of the people, in the People's War for People's Power, in the fight for the liberation of South Africa from the tyranny of apartheid.

(Rashid) Aboobaker Ismail is currently doing a PhD on negotiations and conflict resolution.

Editor's note: While a vast quantity of weapons and explosives was distributed to MK units and SDUs post-1990, the stores that remained in DLBs and caches were handed in to the new SANDF post-1994. The irony was that the ANC's Defence Minister Joe Modise and his deputy, together with General Aboobaker Ismail, working in the Department of Defence, were effectively the recipients.

11

Bogaert & van Hecken – From the Carnation Revolution to Special Ops

LETTER FROM 19 August 1982, two days after the assassination of Ruth First:

> Ruth murdered, the security situation in Mozambique precarious ...
> We will have to learn to live with these things, after all, it is our own
> choice. We are not fools and we do think about our own and our
> children's safety, but on the other hand we are not prepared to let
> ourselves be intimidated, and certainly not by a bunch of inhuman
> bastards in Pretoria! Ruth is the fifth person we know personally to be
> assassinated, four of them in less than a year.

Looking back at this we keep asking ourselves: how does a foreign
couple, from a fairly traditional middle-class background, end up actively
supporting an armed resistance movement of a country that is not their
own; and what has become of the beautiful ideals of freedom, equality –
championed by the liberation movements in the 1970–1980s – don't we
feel disappointed or cheated? Is every revolution doomed to failure then?
And does every revolution inevitably end up devouring its own children,
like Saturn in Goya's painting?

The answer is simple: the decision whether or not to support a project does not depend on the final outcome of that project but is contingent on a broad social consensus regarding its objectives and content, and on the commitment and efforts of its protagonists to make it a success. Like any social project, the transformation of South Africa is work in perpetual progress, in which successes and failures alternate and which is never 'finished'. The observation that after each failure new people and new generations arise to pick up the thread and continue the struggle gives us hope for the future and gives meaning to the efforts we and our contemporaries have made.

This is because we continue to believe in the 'makeability' of the world and in people as agents of change. We believe that everyone has a duty to ensure that the world we have inherited from previous generations is passed on to our children as a place where it is good and safe to live for every member of all future generations. The tools used to achieve this depend on each individual context and situation, and on the opportunities and tools a society offers its members to work for change and progress. Often, nonviolent means, such as consultation and negotiation, peaceful protest and civil disobedience are sufficient to bring about the desired changes, but sometimes 'the time comes in the life of any nation when there remain only two choices: submit or fight'.[25] We shared the ANC's vision of the role of armed struggle as a very last resort in the resistance to the violent oppression and ruthless cruelty of the apartheid regime. We knew the ANC's determination and its great care to avoid human casualties in the use of armed resistance.

On the other hand, we were aware that the use of violence, even for perfectly legitimate and morally laudable purposes, creates violent societies. The reality is that in these situations there are no winners: anyone forced into a life of violent conflict, secrecy, constant suspicion and stress becomes mentally damaged by it; a whole generation is deeply scarred, and one can only hope that the next generation will be able to return to a normal life.

How then did we become involved in the armed struggle against apartheid? The role that a person ultimately takes on in life is determined by a combination of factors: the vision of people and society that one has developed, one's personal character and disposition (partly inborn and

---

25   From the manifesto of Umkhonto we Sizwe, issued on 16 December 1961.

inherited), and a number of coincidental circumstances and events.

As young adults, our parents experienced the destruction of Europe during the Second World War, and its rapid economic reconstruction in the 1950s to the 1970s thanks to massive American aid. While for them the reconstruction of material prosperity and a social security system that offered protection was important, some of our contemporaries began to ask critical questions about the flip side of this prosperity coin. Faster means of communication broadened our horizon and made it clear that the development of a welfare state for a (white) minority was intrinsically connected with colonialism, exploitation, structural inequality and the oppression of the majority of the world population. We refused to accept that this was 'inevitable'.

We remain convinced of the possibility of extending to everyone in the world, regardless of gender, skin colour, origin, etc. the quality of life that our parents' generation had achieved by building a welfare society for the happy few. But this 'awareness' grew at a different pace within each of us and was due to different factors.

Nora's father was a doctor. He lived for his profession and was not interested in getting actively involved in politics and accepted society as it was. He had a set of values that he stood up for, even at the cost of personal risk. During the war and the German occupation, he secretly treated Jews in their homes and in the hospital where they hid. He treated for free those patients who could not pay for his services. He passed on these moral and ethical values to his daughter. Besides, the influence of a progressive French teacher at high school made Nora aware of the impact good teachers can have on the development of an open and critical mind and social awareness. Nora wanted to be like her.

For Guido, the realisation that the world was unequal and unjust came rather late. His parents had left in 1953 for the then Belgian Congo, attracted by the higher salaries and the more affluent lifestyle that the Belgian state offered its civil servants in the colony. They were permeated by the prevailing colonial ideology: they viewed their work in the colony not only as a means to fulfil their aspirations more quickly, but also as a 'civilising mission'. For Guido, the stereotypical colonial world view that he had inherited from his parents was hardly shaken, even when in 1966 his great uncle was shot by the police during the major strikes against the closure of the Belgian coal mines. Until 1969 when on a cultural trip to Greece he found himself in a country ruled by fascist colonels, and dissidence was brutally suppressed. Later that summer he became a monitor at a holiday camp in France for children from orphanages in Paris. They were treated very badly and used as cheap labour. Guido began to realise that in our own Western societies, too, there was great inequality and injustice.

The real turning point for Guido came with the 'discovery' of Portugal in 1971. At university he came into contact with people who were active in the clandestine opposition against fascism, including armed resistance. On his second visit in 1972, he was arrested and questioned by state security, the notorious PIDE, about an article in a Dutch newspaper, which was critical of Portugal.

In April 1974, a military coup against fascism and Portugal's colonial wars ushered in a period of progressive social experimentation, known as the Carnation Revolution. We were so motivated and inspired by the organisation of literacy campaigns, self-government by tenants, workers and peasants, popular clinics, land expropriation and reform ... that we organised active solidarity campaigns with the Portuguese revolution in Belgium – and we decided for ourselves that working for that kind of social change was what we wanted to do with our lives.

By then it was clear to us how we saw our future. In 1976 we joined the Belgian Communist Party and, with Guido's desire to return to Africa, we began to look for work opportunities in Portuguese-speaking Africa. In 1977 Guido met Aquino de Bragança in Lisbon. He turned out to be a special advisor to Samora Machel and director of the Centre for African Studies (CEA) at the Eduardo Mondlane University in Maputo. He invited Guido to the university. We left for Maputo in 1978. At the university, Guido organised a translation course and Nora worked in the Teacher Training department.

When in 1978 Ruth First settled permanently in Mozambique as research director of the CEA and a little later her husband Joe Slovo also moved permanently to Mozambique, we became good friends. Ruth and Joe became frequent visitors. They brought us into direct contact with the South African struggle.

In December 1979, we became directly involved in operational activities of the ANC. Joe told us that he was urgently looking for a place where a few comrades could go into hiding for a while. The next day he brought two men to our flat – Tim Jenkin and Alex Moumbaris, two of the 'Pretoria Three', who had made a spectacular escape from Pretoria Central prison with Stephen Lee the previous week, and who had arrived clandestinely in Maputo. The ANC wanted to be able to debrief them in a safe place.

In the second half of 1980, shortly after the birth of our eldest son Risana, Joe introduced us to a comrade who had lived in Belgium for a while. That was Rashid (Aboobaker Ismail). We became good friends. Due to the nature of his work and for security reasons, he did not have many social contacts, and regularly came to us in the evenings to relax.

After the Matola raid in January 1981, Rashid and Joe were looking for a safe place for Rashid. We were also planning to change houses, as our second baby was on the way and the flat would be too small. For just over three years Rashid was a member of our family and to this day we consider each other as brothers and sister.

Joe was a daily visitor. While we were working in the university, Joe and Rashid used our home as a centre for planning and preparing Special Operations projects. We made a conscious effort to know as little as possible about their work, and since nobody was allowed to know that Rashid lived with us, we kept our own social contacts to a strict minimum.

Joe and Rashid knew that Guido had some experience with clandestine work and that he was a good forger. And so Joe gave him some 'Bantu passbooks' and asked to replace the owner's picture in those dompasses by someone else's. Afterwards Guido specialised in forging the papers for the cars of Special Ops and their drivers. And when he pointed out the possibilities of hiding weapons in our own Renault 4, Rashid asked him to help identify and install suitable hiding places for weapons and ammunition in other cars. Our house became an ammunition depot for Special Ops.

One day Joe told us that Special Ops was looking for people willing to do missions without attracting the attention of the Boers: reconnoitring possible targets for attacks, smuggling and hiding weapons and explosives into South Africa, and other similar activities. Were we prepared to undertake missions and jobs for Special Ops more systematically? Yes, we said.

With Ruth and Joe, who had been confronted with the same dilemma decades before with their three young daughters, we had already discussed at length whether active participation in the armed struggle could be reconciled with the responsibility of parents for the welfare and upbringing of their children. After all, our motivation to act in a certain way stems from our world view and not from a casual availability to devote some of our free time to a cause. And to be consistent, one should also actively seek to contribute to the realisation of one's conviction. It is therefore not because children come into one's life at a certain point that one's conviction and attitudes should suddenly change – that would be very inconsistent and contradictory to that conviction, and first and foremost in relation to the children.

And so we grew closer to the activities of Special Ops, and Guido gradually became Rashid's informal operational sidekick. He acted as a messenger between Joe and Rashid, when the latter was in Swaziland, and together with Rashid he hid the weapons and explosives in the cars that would take them to South Africa and took care of the paperwork. Both of us also carried out assignments for Special Ops in Swaziland and in South Africa, until the Boers found out Guido's identity in 1982 and that part of our work came to an end.

We continued to function as a close team until Rashid and Joe, along with most of the ANC's operatives, were forced to leave Mozambique in 1984, shortly after the signing of the Nkomati Accord between the apartheid regime and Mozambique.

NORA BOGAERT AND GUIDO VAN HECKEN are a Belgian couple who previously worked at the Eduardo Mondlane University in Maputo. In Belgium Nora worked as a language teacher training expert in a university centre focused on the promotion of equity and equality in education. Guido was Chief of Cabinet of the Belgian Minister for Development Cooperation. They currently spend their time between their home in Antwerpen and the South of France.

12

Oscar Marleyn – Stumbling towards Internationalism 1979–1991

SOUTH AFRICA, 25 YEARS after independence from the apartheid regime and the questions have begun. *What the hell were you were doing becoming an MK operative? Was it worthwhile? Did you not learn any lessons from what was happening in neighbouring countries?*

It's hard to explain some decisions to daughters, family and friends.

My granddad Oscar was my greatest political influence. Grandfather Oscar was a trade unionist on the shipyards of Billiards & Murdoch in Oostende (Belgium). He soldiered in the trenches during the Great War and was active in the resistance during the Second World War.

His stories of war and peace were spellbinding for us, the three brothers, during family gatherings. His memories always started with 'a man who has been in a war is never the same again'. He had a hand-size burn on his left cheek caused by a gas used by German troops. The wars had drastically changed his outlook on life.

The French-speaking officers in the trenches did not bother to learn to communicate with Flemish-speaking soldiers and my grandfather was not impressed with the 'establishment', or the shipyard owners represented by the government. The experience turned him staunchly socialist with a thread of Flemish nationalism.

The wars and their aftermath left the family empowered by the Flemish movement but economically marginalised. The government granted concessions to the labour movement in 1918–1921 against the backdrop of the Russian revolution. But there was a healthy distrust for all beings political. My mother thought that once working class, forever working class. My grandfather believed on the contrary that political mobilisation and education was necessary.

As the eldest grandson I got extra morsels of grandfatherly wisdom to sustain the meagre economic and political history diet I was fed at school and socially. A huge wall map in class indicated the natural riches of the Belgian Congo, Rwanda and Burundi. The weekly trade union newspaper was so dense that nobody in the household read it. The daily liberal newspaper informed us that the Congolese were lucky to have us thanks to the enormous efforts of Flemish missionaries.

In 1967, aged 19, I worked and studied in Liverpool to finalise my BA degree. I assisted working-class families to find jobs and improved housing outside the densely populated inner city. I detected very little empathy for the Scousers coming from housing slums in Everton and Scotland Roads near Liverpool's Anfield stadium. These families – similar to my own in Belgium – were considered by the middle-class professionals with whom I worked as a loud and troublesome lot. Working-class housing was shocking, and unemployment was high, so why didn't these blooming families want to move?

One Friday night I met my future wife Bernadette Nee and was introduced, through her, to the Irish-Catholic immigrant community, the Catholic Church, St Patrick's parades and the Irish Club. Again, the Irish-Flemish similarities struck home. Here were a people who because of culture, language and religion had been relegated to second-class citizens. When invited to work as a senior environmental planner in Portadown, Northern Ireland, I refused.

In 1972 I opted to work with private architects and planners in London and Edinburgh. I was uninspired but earning some serious money. I assisted in camouflaging mining enterprises' eyesores in national parks and beautified urban spaces. Sultan Qaboos bin Said Al Busaidi was in power with British support and British architects were invited to work in Oman. Designing the outer courtyards of the sultan's new palace brought me into contact with Islamic traditions, art and design. Lovely – but the wastage of building funds due to the sultan's whims sickened me so I left.

I'd read Rachel Carson's *Silent Spring* and headed into the environmental movement but was kicked out for supporting and promoting radical ideas on inner city housing development.

I wound up in the Architectural Association's planning department and got a sniff of the underlying tangents of development policy. I tried to make sense of Marx, Lenin, Althusser, Balibar and Samir Amin, guided by academics Ben Fine and James Anderson. In 1977 the department invited Albie Sachs to explain developmental challenges in Mozambique – it was a recruitment drive. Albie painted a colourful picture of the country in a challenging post-colonial environment.

Before we knew it, we were in Maputo with a new philosophy in the back pocket, a six-month-old daughter and £50 in the purse. Settling in took time because of shortages of accommodation and food but I did not expect first-class treatment arriving to assist a newly independent country.

If I wanted to be involved in broader development issues, that is exactly what I got when I was assigned to the Communal Villages Planning unit (CNAC). Villagisation was based on a centrally planned economy supposedly to provide the rural population with essential services like education and health. Small-scale producers with hundreds of years of farming experience on ancestral lands were considered 'backward'. Their means of production were confiscated as they were resettled to work on state farms or in state cooperatives.

Field research organised by the Centro de Estudos Africanos (CEA) under Ruth First showed that both state farms and the agricultural services were badly managed. You can take over an enterprise, but it doesn't mean you have the necessary skills to run it profitably. The costs of state enterprises peaked, food production plummeted, and small farmers forced off their land reacted by joining the South African-backed RENAMO in the ensuing civil war.

I was considered pro-government and pro-FRELIMO but my hours of patient listening to opposing political views of workers in my brother's café in Oostende had prepared me. Yes, the farmers previously supported FRELIMO and no they didn't want to lose their land or trees, but they were never listened to. Their objections were considered to be antigovernment, as signs of political dissent. Elders showed me the damage soldiers inflicted on houses and livestock. I worked with farmers who were FRELIMO supporters during the day and RENAMO insurgents at night.

The Mozambican elite despised these able, small farmers and instructed them in farming methods to produce a surplus 'for us to eat well', even if they [the elite] had only ever grown tomatoes in their own backyards. None would adjust the approach – the party line determined the framework. My new back-pocket ideology had seen live practice of the advantages of democratic centralism and needed revision.

Meantime, direct contact with ANC exiles was inevitable. Sue Rabkin, who had two children in the Maputo International School, took it upon herself to 'instruct' us on a weekly basis on South Africa. We got involved in delivering ANC pamphlets to Swaziland on a family vacation. Sue's car was so packed she couldn't open her window when asked to do so at the Namaacha border post.

The ANC's safe house in the Rua Mateus Sansão Muthemba was out of bounds for people like me, but I had plenty of occasions to meet my neighbours and discuss their homeland and the lives of black South Africans under apartheid.

When Joe Slovo (J.S.) asked in 1979 if I was willing to support the ANC's armed struggle I had been thinking about this possibility. I felt that some of my ancestors might well have been responsible for establishing the regime besides having conducted themselves barbarically in the Congo. Something needed to be done. My answer was positive.

I thought it opportune to raise some concerns about the political system he envisaged for South Africa. J.S. must have been thinking about this issue. His article titled 'Has socialism failed' only appeared in an SACP publication later, in 1989. J.S. knew I wasn't a communist and listened patiently. His response that 'working class internationalism was one of the most liberating concepts in Marxism' sounded rather flat but seeing my discomfort he picked up speed. He noted that with a 'broad church' such as the ANC anything was possible and could produce different types of democracy. He emphasised the economic failures of the Soviet-type system as well as the enormous human costs related to forced collectivisation. I thought he had been prepped by his wife Ruth First.

My first task was to reconnoitre a way to attack the Sasol pipeline starting from the Durban terminal, going through Pietermaritzburg, Ladysmith, Harrismith, Kroonstad to Sasolburg. In July 1979 off I went with my camera and topographical maps of the region to Swaziland and then South Africa for two and a half weeks. I reported that the oil pipe was not very accessible for MK operatives at those particular locations due to the pipeline either being well guarded or underground. An MK unit would be much too exposed if it intended to do more than exploding a device. It later became evident that an MK unit exploded eight fuel tanks inside the Sasol plant terminal on the night of 31 May to 1 June 1980 by cutting through the perimeter fence.

From 1980–1983 I became involved in a number of supply missions between Maputo and Swaziland carrying ammunition. Probably limpet mines but I am not sure because the 'stuff' was hidden in a vehicle which I left behind in Manzini and collected later. Only once did I know what I was transporting because I had to fix the 'stuff' underneath the car myself with the help of two Belgian comrades.

The vehicle was a massive Ford F-100 pickup truck, not exactly one that could easily be hidden away in a public car park. It had to be 'fitted' a day before I left in the backyard of the family home in Sommerschield in Maputo. When I arrived at around 17:00 I realised that the 'stuff' was a 2.54-metre-long artillery piece. It was probably used in the Voortrekkerhoogte attack, but I am not sure.[26] It was crazy to have to fit the pipe underneath the truck at night because the clanging and banging could probably be heard three or four houses away in this quiet residential neighbourhood of Maputo. To my surprise nobody came to check.

In September 1987 we returned to Zimbabwe, and I worked with Riaz Saloojee and Muff Andersson, whom I then knew as Cal and Yasmin, in MK Ordnance. One project was to secure a regular supply of ammunition from Beira Port through the Beira Corridor, but this didn't come off the ground because of the imminent National Peace Accord of 14 September 1991.

South Africa has had a democratic government for more than a quarter of a century. There have been improvements in housing, health and education but not an economic transformation that has transformed

---

26   The commander of the unit who carried out the operation, Barney Molokoane, later confirmed that the rockets and GRAD-P rocket launcher for the operation on Voortrekkerhoogte was brought in via Swaziland.

the lives of the majority. How quickly a local elite has organised itself with the assistance of the private sector to cream off a large slice of its wealth through contract fixing and down right fraud and money laundering. Amazing that some still point to the 'apartheid regime and its allies' as being responsible for this. I'm not surprised to receive the scathing comments I mentioned before.

I think back on the gains in my own country where universal manhood suffrage was first attained in 1919 and for women in 1948. Seventy-odd years ago. The damage done by Belgium's elites during its colonial past has never been dealt with. It's barely official history. At least 12 American presidents were slave owners, including five of the founding fathers after the abolition of slavery in 1865. People of colour there are still not treated as equals. Unequal power relations between elites and 'other citizens' are maintained by race, ethnicity, religion, language, culture and origin.

As I write this, the architect of state capture questions the legality of the constitution that underpins the rights of South Africa's citizens, and whether an African head of state should be convicted for his crimes. The ANC is gradually losing its international and local support. Democratisation, the attainment of citizens' rights, is not an act of liberation but an ongoing process in which citizens are continuously mobilised to maintain and realise their economic and political rights.

Many I meet are disillusioned. I would argue that change is not linear and needs measurement over a longer period. Political liberation was a worthwhile cause but stopped short of the necessary political empowerment and economic transformation. Liberation was class-captured together with the institutions of the state. A second phase of liberation must go well beyond the creation of a black middle class. We need to transform the 'economy of the majority' which lies well beyond the enterprises now considered the mainstay of economic activity. This transformation has to go together with enhanced political empowerment of the majority of producers to challenge those who now wield power from the doorsteps of state institutions. Can the ANC be the vehicle for this? It is up to each of us to take a moral decision whether to support such empowerment efforts or remain untouched.

So, were my efforts worth it? Well, I'm waiting to see. I'm a patient man.

OSCAR MARLEYN is a development planner/organisational change agent, researcher and writer. He has two daughters Rebecca and Els Marleyn. He now lives in Johannesburg with his partner Muff Andersson.

13

Hélène Marinis Passtoors – Words and Blasts

EARLY 1990 AND MANDELA is not yet released as I arrive at the university campus in Harare for the ANC workshop on the future language policy.

It is my first time back in Africa since my deportation to Belgium straight from prison in May 1989 and it's a joy to return to the ANC family. After my years in the military (1981–1985), I am delighted to contribute to South Africa's future as an African linguist of some experience.

In 1990 the ANC in exile had reached the heady stage of preparing concrete policy options for a free South Africa. Internal commissions were set up in all fields of policy with delegates from the different structures and departments of the ANC in exile. Louise Colvin aka Angela organised and led the debates with a strong, very inspiring hand. I was thrilled to find I represented MK on the language commission.

Language policy was a field I had been working on at the University Eduardo Mondlane in Maputo where Ruth First's assassination – and later the attempt on Albie Sachs's life – had shown how the enemy regarded the mind as a powerful and fearful weapon.

While I had gladly participated in the armed struggle as a necessity, a duty even, the military never reached the stage of a calling for me. What did come naturally to me was reconnaissance, communication/liaison, intelligence, i.e., the métiers of the mind that I found quite similar in logic and reasoning to linguistics. And I liked the underground, the mice deceiving the puffed-up cat.

In the workshop, through intensive debate, the experience and arguments of the role of language in the various fields – language and oppression, class formation, education, culture, emancipation, development – converged fairly easily. We agreed that equal status of all major South African languages, including English, Afrikaans and the major African languages, was the best way to reach our political and socio-economic goals.

A complementary proposal was the re-standardisation and unified spelling of the Nguni (Ndebele, Swati, Xhosa, Zulu) and Sotho/Tswana (Sotho, Sotho se Leboa, Pedi, Tswana) in which dialect clusters were seen as two major languages with dialect variations. Much like British, American, Australian, South African and other versions (or dialects) of English have one standard with accepted variations. Stalwart activist and academic Neville Alexander, who came from outside the ANC, was in favour of this approach to reduce the number of official languages, promote unity and nation building. However, in the end this proposal didn't make it.

After the workshop I went to Lusaka for the debrief at Military Headquarters (MHQ). I was registered by ANC bureaucracy and made a card-carrying member after almost nine years. The debrief before the full MK High Command was led by Chris Hani, the chief of staff. It lasted for hours. Joe Modise offered a choice of transfer to another department. I left that up to them. They decided I should stay in MK and go for additional training in Cuba.

Jackie Sedibe, our only woman commander in MHQ, had organised a 'welcome home' party with MK women; I never knew there were so many women commanders! Strong personalities. The first thing Joe Slovo said when I saw him again after almost five years was, 'What have you guys proposed for the language policy? Why not just English?' That had been the ANC's general idea. We sat down and I explained. To my surprise the big Slovo changed his mind! Others followed suit.

Cuba never happened. Within months everyone in Lusaka packed their bags and went 'home' to South Africa. Once negotiations started, the ANC applied twice for indemnity for me since I had tasks relating to the future language policy, a hot issue.

Twice the regime refused indemnity at the last moment. Meanwhile not only was there the horrible 'Third Force' violence but many returned comrades were harassed and even murdered. One of my closest comrades, Trevor Nkululeko Vilakazi aka Socrates, was ambushed and murdered in front of his kids on the Cape Flats.

In 1992 I received an order from the ANC not to return to South Africa for the time being because the ANC couldn't guarantee my safety and there were not enough bodyguards available, they said. As if I'd want a bodyguard. But yes, I had a rather high profile, especially among those conservatives who couldn't forget that I had delivered the car with the bomb in Mamelodi for the attack against the Air Force headquarters in Church Street in Pretoria in May 1983. This biggest and bloodiest of MK attacks struck the heart of Afrikanerdom. For lack of evidence, I hadn't been indicted for that operation in my 1986 trial, but they again opened a docket in 1996. I applied for amnesty at the TRC.

I was back on the road as a cosmopolitan. I don't care for nationalities and national borders of inclusion/exclusion. In prison I had decided I'd settle in South Africa at liberation and give the best of myself to the transition. After all, South Africa was – and is – the only country I ever fought for. But it could not be.

With my struggle profile, jobs proved to be hard to come by – even in Africa which I favoured. I turned to journalism and in 1992 accepted an offer to go to Chile as a correspondent for Belgian national radio but the friends of apartheid didn't leave me alone. I found some peace on a small farm in the mountains. When I was granted amnesty in 2001–2001, I took an editor job in Belgium and prepared my first return to the 'new South Africa' in 2003 as a journalist.

As a child I was called a restless dreamer by my father. He said I would go into the world and not turn back. He was right. It's hard to say why I always felt – and feel – claustrophobic in Europe. Wings clipped, wrapped in cotton wool, that's how I expressed it in my teenage poetry. The Suez crisis in 1956 when petrol shortages caused spectacular bans on mobility in Europe, opened a window to colonialism. But it was only when I turned 21 that my dad let me go out into the world.

I took the first opportunity that came my way with a visa. It happened to be the US of the Vietnam war and civil rights uprisings. I came across abject poverty as I'd never imagined – a baptism of fire. I met my husband anthropologist who took me to Congo where he had already lived in the early years after independence.

The years there were defining years. We founded our family of four children, I took up the study and research of African languages and linguistics, and lived through two uprisings of my fellow students at the University of Kinshasa. We left with a heavy heart when Mobutu's dictatorship had crushed all resistance and became unbearable.

Then followed additional study in Europe, research in West Africa, mainly Ivory Coast and Ghana, and the pioneering post in linguistics at the university in Maputo in 1981 where I met the ANC and MK. By then I had strong leftist convictions from an African perspective. But no known Western political profile.

I met Joe Slovo as the husband of Ruth First, a very impressive and warm woman who was like a mentor to us researchers in human sciences at the university. In late 1981 Slovo recruited me and later my then husband Klaas de Jonge as a reconnaissance team for Special Operations. Joe and Aboobaker Ismail aka Rashid were the commanders and our early trainers.

From Christmas 1981 till May 1983, we did a fair number of reconnaissance missions in South Africa on economic and military targets. We often also brought the weaponry in for the selected targets but unlike Klaas at a later stage I was never into 'gun running' proper. In 1983–1984, after separation from Klaas, I worked intensely with Rashid mainly on communication/liaison between him in Maputo and our unit's command in Swaziland.

They were Ernest Lekoto Pule aka T-man, still a dear friend, Johannes Mnisi aka Victor Molefe and Lester Dumakude aka Chris, who saved my life in Swaziland by not giving me away under torture. They were incredible soldiers and genial, good-natured personalities. They were brothers closer than my real brother. I last spent an afternoon with T-man at Chris's bedside in Military 1 Hospital. He joked and laughed as always and didn't tell us his death was near. Trevor Nkululeko Vilakazi aka Socrates was a student and Special Ops operative in Swaziland. We had incredible stories about my tracking him down when the others were deep underground and communications cut. We found each other again in London after my release. When Rica Hodgson, the remarkable stalwart with whom I usually stayed in London, phoned me to tell how he had been murdered in the Cape, I howled.

1983/84 were very tense, mad times with a real manhunt on in Swaziland especially for Special Ops. Then Special Ops went to Botswana, and I was deployed in Johannesburg where I was in the linguistics department at Wits University finishing my PhD and about to start teaching when I was arrested on 28 June 1985.

Most often, getting arrested means you've made mistakes. I surely had. I had a tendency to take risks and I did do so once too often. I was eight months to the day in solitary confinement with the SB at John Vorster Square. In May 1986 I was convicted of high treason as a resident in South Africa and sentenced to 10 years. I stayed with the white women political prisoners Barbara Hogan, Marion Sparg, Jansie Lourens and Trish Hanekom in Pretoria Central prison. In 1988 I was again isolated in Kroonstad prison for about eight months when the SB tried to 'break' me and get me to give evidence against my romantic partner since 1983, 'Ebe' Ismail Ebrahim. He had been kidnapped from Swaziland and was on trial for treason. After my return to prison in Pretoria, the Belgian government negotiated my early release in May 1989.

HÉLÈNE PASSTOORS, MK operative, grandmother and occasional writer lives in a small village in the province of Namur, Belgium. She and Jan Vanheukelom would like to pay tribute to their late friend and compatriot Paulette Pierson Mathy's important contributions to the liberation struggles in Algeria and Southern Africa. Paulette and Hélène are recipients of the Companions of Oliver Tambo Award.

14

*Klaas de Jonge – The Daring Escape of a 'Damn F**king Foreign Terrorist'*

Lieutenant Botha (SAP interrogator, 1985): 'Did you ever meet Klaas or Hélène?'

Mo Shaik (ANC and South African government senior Intelligence officer): 'Who are they? I don't know any Klaas or Hélène. No, I don't know either of them.'

Lieutenant Botha was a skilled interrogator. He looked at Shaik and said, 'I believe you. The woman's name is Hélène, and the guy is named Klaas, damn fucking foreign terrorists. But we have them locked up.' His contempt was palpable and undisguised.[27]

Hélène and I were part of the Special Ops unit under Rashid. Since the end of 1981, our activities for the ANC – carried out in addition to our regular jobs – consisted in occasionally bringing weapons and explosives into South Africa and conducting reconnaissance of potential targets. We operated from Maputo. After our divorce, I operated from early 1985 from Harare where I taught at a secondary school, and Hélène from Johannesburg.

Hélène was to 'take it easy' for a while after moving to South Africa.

---

27   Mo Shaik, *The ANC Spy Bible: Surviving across enemy lines*, Tafelberg, Cape Town, 2020.

If necessary, I could call upon her for help. I did so in June 1985 when I had very little time to install an arms cache (a DLB) somewhere between Johannesburg and Pretoria. It was to be our last one.

Although we had been trained in Maputo by Rashid and Ronnie Kasrils, MK's military commander in Swaziland, to ascertain whether we were possibly followed or not while carrying out these operations, I did not manage to do so. At the time I thought it was just paranoia. However, we were indeed followed and observed by agents of the South African secret service while we were working on the DLB at night.

Soon afterwards we were arrested and taken to John Vorster Square (JVS) in Johannesburg; to me it happened on Sunday, 23 June 1985 on my return trip to Harare. Hélène was arrested five days later. I could have kicked myself for not taking seriously the feeling that I was being followed.

I was detained in solitary confinement (Section 29). From the first day of my detention, I was regularly interrogated at length, usually by two secret service officers who occasionally insulted and threatened me, but I soon realised I would not be physically tortured. I thought this was because I am a Dutch national, but later I heard that they thought I might have been connected to the Dutch secret service.

Someone made the threat, when I was walking down a concrete staircase with my hands cuffed behind my back, 'If we give you a push now, you'll break your neck.' Or, 'We know where you lived in Harare, so we can hurt your family and kill your dog.' That type of thing, but they never laid a finger on me.

I wanted to buy some time and intended to admit certain things that I thought couldn't do any harm, e.g., point out some DLBs that I assumed would have been emptied by then. After all, we were caught installing a DLB. I took the policemen to a number of empty DLBs where I exaggerated the number of explosives and weapons that had been hidden there, which often scared the hell out of them: 'with that, you could have blown up the whole of Pretoria' – reactions which made me feel good.

I planned to escape from the first moment. This was always in my mind. Escaping from John Vorster Square would be impossible. It would not even be possible to flee during one of the 'pointing out' sessions. There were always at least three armed policemen with me: Captain Du Preez, the boss of the trio, a nervous-looking man; Lieutenant Herbert, a commando-type policeman built like a rugby player; and De Villiers, who took the photos. They were arrogant as hell and compared themselves to the best intelligence services in the world, which, according to them, was the Mossad in Israel. I always wore ankle cuffs and sometimes handcuffs, attached to a bench of the car during transport.

I remembered that in September 1984, six anti-apartheid leaders had taken refuge in the British consulate in Durban to avoid arrest. The refugees received some temporary support. If I could do something like that, then at least my family and friends, and also the ANC, would know what was going on. I knew that Rashid would then immediately declare all DLBs in which we had been involved to be taboo.

I knew Pretoria quite well. The Nedbank building in the city centre housed various companies as well as an office of the Dutch embassy. I would have to take the policemen there with me. Running away fast with leg irons was not possible, so I needed a piece of rope to pull up the chain between the two ankle cuffs.

I decided to tell my escorts that the ANC planned to take tougher actions against military targets and companies that didn't respect the boycott and that we were planning an attack on an office in the Nedbank building in Pretoria. They might fall for the trap; they came from Johannesburg and didn't know Pretoria well and surely did not know the Dutch embassy was in that building. I hesitated, afraid that Du Preez would shoot at me in panic if I ran, even inside a building. My three wardens thought I was cooperating quite well. Once they left me alone in a café (without removing my leg irons). I didn't move at all and waited quietly until all three came back. After that, they were no longer very vigilant.

A few days later I told them that I had installed a DLB in Mamelodi, a township near Pretoria, and indicated where. A lot of excitement, but I knew the DLB was supposed to be empty. We went with more cars and personnel than usual. When we arrived, they had already started excavating and there were some bags of firearms and limpet mines next to a pit. I was startled. Had the DLB not been emptied a few months ago? Could the secret service itself have planted something there in an attempt to break me? I will never know. Rashid later told me that if a guerrilla unit likes the location of a DLB, they sometimes remove only part of its content, leaving the rest for later.

A senior police officer told me: 'If we release you now, the ANC would consider you a traitor and kill you.' I knew it was not true, but at the same time I saw this as an opportunity. Sounding as devastated as possible I muttered, 'OK. Now I may as well tell you everything,' but I also decided, that's it. Now I'm going to get the hell out of here!

During my next interrogation, I told them I had photographed a military airfield from the Voortrekker Monument, which meant we should pay it a visit. I said I did not want to walk around crouched and that I needed a piece of string to pull up the chain of my ankle cuffs. They gave it to me.

I told them that my unit had planned an attack on a company in a Nedbank building and that I had participated in the reconnaissance. This company (I invented this) didn't respect the boycott and so we were planning to attack its office. I said the entrance of the company was on the second floor (this was one floor above the entrance to the embassy).

Arriving at the Nedbank building, De Villiers wanted some photos. He ordered me to stand in front of the doorway of the building at Andries Street entrance. I saw NEDBANK above the door and above that the blue weapon shield with lions of the 'Embassy of the Kingdom of the Netherlands'. No reaction from De Villiers.

We walked in and I thought 'VERDOMME!'. A wall in the hall listed the indoor companies and organisations, including the embassy. It escaped Du Preez and the other two.

I took the stairs, telling them the 'company' entrance was on the second floor. On reaching the first floor I pointed to the right to indicate something the ANC was planning there. An instant later they saw me 'running' to the left, holding up my ankle chain with the string. The Dutch embassy was further away than I remembered. There were screams behind me, but no shot. I reached the door which wasn't locked, shouting, 'Help me', as I stormed into the visitor's room.

'I am a Dutchman, a political prisoner, my name is Klaas de Jonge,' I yelled. I was followed by two policemen. Behind the reception glass two young women looked shocked. Herbert tackled me to the ground, and a swearing and screaming Du Preez brandished his pistol. He vowed to kill me: 'Ek moer jou!'

I was dragged out again by the police officers. Outside, a Dutch diplomat demanded they identify themselves.

My escape triggered a diplomatic crisis. Du Preez reported quite a different version of what had happened: that I hadn't entered the embassy and nor had the police.[28] To my surprise, I was suddenly told I would be released. The South African government returned me to the Dutch embassy ten days later. Mo Shaik wrote that the police generals in charge of investigating Hélène and me were furious. The incident had become an embarrassment to the apartheid regime.

In 2019 CCB's imprisoned apartheid assassin Ferdi Barnard told me that he had been tasked to organise my killing in Amsterdam in 1988. The words were 'The cunt must die'. This came from the president's office. According to Barnard these kinds of actions were stopped when De Klerk took over from P.W. Botha.

I only spent 26 days as a prisoner in John Vorster Square. However, it would take nearly 26 months before I could leave the 'old' deserted embassy in Pretoria. The staff had moved two years before to a smarter part of town and two Dutch military police officers kept me company. Around the perimeter, armed riot unit policemen in plain clothes kept watch.

On 7 September 1987 I was exchanged, along with the French anti-apartheid activist Pierre-André Albertini and 133 Angolan prisoners of war in a swap for a soldier of the apartheid regime Wynand du Toit, who was imprisoned in Angola. In Arusha in December 1987 an ANC functionary (I forget his name) approached me, hugged me and said, 'Hey man, you really fucked the Boers.' The best compliment I ever received. I also liked the comment Andries Treurnicht (head of the conservative opposition) made in Parliament when we left the country: 'Good riddance to bad rubbish.' I also took it as a compliment, coming from his lips.

On that note, I feel honoured that I could take part in this huge mass struggle to end apartheid.

KLAAS DE JONGE is a social scientist and has worked in Africa and Latin America He also worked as a journalist for *De Groene Amsterdammer* and in the field of transitional justice. Klaas has three sons and lives in Amsterdam.

---

28   Holtland, Jenne Jan Holtland *De Koerier van Maputo: Een Nederlander in de Zuid-Afrikaanse Revolutie*, Podium, 2021.

FURTHER READING

Jonge, Klaas de Jonge, 'SA's fight for freedom was hard won, but some don't feel free at all', *Sunday Times*, 9 September 2020.

Klaas de Jonge, 'Two years in Pretoria: A journal'. Unpublished translation of Dagboek uit Pretoria, Van Gennep, 1987.

15

Saloojee, Smith, Andersson, Evans & Harper – The Truck Safari: 1 Trip, 1 Tonne

To DATE, THE FULL STORY of African Hinterland, or to use the correct MK name, Operation Laaitie, has not been told – except in part by those who do not know the details and scale of the successful seven-year infiltration of 40 tonnes of arms by safari without a single casualty in the years 1987–1993. Now the team directly involved in the daring operation tells the tale.

The origin of Operation Laaitie is this: the idea for the project originated with Rodney Wilkinson, who had fled South Africa after the December 1982 sabotage of the Koeberg nuclear power station. He met leading ANC official Aziz Pahad twice a month in a London pub, coming up with various ideas to transport arms – initially for a smaller convoy of vehicles. Says Rodney:

> I shared the concept of using paying tourists as a cover for cross-border sanctions-busting ... The problem faced was the ratio of weapons going into South Africa compared to the number of comrades getting arrested. Thus was born the concept of a large vehicle with a small team rather than lots of small vehicles. Less risk. It took years for me to

research, design the truck and write up the business plan for the truck and many meetings with Aziz before it was submitted to J.S. [MK chief of staff, Joe Slovo]

The reason for a Bedford was that both the British and South African armies used those vehicles, and overland tour companies could buy them cheap at state auctions so they were common and would not raise eyebrows. 'When we ordered that one ... I asked for a specially made steel drop-side body to fool the metal detectors. The military trucks had timber decks. It took me most of a year to physically adapt the truck: extra petrol tanks, extended chassis, extra spare wheel, military roof platform, compartments, underfloor lockers, personal lockers, camping gear, tools, spares, trailer, etc.'[29]

Slovo assembled a team called the London Traders, and appointed Mannie Brown, a long-time fellow exile, to manage the project along with Laurence Harris, a British comrade close to the ANC. It met many times, with Rodney, and occasionally with Aziz and Slovo.

Overall charge of the operation was given to Job Shimankana Tabane aka Cassius Make, the Ordnance chief and member of Military Headquarters. He deployed MK cadres based in Zambia to handle operations and liaise with London. Among these were Cal (MK name for Riaz Saloojee), Yasmin (Muff Andersson) and Chips (Govind Chiba). Ronald (Benno Smith), Henry (Winston Harper) and Kate (Jenny Evans) were recruited a bit later.

To maintain operational security, Cassius separated the tasks. Those he sent to London working under discipline from MK, Cal and Muff, were the link to Lusaka and the covert aspects of the operation. Others already in London dealt with the office, the finances, staff and drivers, which Mannie and Laurence did superbly. On 30 June 1986 Mannie registered Africa Hinterland as a tourist company aimed at backpackers looking for a cheap bumpy camping adventure. The office was in Greenwich, South London. Here unsuspecting customers responding to advertisements could book tickets to travel overland through Heather Newham and Jenny Harris. Backroom 'boys' in London were extremely dedicated. The young Chris Kasrils spent two years sitting in a matchbox office servicing coded calls from the drivers and enquiries for Mannie.

---

29   Rodney Wilkinson in correspondence to Muff Andersson, 19 August 2021.

Although six-weekly tours for the safari were initially booked by the Greenwich tourist office, command and control of the operation were located in Lusaka. Outside of the drivers involved in the operation, the comrades on the 'tour' side had no idea of the scale of the operation or of the operatives in Lusaka, Zimbabwe, Botswana and South Africa.

Comrades in Lusaka had to figure out the logistics around the movement of material, and further on, others were responsible for the movement of the material inside the country.

Hence those authoring this article and one or two others dealt with the covert side of Laaitie; we started in 1986 when we were young and raring to go, in our twenties and thirties. We worked from the time Cassius Make commanded it, through the period it was commanded by Aboobaker Ismail (Rashid) after the assassination of Cassius in 1987, and until it ended with the demobilisation process.

Laaitie developed faster and faster turnaround times as material was loaded not only from Lusaka but also from Bulawayo. It was an operation with multi-dimensional networks well compartmentalised to ensure security at all times.

The operation successfully tied internationalist support — including southern African – with that of MK comrades based in Lusaka, the forward areas (Zimbabwe and Botswana), and inside the country. It was efficient because it built on existing experience and infrastructure developed over the years in partnership with the internationalists who worked as drivers and internal operatives. It reflected the non-racial content of the struggle and could deliver material to MK units more tailored to their needs and more responsive to demand. We are proud that, over seven years of operation, there were no casualties or exposures.

WHY DID WE USE INTERNATIONALISTS?

Let us historicise. The period we talk about is the mid to late 1980s, post-Nkomati when Mozambique had closed up as a safe haven for MK, and there had been raids by the SADF on all of the forward areas (Swaziland, Botswana, Zimbabwe). It was increasingly difficult to move material across the border. So asking people from other countries to carry weapons across borders on behalf of the South African struggle became a very logical solution to solve this problem. Using internationalists inside the country to store and distribute weapons was a pragmatic choice. Freedom of movement for the vast majority of South Africans was inhibited. A relatively small number of white South Africans sided with the armed wing of the liberation struggle. They were hard to reach and recruit. However, we would not often use people with left-wing profiles in Ordnance as they would likely be searched. Our commander Cassius Make asked us to look for individuals who would not attract the attention or suspicion of the enemy.

People in other countries had strong views against apartheid, and they were unknown to the apartheid regime. Foreigners, particularly whites, moved relatively freely across borders as tourists and were welcomed with open arms. We met internationalists via the Anti-Apartheid Movement, Communist Party formations, student movements, disinvestment- and direct-action groups, or befriended individuals independently.

However, in talking about internationalists, we cannot forget our African brothers and sisters who helped with Laaitie. In Masvingo, where Winston and others loaded the truck once we had the Joburg Hinterland office, we used the premises of a Zimbabwean farmer. He is a former ex-combatant, who does not wish to be named. He was a contact of the late former regional Ordnance commander in Zimbabwe George Sibanda, aka Moss.

THE TRIP

Underground ANC funding paid the start-up budget for the truck and office in London, which was just under £80,000 – though this amount did not cover the costs incurred in the other regions. Rodney and Cal fine-tuned the size of the compartments so that the weapons were exceptionally well concealed and undetectable.

Tourists flew to Tanzania to board the Bedford overland vehicle, which was shipped to Mombasa in December 1986. Then would begin the long bumpy seven-week trip along sinuous roads from Nairobi to Cape Town.

The trips from Nairobi would wind through Tanzania, Malawi, Zambia and Zimbabwe, and then from Botswana to South Africa. Drivers had to entertain the passengers – the majority of whom were backpackers who had never been to Africa before – and answer their questions along the way.

Stuart Round, one of the drivers, has described the experience. He got his driver's licence weeks before the trip started:

Some days I would be driving for 18 hours, and then do routine checks and maintenance on the truck afterwards. The responsibility weighed very heavily on my shoulders; the dangers weighed on my mind. The roads were treacherous, pot-holed and narrow, there were wild animals to contend with, there was a whole catalogue of diseases to catch – all with life-threatening consequences – and southern Africa was on a war footing with armed soldiers and police checkpoints everywhere. As each day passed though, my confidence grew. Every other overland driver I came across was a source of valuable information and advice and I would pick their brains ravenously. I became familiar with the truck, its size, and handling, how the various systems on it worked, and the Bedford manual was never far from my side. Somehow, I reached Lusaka on time, in one piece and with a fairly contented full complement of passengers.[30]

In Lusaka, Zambia, the driver would tell the passengers that the truck had to be serviced at a garage but really the vehicle was being 'doctored' – loaded with weapons. While tourists visited the city of Lusaka, the MK comrades would pack the custom-made boxes of material.

Shortly after the August 1990 Pretoria Minute when armed action was suspended, Rashid had the London African Hinterland office closed, and another opened and run in Johannesburg by Menno Schreuder. For the final part of Laaitie, trips offered were only in southern Africa, no longer on the Nairobi to Cape Town stretch. African Hinterland drivers were Mike Harris and Jo Lewis (1986–1987) and Stuart Round (1986–1991), all from the UK. The Dutch Menno Schroeder and the British Roger Allingham were the final drivers for the internal office (1991–1993).

Besides Stuart's hair-raising experiences as a first-time driver, other drivers also had scary moments.

On the very first trip when Mike and Jo Lewis were the scheduled drivers, Cassius advised that the border gate officials were planning to search an orange truck with the word 'Africa' on it. The intelligence came from the Soviet embassy. Laaitie then had an orange canvas covering over the load area. We decided to proceed with an empty vehicle. Border officials searched a truck, but it was one from a Truck Africa fleet, with orange branding. Africa Hinterland sailed through.

---

30   Stuart Round, 'Safari of a special type', *The Thinker*, Vol. 58, 2013.

Another incident affected Roger Allingham and Menno Schreuder in Bulawayo. Roger went into Bulawayo to get the truck loaded [by Winston, etc]. Once this was done, he parked in central Bulawayo to buy food. Returning to the truck, Roger found it had been broken into and his passport, in a false name, and some money stolen. He and Menno reported the theft. A Bulawayo police officer produced a letter explaining the circumstances, requesting the South African authorities to assist Allingham to get back to the British consulate in Johannesburg. The pair drove on to Great Zimbabwe with the tourists. The following day at Beit Bridge crossing they convinced South African border officials that Roger was an essential driver on the trip and that some tourists had to catch flights. After some tut-tutting, the truck was allowed to proceed.

Within South Africa, after the drivers had dropped off the passengers to do their own thing, they would park the truck in a safe place and hire a closed van. Next, they would pack the boxes into the van, use prearranged stickers and fluffy toys and park the van in an agreed spot for collection by an internal operative. The operative would collect and stash the boxes until it was time to hack away at the hard earth to build a DLB to house the combination of material that had been ordered. For security reasons, it was necessary to ensure a complete break between those bringing in material, burying it, and the MK operatives using it for operations in South Africa.

This was roughly the process, albeit with variations depending on factors like security, problems faced by various comrades, and the need to alter the routes, and so on.

The boxes contained AKs, limpets and grenades. The packages were sealed in plastic and heavy tin foil, fitted into each box. The entire box could be stored easily. Why this particular choice of hardware? The contents of the boxes reflected the particular stage of our armed struggle to hit legitimate targets.

POLITICAL ISSUES

In the early part of the struggle, the targets were economic. Post the 1985 Kabwe conference, when Operation Laaitie was conceptualised, we were in a different stage of struggle. We were preparing for People's War. Operation Zikomo was launched to speed up the infiltration of MK units inside the country. The training of comrades was taking place inside the country. It was critical to provide arms to the ever-increasing numbers of self-defence units set up, as the townships in South Africa were occupied by South African Defence Force troops, and people were living permanently in a state of siege. The IFP was also working closely with the SADF, attacking hostels and communities with impunity. So the AKs were there for self-defence, limpets for armed propaganda, and grenades to attack the enemy.

In addition to that, in what was defined under apartheid as Indian and mixed race or 'coloured' areas, stooges of the regime had opted to join in with various National Party parliamentary structures – the President's Council, the House of Representatives, the House of Delegates, and urged their communities to do the same. There was a lot of resistance in these areas to show that they could not get away with dividing the black majority.

Typically, limpets and grenades were used as scare tactics in such structures. They were also used in support of various workers' strikes. Jameel Chand, the former commissar of the Ahmed Timol unit who used a tonne of weapons brought in by Operation Laaitie, recorded in his TRC application that of 40 operations, none caused loss of life or injury. There was only damage to property because the operatives were so careful. However, two members of the unit died during an operation.[31]

We in Ordnance were not necessarily privy to which operation would take place. People from other MK structures and units did these, but we communicated what was buried and where.

MODUS OPERANDI

Initially, Muff and Cal recruited and trained the internal comrades and Jenny joined in these activities once she was set up in Botswana. Cal helped Rodney with the truck specifications and scale of compartments. The late Chips was responsible for the packaging of materials together with Ronald, Abie, Douglas, Henry and Flo, among others, in Zambia and the regional side. Packing did not always go smoothly. In Zambia foam from London to spray into the boxes to keep the stuff stable turned into a sticky mess. Ronald also oversaw the team constructing the boxes; various

---

31 Prakash Napier and Yusuf Akhalwaya died when the limpet mine they were carrying prematurely detonated on the way to an operation at a goods train at Johannesburg Park station on 11 December 1989. Jameel Chand is currently writing an account of the unit in his own memoir to be published in 2022.

other comrades gave information about the traffic at the border gates. Muff, Cal and Jenny dealt with the internal comrades and establishing those units.

Chips once suggested that the team saw bits off the stabilisers on the RPG7s to fit more stuff into the boxes. The response of JM, MK commander Joe Modise, was, 'The Ruskies had a good reason for the shape and size of those stabilisers, leave them as is.'

Many different comrades transported material over borders and inside the country, kept it in safe houses, dug DLBs, buried arms, drew maps. Many others did the same. Of those who have written, James Garraway and Sue Godt worked during the era of Cassius Make. Andrea Meeson, Pierre Koster, John Spyropolous, Martha Gordon and Peter Craig were under Rashid's command. In most cases, the international comrades settled in South Africa afterwards and became permanent residents or citizens. The operation began in 1986 and terminated in 1993.

Cached materials not used were handed in to the newly established SANDF after 1994, under Defence Minister Joe Modise.

All these comrades reflected the values of MK, often at tremendous cost to themselves as individuals. These comrades were prepared to face loneliness and isolation and sacrifice their own lives to contribute to the freedom of our people. We admire them and salute them. Sadly, we cannot name all the African comrades who helped Laaitie in the same way.

For the first time in the history of MK, we were able to successfully infiltrate large quantities of arms in support of our combatants.

RIAZ SALOOJEE is now a retired brigadier general from the SANDF and until recently a CEO of defence and aerospace technology companies. Currently a strategic defence and security consultant, he lives in Johannesburg.

BENNO SMITH is retired and lives in Mtunzini, KwaZulu-Natal.

MUFF ANDERSSON is a writer and editor living in Johannesburg with Oscar Marleyn.

JENNY EVANS is now happily retired in Durban with her partner Diana.

WINSTON HARPER is a farmer and farm watch with Buffalo Protection Services for the properties in the Matatiele area, Eastern Cape.

16

James Garraway – This Is No Picnic, It's War!

As an adjunct professor of higher education at a South African university, I supervise Master's and PhD students and research improvements to the teaching and learning system. Yet as I write I feel anxiety, even now, a return of the fear of what we were doing under the noses of that regime.

It is 1984. I am filling up my Renault 5 at the Shell garage in downtown Bloemfontein (Mangaung) before the long drive back to Johannesburg. Bloemfontein is a major military town so unsurprisingly there are soldiers everywhere. It's a chilly day so I grab my hairy, green Woolworths jersey from my suitcase. As I walk around the car, I notice a shiny metal cylinder hooked onto the front of my jersey. Only half an hour previously I had been feverishly digging a hole up on Naval Hill, concealed under a thicket of bushes, and burying two AK47s, two Makarov pistols, two limpet mines, spare magazines and eight grenades. The shiny attachment was a grenade detonator which had somehow latched onto my clothes.

The night before I'd been staying at my friends' house, Dick and Gay, having supper, drinking wine, listening to music, singing and waiting (unsuccessfully) for them to go to bed so I could transfer the weapons from my car doors to a holdall for burial as a cache the next day (digging and waiting turned to be a dominant theme of my ANC work). Every time

I snuck out to the car loud singing forced me back inside, and only in the small hours was this transfer possible.

How did I get to have arms in my car doors and a detonator on my jersey (if it had fallen off and detonated would that have been the end of my underground career)?

The story starts in 1981, when a group of teachers moved from Johannesburg to Gaborone, Botswana, to teach at the local high school Maru-a-Pula (MAP). I was British then, having emigrated with my parents 13 years previously. MAP was a non-racial alternative to apartheid schooling in South Africa. For three years I was the biology teacher.

Gaborone was a thrilling experience, a melting pot of different nationalities – Russian, Libyan and Swedish diplomats – and a haven for some of the best of South African music since exiles Jonas Gwanga and Hugh Masekela performed alternatively almost every weekend.

We met and spoke to South African exiles at parties about the injustices and horror of life for the majority of black South Africans, and the possibilities for a newer, brighter, more democratic future – discussions not possible within the restrictive structures and culture of apartheid South Africa. I invited South African exiles to talk to my students. One such person was Muff Andersson, who became part of my circle of friends.

Later in 1983, when I decided to return from Botswana to South Africa, Muff approached me to carry ANC cultural materials across the border to South Africa. With some trepidation I agreed. Carrying anything across the border for the ANC was extremely dangerous. Lots of discussion ensued. Before I knew it, I was carrying a different sort of *magazine*.

The night before departure, I parked my car at a close-by restaurant for packing to avoid detection at the South African border crossing. When I retrieved my car and felt under the door lining it was hard. My car (then a Renault 9) resembled a mobile second-hand furniture store, with a cupboard and two chairs on the roof, my hi-fi, gas stove and dismembered bed, carpets, clothes, kitchenware and everything else inside. There was a small nook for me, the driver.

Without any fuss, I was waved through the border, past the South African military machine gun nest and on to Mahikeng.

The plan was that I would drive to Johannesburg (4–5 hours away), offload the furniture and park at a predetermined spot to be picked up by

MK. To my shame, I was so relieved to have made it across the border that I stopped to visit a friend in Mahikeng, and after large amounts of wine and whisky failed to make my assignation in Joburg on the dot.

So there I was in Johannesburg in a state of emergency with a carload of weapons. Not long after, I was summoned back across the border, and given brief training on timekeeping, sobriety on the job, concealment, counter surveillance and coding, and then sent to Bloemfontein. (Bloemfontein seemed to be generally where you were sent for poor behaviour – the friends I stayed with had been sent there from Durban to work on the local newspaper after puffing something they should not have.)

During this time I worked at the South African Council for Higher Education in Johannesburg, writing science materials for part-time, black matric students and was asked to perform one or two other jobs for MK.

In 1986 MK Ordnance needed an additional hand in the south of the country. After some more training in Zimbabwe, and without much resistance, I relocated to what is one of the most dramatically beautiful cities in the world (if you live in the right part of it), a city of the outdoors, picnicking, cycling and camping. I became an operative in the deeply secret, large-scale and very successful arms smuggling initiative of MK's African Hinterland Project.

It is around 10:45 on a weekday morning, the site is the busy parking lot behind Checkers supermarket in the largely white, middle-class suburb of Claremont in Cape Town. I am cycling around the parking lot.

I spot the panel van with the required bumper sticker 'surf's up!'. It's important that I don't arrive too early. I must not meet those delivering the van, a measure of security in case either party is picked up. It is necessary to do one more, relaxed, ambling circuit, to check if there is something hanging from the rear-view mirror.

If it is a red devil, it is all clear and I can go ahead; if no red devil, get out of there quickly and disappear. It's all OK. I chain my cycle to a tree, reach under the van's back fender for the magnetic key case, open up and I am off!

In the back of the van are eight boxes, each about 1x0.75 metres, weighing about 30 kilograms, covered by blankets (I still have one, much appreciated in the cold Cape Town winters). Each box contains AKs, pistols, grenades, limpet mines and ammunition.

Two weeks or so earlier, somewhere in Lusaka, MK comrades packed these boxes and loaded them into compartments in Africa Hinterland's large touring Bedford. The courageous driver had transferred boxes of weapons to the panel van and I was collecting the van.

After lots of twists and turns to check if I am being followed (it probably would have been quite easy to follow me), I head to the garage I have hired in an adjoining suburb. It's a tight squeeze but I heft the boxes out and hide them behind the old furniture cramming the space, then return the van.

Now to distribute the arms to MK operatives in the Western Cape. Once a month I search for a suitable secluded spot with nearby cover of dense bushes along the scenic passes of Du Toit's and Bains Kloof, Chapmans Peak Drive or alongside Cape Point Nature Reserve. I return to load the boxes covered with camping gear, a picnic table and chairs, cooler box, folding spade with saw-edge (critical). On top is my bicycle (extremely useful in my underground work). This is after all Cape Town, where outdoor activities are de rigueur.

At the chosen picnic site I set out my bottle of wine, gas stove for tea, plates and food and my novel. When I am sure I am alone I rapidly dig a metre square 50-centimetre-deep hole, grab a box or two from my car, drag them to the hole and bury them. I mark the spot with nails on nearby trees or a splash of paint on a rock on top of the cache. It is never easy. There are always rocks in the way or tree roots to cut away. I pack up and head home to send the cache location in book code to my commanders.

Digging approximately 21 arms caches around Cape Town in 1987–1990 was exhausting and scary. Twice I remained motionless and waited next to a large hole and pile of weapons as people suddenly appeared. Once the then feared South African Police stopped next to my car and peered through the bushes in my direction as I nervously clutched my Swiss Army Knife and a toilet roll. (Hint: what the hole could be for.)

In Zimbabwe MK operatives modified the boot of my Renault 5, creating a secret compartment for AKs, pistols and other weaponry. I felt more secure driving around and safely delivered a load to KwaZulu-Natal.

I was hitched up with a Canadian comrade who accompanied me on arms collection runs. This felt so much safer. With the moves towards a political solution to South Africa's low-level civil war, we were asked to stand down and consolidate our weapons caches into one site. MK sent us a builder and the three of us constructed a false wall at the end of a garden cottage, creating a secret storeroom. To gain access we smashed a hole through the foundations which led into a 10-metre underground tunnel, supported with a wooden frame and opening with a trapdoor in the nearby vegetable garden – claustrophobic. Our consolidated cache contained approximately 80 AK47s and pistols, hundreds of limpet mines and grenades, light machine guns, anti-armour weapons (RPGs), piles of TNT and thousands of rounds of ammunition.

With integration our final waiting was over, and my Canadian comrade facilitated the handover of the cache back into a Bedford lorry. This time it held no Australian tourists and belonged to the SANDF, as part of the peace deal. No more waiting! No more digging!

JAMES GARRAWAY walks the Cape Town reserves and mountains with his dogs, cycles country Karoo roads with his friends and kayaks to appreciate the beauty of the coastline and the underwater kelp forests. In his spare time he also supervises students and thinks about what would make a better, future university. (He is an adjunct professor at the Cape Peninsula University of Technology.)

Editor's note: James Garraway was the first internal operative with Operation Laaitie (trading as Africa Hinterland). Under the command of Cassius Make the boxes of weapons were buried whole. Under Rashid operatives were instructed to break up or burn the boxes and bury the contents without them.

17

Pierre Koster – Of Fish Eagles and DLBs

I WAS RECRUITED INTO the MK underground in 1987, at half past one on a sunny June afternoon.

I grew up in an Amsterdam working-class communist nest, as they used to say. During my teenage years, the family home was a distribution point for *De Waarheid* ('Truth'), the daily newspaper of the Dutch communist party, the flat often being visited by comrades and other friends. I cut my political teeth in the Dutch Young Communist League and other progressive political mass movements.

Young progressive people – as is their responsibility – stood up and became radicalised in the political turbulence of 1970s and 1980s Western Europe. Naturally, I was one of them. And the politicised youth had a rich legacy to draw on: we could be proud of our history of anti-fascism and anti-racism, our steadfast solidarity with the anti-colonial and anti-imperialist struggles of the oppressed all over the world.

In my teens and twenties, I found myself surrounded by quiet giants, quite a few of whom I knew personally as comrades of my parents and my family, like Karel van Dillen, one of many comrades who, in the mid-1930s, joined the anti-fascist International Brigades, fighting fascism in Franco's Spain.

Elske and Jo de Smit were Party branch members as well, and neighbours. Jo also fought in Spain. Elske, a small, gentle woman with a fierce spirit, was part of the communist armed underground resistance during the Second World War. Her underground work, like that of many brave men and women in occupied Holland, kept alive the spirit of anti-fascism and resistance. Unlike many others, Elske accepted the responsibility of executing Dutch Nazi collaborators and plain traitors.

And after the war, the anti-colonial struggle bred quiet heroes like Ratio Koster – whom I knew – Piet ('Pitojo') van Staveren and many others, young workers who refused enlisted military service in the bloody oppression of the struggle for national liberation of what was then the Dutch East Indies, Indonesia. In my youth I learnt to swim in politicised waters.

On that afternoon in 1987 the front door bell of our squat in Amsterdam rang. Looking out, I recognised my old acquaintance F, an activist in the Dutch Anti-Apartheid Movement. We talked and I was recruited into the Umkhonto we Sizwe underground before sundowners.

I was in a relationship at the time with a fellow activist whom I shall call Naomi, at her request. Naomi decided to join me in the new struggle. The tone of my life was set.

After setting up a shaky 'legend' (plausible cover story) for friends and family and a minimum of practical preparations for our potential life-threatening underground work, our recruiters booked us in the smoking section of a Luxavia jetliner, and sent us on our way to South Africa, where just the year before, a second state of emergency had been declared.

Our contact in Gaborone, Botswana, was Kate (Jenny Evans), a great, brave and compassionate comrade full of strength and fun. True comradeship, political and philosophical, can only be tested and proven in the active struggle.

At the core is the unit, it is everything and *alles*. There was nothing beyond the unit. No names, no faces, no connections. It is a safety thing of course. When the unit functions, the operation works. And under Kate's wings, politically and military, we started our mission for real in the MK underground.

We were based in Gaborone, Botswana. The mission was clear and daunting: we were to smuggle arms and ammunition across South Africa's borders, in a specially modified vehicle, and drive 1200 kilometres to our operational terrain, the Eastern Cape.

The modus operandi: two ignorant tourists having a picnic next to the road, blanket spread out, food at hand. When the road was deserted, we would open the DLB – the hiding space – in the car, pack the weaponry brought in with sports bags and carry these into the bush, then start digging. In rock hard Eastern Cape soil. With our little camper's fold-up spade. While what we really needed were explosives or a full *bakkie sakkie*. Or the NUM. But eventually we managed.

We would make and encrypt maps and return to Gabs. The arms caches would later be retrieved by underground MK units *in situ*. Nerve wracking, but the first trips went well.

Two events caused our unit to change the mode of operation.

On our third mission, after passing the border at Ramatlabama into the puppet Bantustan of Bophuthatswana, we ran straight into a huge roadblock. Unshaven, aggressive 250-pound khaki-clad white gorillas, shoulders and hips hung with guns and ammunition belts, looked set to start tearing us apart limb by limb. They were backed up by black soldiers in armoured vehicles, equally vicious looking, with mounted machine guns aiming at our poor Nissan.

The car was subjected to a thorough search, but they didn't find the DLB.

Later we learnt that we had made the acquaintance of the combined Koevoet and 32nd Batallions, freshly withdrawn from the Namibian occupation war.

We were renting accommodation in the desert-edge village of Molepolole, outside Gaborone.

But after the 1985 and 1986 SADF raids on Gabs in which 15 people were killed, the Batswana became suspicious about two whites hanging around, outside their capital. On a late summer morning we were raided by Botswana's finest. Police, Security Police, Special Branch, Military Police, Customs. There was nothing to find, but from both incidents it was clear that the unit needed to change tactics. Naomi and I then proposed to work from inside the country, South Africa. We rented a house in Port Elizabeth. As a cover and to get us visas, I enrolled in the university, leaving us plenty of time to do reconnaissance and the actual drops.

Operational procedures were now as follows: at a pre-arranged time and place we pick up a van, loaded with 30 steel-plated boxes of arms and ammunitions. Each box contained AKs, hand grenades, limpet mines, mini-limpets, detonators and hand guns with their ammo clips. Sufficient to establish one arms cache, to equip one underground MK unit. We unpacked these boxes and then hid the arsenal behind a false wall that I had built in the attic. We took the boxes apart and carefully disposed of them, as they could form a link to their source, Operation Laaitie, the Hinterland truck safari.

Loaded with camping gear and our picnic stuff, off we went to recce potential sites all over the Eastern Cape. Those Cape dirt roads hold no secrets for me, or surprises, I've driven them all, or so it seems, and dreamed about them all, for years and years and years. Between March to October 1988 we established 30 arms caches in our operational area. When we were done, we asked and pleaded for another truckload.

We had to be well aware and prepared, politically and psychologically, to be active in those rural areas. Never to let your guard down. Always to be that other *persona*. Farmers in those days were all part of the paramilitary local commando networks. These were part of the apartheid regime's apparatus to maintain military and political control over the rural areas and, as such, they were legitimate targets, and they knew it. Maybe it was death-defying audacity and a certain 'What's the problem, come, let's get on with it!' And maybe it was just blind luck. But we never ran into trouble during those drops. Not once.

There were scores of them, those holes in the ground. Many of them around Port Elizabeth, many near Grahamstown and Port Alfred. Then there were Cape St Francis, Sedgefield, the beach at Keurboomsrivier, Stormsriviermond and Van Stadens River Mouth; Knysna and George in the Tsitsjkammaberge and Outeniquaberge; Riversdale, even as far as Bredasdorp in the shadows of the Overberg and Prince Albert and the Swartbergpas and Schoemanspoort in the Groot Swartberge. We dropped in Middelburg, near Molteno and Dordrecht, and in the area of Noupoort and Steynsburg.

Steynsburg was an evening drop. On a dead-quiet winter evening we parked the car next to the road and set out our trusty picnic blanket with gas stove, food and blankets, tent at our feet, apparently ready – for the observant passer-by – to do some ill-advised by-the-road camping. Fields ran off to ranges of low grassy mountains and on the other side of the road the blades of a wind pump croaked their complaints to the dry skies.

As dusk fell and the already sparse traffic dwindled, we started preparing the drop. With one of us on the look-out, the other unscrewed the bolts that secured the DLB in the car. Night falls quickly in the Eastern Cape, more so in winter, and we moved fast. The sealed arms and ammunition were quickly loaded in sports bags, waiting to be moved to the hole being dug. It was quiet there at night, in the Suurberge (Sour Mountains). While Naomi was finishing the DLB hole behind bushes off the road, I stood guard next to the car, a loaded rapid-fire Soviet-made Stechkin automatic pistol at the ready. Then, footsteps on the road! In a normal sounding voice, I loudly asked Naomi: 'Do you need more tissue paper?', our arranged warning sign for her to stop making noise. It gave an embarrassing but legitimate reason to be behind the bushes. The footsteps approached and as I prepared myself to employ the gun, a black farm worker walked by on the side of the road, looked at the bizarre scene in front of him, mumbled a greeting and, obviously bewildered, hurried on his way. We finished the drop quickly, having decided to bury the hand gun with the rest. I really didn't want to be caught carrying a gun anyway and pointing a gun at innocent workers was just not me. Having closed off and camouflaged the DLB we would code name 'Windmill', we left the scene quickly, driving too fast, adrenaline and nerves pumping. We camped that night far away from the drop zone.

Once every so often there was the planned 'vacation'. In the late spring of 1988 we travelled to Gabs for our scheduled meeting with the unit – Kate our handler, Rashid (Aboobaker Ismail) the political commissar and Alex (Benno Smith) the technician – for a debriefing and some R&R time. But there were issues.

The violence and pain of apartheid did not – and could not – stay in the townships: the war was brought to the whites, with a vengeance. One of the recommendations of the 1985 ANC Kabwe conference, in exile in Zambia, read that 'We should shift the struggle from the black ghettoes into the white areas'.

Daytime attacks on apartheid's security forces were planned and executed, with recruitment offices, personnel transport, cafés and recreation centres frequented by soldiers and police the target of grenade attacks. But then some cadres started blowing up Wimpy restaurants with limpet mines. The attacks caused shock and uproar, as was the intention. But many of the casualties were black workers and other civilians. Something had changed. Back in Gaborone, we put it to our unit: if the Wimpy attacks and other attacks on civilian targets didn't stop, then we refused to continue the mission. Technically, this was refusing to take orders and insubordination in a war-time situation. We could have been severely disciplined for this, but we stood our ground. And our unit stood with us. We were not the only ones: voices from the underground rang out with the same appeal to MK High Command – Stop the Wimpy attacks! They are counter-revolutionary! And Military Command listened to its cadres: they did stop.[32]

And so, we continued with our drops. From late summer 1989 until September of that year, we dispatched another truckload of 30 boxes, all over the Eastern Cape, reaching outwards further and further from our base. Longer on the road meant more risk.

You don't get used to life in the underground. You shouldn't. Because if you do, then that could be fatal. High alert all the time. Every step you take must be considered being under observation, every innocent action being scrutinised by suspicious eyes, every telephone call considered reaching listening ears. Every newspaper you buy being recorded. Why is that car parked in that driveway two houses down? How often have I seen it in this neighbourhood? And aren't there too many delivery vans coming down this quiet road in which we live? Memorising number plates. Paranoia and suspicion feed on themselves. Just like depression. The life we lived was a life of isolation and stress. We made the occasional phone call to family in the Netherlands from a clean tickey box,[33] a call in which nothing could be said apart from the bare, bland formalities.

Over time, we had secreted an estimated 3000 kilograms of arms and ammunition in the attic. Sixty arms caches. We travelled thousands of miles in enemy territory in a car packed with weaponry. Obviously, we couldn't sustain this in the long run, and it was decided that at the end of

---

32   Editor's note: This was never ANC policy but misinterpretation by some units within the country of 'taking the armed struggle into white areas'.

33   Tickey was a South African 2.5-cent coin originally used in call boxes and the name stuck even when the coin went out of circulation.

1989 we were going to be pulled out.

For me, leaving South Africa was painful. I had fallen in love with the beautiful Eastern Cape and its history, its lessons from aloes and the legacy of Sizwe Banzi and the Cradock Four, with the mountains and the fish eagles and the dirt roads, the quiet in my soul that I experienced there. And I couldn't handle the idea of retreating while we were advancing, of leaving my comrades, of no longer being involved.

And returning to the Netherlands was alienating. There was no debriefing from our former recruiters, no psychological support, no political connecting. The hole was deep, and I was too close to the edge.

As it turned out, Naomi had made the decision to call it 'Finish en klaar'. I respected her decision, but I could not 'come out of the bush', as they say. My story had not finished. Without being part of the South African struggle I was in danger of losing my soul. I put my case before my former recruiters and pleaded to continue my underground work.

The next year, in October 1990, against the advice of some of my most trusted friends and comrades, I was back in South Africa as part of Operation Vula. I worked in Vula for almost three years, with great comrades, until August 1993. But that is another story.

PIERRE KOSTER now lives in Mpumalanga with his South African wife. He is a woodworker, who regularly hits nails on the head.

18

Gordon, Godt & Craig – Crossing Borders

ONE MORNING IN 1989 we were driven blindfolded in separate vehicles through suburban Harare. In the cool air you could smell the plants and trees as the car wove to an unknown safe house. We were meeting for the first time as a Canadian trio to plan what would be several missions from Zimbabwe into South Africa over the next two years, under the command of Muff Andersson and Riaz 'Cal' Saloojee.

Though from different cities, we had an immediate bond of a shared history and references, and our shared commitment to internationalism – united in doing our utmost to support the liberation of South Africa and our MK comrades. Our mission was to transport and clandestinely bury arms and other materials inside South Africa. Our cover lives were university student, educator and NGO worker. We were in our twenties and thirties. Our 'legends' were real, we enjoyed and were committed to our everyday work, while leading a double life. Our aim was not to get caught and to keep our cover stories intact.

Zimbabwe, a frontline state, was on high alert with several assassinations by the apartheid regime. There were numerous MK operatives there, as well as would-be infiltrators, mercenaries and diverse intelligence services. We were forbidden to associate with comrades and asked to keep low profiles.

So we moved in liberal circles, making friends carefully while trying to have semi-normal lives.

Back at the safe house, over fresh bread, cheese, fruit and nuts, washed down with Mazowe orange cordial, we scrutinised maps before setting out the next morning. In the late 1980s communication technology was very basic. Most of our maps were purchased at CNA stationery shops; typical road atlases with at least reliable details of secondary roads and topography.

The Bantam bakkie had a hidden compartment built behind the seat, and was fully packed with various guns, explosives and ammunition. The loose weapons were individually sealed with special foil paper and tape to prevent dogs from sniffing them out at the Messina border post. Or so we hoped!

From Harare to Johannesburg was a 14-hour journey, via Masvingo and the lowveld, where we crossed the border along with freight trucks, hawkers, holiday makers and others at Beitbridge. The Limpopo, the second largest river in South Africa, nourishes a semi-arid landscape, with wildlife as likely to cross the road as local villagers. With the vehicle laden with arms, Beitbridge itself was one of the most dangerous points on the mission.

It was always stressful when border security commanded the German Shepherds to sniff the vehicle in the border post parking lot. Muff and Sue had trained Martha and Peter individually and meticulously in secret work, including staying focused and keeping calm under pressure. So we'd go through the Zimbabwe border, get the exit stamps, drive across the no man's land as you cross the bridge, see the rigid order on the South African side ... then when we finally saw the baobabs, we were clear and we would holler with relief, a few delicious stress-free minutes.

Sue stayed in Harare. She was our command node and it was critical to check in with her at precise moments on the trip. Should something go wrong, she took action back at base. She worked closely with Muff and Cal, providing regional support. She met, oriented, recruited, trained and supported other internationalists, particularly Canadians, as they arrived, and managed, stored and moved weapons within Zimbabwe.

Martha and Peter each had a few solo missions under their belts, so it was a relief to work as a team inside South Africa. With a new set of legends for being in South Africa, we were for all intents and purposes now a typical, innocent-looking, white couple on holiday in their bakkie.

We practised how to open and close the secret compartment quickly so that we could operate under pressure. It was usually a seven-day round trip to the destination area, reconnoitre and plan digging places, and return. Some missions required 24 hours driving non-stop, constantly swapping drivers. Drops were usually at night, which meant day reconnaissance, then night reconnaissance and then the drop. Sometimes there were smaller DLB drops besides the main one the same evening.

As neither Peter nor Martha had lived in South Africa, every mission required learning about geography, highways and byways, and as South Africa was designed with apartheid as its main logic, it meant white people would only be seen in white areas, whereas drops had to be accessible to people of colour. It was important not to rush or to become too exhausted as that was when mistakes were made.

Peter was good in working out the phases of the moon. A full moon meant we could be spotted, and a small moon meant it would be too dark to dig without a flashlight. Cloudy or rainy weather was another challenge.

We used a lay-by picnic spot at the side of the road in the rural or semi-rural area accessible for anyone to stop. We would try to find a secondary road, not too far from a highway or town, remote enough that we would not attract attention. Around Johannesburg was more complicated, and we had some tricky times near Kliptown.

A site must not be too busy or close to farm buildings or settlements. The highveld soil was extremely hard and stony so we pretended to be having a romantic picnic and put out the blanket, basket and food and took turns digging with the pick and shovel while the other comrade was on watch. Sometimes it took one hour to dig 5 centimetres.

Once the hole was 2 metres deep, we opened the vehicle compartment, took out the 'goods' and buried the lot while remembering and measuring the exact location. This was the most vulnerable point as if anyone came then we would be caught red-handed. Of course, we had lots of stories in case someone surprised us – we were burying a dead animal we accidentally hit on the road, etc. If we got caught, we would likely be tortured, and it would put the whole team at risk. We had to maintain impeccable vigilance.

Martha usually wore a dainty dress in the day time, like any rural

Afrikaans lass. Peter wore shorts and long socks, and typically sported a pair of veldskoens. For good measure, he sometimes tucked a comb in his sock. At night Martha had on black slacks and a shirt and somehow found the strength in her slight frame to carry hefty bags of weapons up a hill, dig holes, clean up and get out of there.

One close call was during a drop one night south of Johannesburg, when a police bakkie drove slowly by. Peter and Martha leapt into a passionate embrace on the front seat of the bakkie, fogging up the windows. The police vehicle cruised on by.

Before a mission, we went over the legends, addresses to use and biographies to repeat. Peter had devised coded greetings and messages to say when we called Sue Godt from pay phones at prearranged times, to let her know our progress. It was so wonderful to hear her voice.

On one return trip back in what is now Limpopo province, there was no working pay phone in the entire little town. Out of desperation we broke the rules and went to an old hotel and used the reception phone. We later received a severe ticking off by Cal.

We made our commitment to MK and the liberation of South Africa without a time limit, without an idea when things might change. Before we knew it, Mandela was released. By 1991 we relocated to South Africa to be part of different units – Peter to Cape Town and Martha to Johannesburg where they remained active in clandestine ordnance and reconnaissance work. The missions were now more dangerous and involved keeping safe houses, and car and truck swapping during one of the most violent times in our history.

Africa Hinterland – Operation Laaitie, the Joburg view

In January 1991 Martha had to get both employment and a garden cottage with a separate entrance and lock-up driveway out of view of the owner or neighbours – a tall order. She found an ideal cottage on a quiet street in Parkhurst suburb. It was a renovated former servant's room at the end of a car park big enough for one vehicle. The front door led to a tiny open-plan lounge and kitchen, with an interleading (locking) door to a small bedroom and bathroom. The bedroom window looked over the owner's courtyard full of plants and trees.

This suburban bedroom became an armoury so full at times that

Martha had to stack the wood framed arms boxes with metal sides under her bed in 10x2 columns. These lifted her mattress so high she had to use a step to get on the mattress to go to sleep. The built-in cupboard could fit six boxes, but they were so heavy they eventually broke the bottom. Martha had a blue metal trunk full of individual pieces locked with a padlock. It took hours at night to unscrew the metal sides of the boxes to open the sealed packets which had to be opened and sorted depending on the order and put into sports bags ready for delivery either in a DLB or boot of cars swapped at mall parking lots in Gauteng or KZN. The bedroom sometimes reeked of oil and weapons so much that Martha regularly burned incense to try to cover it up. To this day the smell of incense makes her nauseous.

She had no clue where the boxes came from. Every so often she had to rent a panel van and leave it in a parking lot at a given time and place with a bumper sticker on the rear in the required colours and an agreed keychain on the rear-view mirror. She also bought a lot of blankets and left them in the back. A few hours later she would collect the van full of 30 boxes covered with blankets to take back to her cottage, which required the help of her new unit commander to unload. She would return the car to the rental on the other side of town.

Once she had to collect a BMW from Eastgate parking lot, drive it home, load the boot with a bag and return it to Eastgate and disappear back to work. Once, however, when she went to collect the BMW it was not there. Her heart skipped a few beats when she spotted police hiding behind a pylon. She rushed back to work and there was a message that the mission had been aborted due to a security risk.

Her first trip to KZN was in a bakkie that had no driver's window but a piece of taped plastic which made such a racket the whole trip. It was going to be a tight squeeze to get there in time. The bakkie was to be left at a parking lot near the beach. She reconnoitred the place, and two policemen were having refreshments at the canteen. She drove around and returned, found them gone. She parked and tried to put the car key near the front wheel with Prestik as instructed, but it would not stick. Sweating profusely under a wig, she heard a voice over her shoulder 'Just leave the keys in the car'. We discovered later it was Jeff Radebe.

Forbidden to ever make contact with any comrade let alone have a conversation for security reasons, she simply said 'OK' and left the keys and dashed off.

We were immersed in South African life with politics swirling around us. We all felt committed and attached to South Africa and its destiny. In Zimbabwe, it was relatively easy to keep out of political issues and networks. Inside South Africa it was very different. Everything was political during the transition period. South Africans were often quite vocal about their political alliances and if you did not declare your allegiance, you were often considered suspect or at least an outsider. We all settled permanently in South Africa, became citizens and remained committed to the NGO and civil society movements building the new democracy. It was a transition for us as much as for the country. One type of struggle transformed into new commitments. We moved from fighting for democracy to actively working on its development and understanding.

Those years as a unit were turning points for the three of us as it was an honour to be called and to serve the ANC as internationalists, doing dangerous work to support the liberation movement (and South Africans as a whole) in ways it directed. Race was always an element of our experience. Given that racism was so dominant in apartheid South Africa, the MK leadership recognised that white foreigners would be able to do the work that many were not in a position to do. We too could see that despite our accents and our foreign passports, our skin colour would facilitate our work. This only committed us further to helping build a truly non-racial, non-sexist, democratic country where everyone can enjoy equal opportunities and human rights.

We also realised that our work with MK was very different from international solidarity work (which could be energising, dynamic, out in the open) compared to secret lives, false identities and all that goes with that. Both were needed. But moving from solidarity to MK was a process of becoming an internationalist rather than a supporter in solidarity. This brought a profound internal change and devotion to the cause and to our international and South African comrades – whom we would die for.

This brings many lessons for today's struggles – it is a new era with the impact of 30–40 years of neoliberalism which has undermined concepts of social solidarity and increased further the precariousness of people's lives. There is so much work to be done in the fields of peace and justice. Whether it is world health, global warming, human rights or anti-poverty campaigns, international solidarity and internationalism have a major role to play in our present and future for South Africa, Africa and the world. In writing this, we all felt that it might speak to a new generation about not standing on the sidelines of world events, but being a change agent oneself, not doing this alone but as part of a team, part of a movement, part of a vision of a more just and respectful world.

Martha Helen Gordon spent most of her professional life in various media, educational and health organisations and is now a full-time Anglican priest in Johannesburg.

Sue Marie Godt became a citizen of South Africa, married and raised two children. She worked in development for the past 30 years and is now engaged in development advocacy.

Peter Craig is a recluse in Cape Town, currently writing a memoir.

19

Andrea Meeson – In Each of Us Lives a Revolutionary, a Fighter for Better

I WAS BORN AND RAISED in Toronto, in a house full of art, literature, theatre and conflict. Mine was not a radical political upbringing, but I grew up among people who were curious, conscious of the world around them, social democrats who exposed me to like-minded people and ideas. From the age of 12, I developed a fractious relationship with my parents, whose childhood traumas played out in front of me and my siblings, while they insisted there was always someone worse off. At age 16, I left the family home.

I finished secondary school in the late 1970s and chose to travel – first in Brazil, where the disparities of wealth spill over every street corner, along every beach front from Recife to São Paulo – and then alone in and out Guatemala, at a time of intense repression aimed primarily at indigenous people. Even from the periphery, and in the relative safety of my skin, the violent injustices of a military junta were palpable. I returned to Canada and, despite the distance, the impact followed. I became involved in Latin American solidarity, as well as feminist struggles.

My introduction to the ANC was through my friendship and work at York University with a Rwandan graduate student, who convinced me to join him in the leadership of the Anti-Apartheid Committee to campaign mainly on Boycott Divestment Sanctions issues. A longer story is my meeting the late JoJo Saloojee, then ANC rep in Toronto, and being recruited to join an MK Ordnance unit in southern Africa. In a nutshell, I was attracted to the practical aspect of the work and quite happy to be considered a potential recruit for it. My friends at the time were students immersed in revolutionary political theory – the works of Marx and Fanon. I struggled to articulate and hold my own in these spaces, so the opportunity to do hands-on work in underground structures seemed potentially a good fit for me. Moreover, I was a young, white woman with no responsibilities to family, no obvious or overt connections to radical movements in Canada, and very comfortable operating independently. I was told I could make an important contribution. Within six months of meeting JoJo, I committed to leaving Canada again, this time indefinitely.

I arrived in Gaborone, Botswana, after a week of briefing and training in London, and settled into a routine under the command of the remarkable Comrade Kate (Jenny Evans), who ran the Ordnance cell that I was now attached to. I soon secured a full-time teaching job at a local private school, with no qualifications and no proof of any required. This gives you some idea of the ease with which white expatriates lived and operated at the time in countries like Botswana.

The teaching job and engaging in the social activities of a white expatriate community became my cover, my legend, the foundation of my overt persona. Living the legend was living a lie, something my furtive imagination from childhood made easy; maintaining strict and often complicated security protocols with regards to my house and personal life was a more difficult job. Meanwhile, my covert persona was immersed in a laundry list of tasks, among them:

- regular reconnaissance in South Africa: identifying appropriate dead letter box (DLB) sites where I would eventually bury arms caches
- storage and preparation of military hardware
- crossing highly militarised borders in a vehicle full of weapons
- assessing security situations wherever I found myself
- driving in militarised zones/through military checkpoints
- developing legends: plausible reasons why a young, white woman would be travelling alone at any time of the day or night, often in isolated areas

- digging DLBs – sometimes in broad daylight and often in the middle of the night
- recording coordinates and other specifics of caches/DLBs
- coding maps of DLB locations for dispatch to operational units
- meeting tight communication deadlines/being precise
- returning to 'overt persona' activities – the day-to-day deceit

All of the above was on rinse and repeat for seven years and resulted in 38 successful drops. Thirty-five of them I completed as a solo operative. However, the success of all missions was dependent on a team of people, dedicated comrades who lived in extremely difficult circumstances in frontline areas/communities. Each of us was a vital part of the machinery that drove the mission. One didn't happen without the other.

Comradeship, particularly the times of coming together to do the work – to prepare me to travel, to welcome me back – were critical to keeping me going, to helping me to maintain discipline. Comradeship also offered some reprieve from the schizophrenic-like existence that is inherent to this kind of work. There is a persona/lifestyle that is ever parallel, ever-present, yet hidden, revealed to no one. It takes a lot of mental energy to control that environment, and it is a life that can mess with your head over time. I was a successful solo operative, but on reflection, it took some toll on my mental health.

I recall a night 'drop' when I slammed the digging pick into a finger, breaking it badly. I completed the DLB in intense pain, the finger needing medical attention. The then JG Strydom Hospital was around the corner from my house [in Johannesburg], but I was riddled with anxiety that a doctor would take one look at my finger and expose my story of being clumsy with a heavy skillet for the lie that it was. There was no one to talk me out of this deluded thinking, so a slightly warped pinky finger remains a war wound. In considering acts of solidarity, recall and celebrate the courage of people who fought, and continue to fight for social justice, but let's not accept this as the status quo that we 'hashtag' into the future. The life of struggle, and in the struggle, is not romantic. It is detrimental to the wellbeing of individuals and communities. It is exhausting and contributes to intergenerational trauma, as is evident in South Africa, in Canada, in Palestine and other countries that have long histories of colonial violence.

Solidarity, in my mind, begins with examining, through a critical lens, your history. If you are white and of European decent identify and challenge our history, the ways it contributes to blatant injustice, beyond borders and also just outside our front doors. I was raised with little awareness of Canada's contribution to the foundations of apartheid and the horrific legacies of genocide committed against indigenous peoples, who died violently on the stolen land I grew up and still live on. Understand how insidious colonial violence is. Connect the dots to its universal reach. We all have to do this consciously to live principled lives.

Understand and accept your limits because everyone has them. Arenas of struggle have evolved and so have the threats. There are many ways to work for change: decide what you are able to contribute/sacrifice and commit to it. In each of us lives a revolutionary, a fighter for better.

Do solidarity well, do it collaboratively, do it as an ally, not with a need to be in the spotlight, to have the most likes on Facebook, or retweets on Twitter. Share your experiences, but also know when to put down the microphone, stand back and listen.

This is an edited version of a presentation for 'Solidarity in practice. Memories of international recruits on undercover missions in the fight against apartheid,' a webinar exchange hosted by the University of Vienna and the Documentation and Cooperation Centre Southern Africa (SADOCC), Vienna, 1 June 2021.

ANDREA MEESON is a freelance editor and administrator currently based in Toronto, Canada.

20

John Spyropolous – The Adventures of a Wandering Greek

I WRITE THIS STORY as a contribution to a particular period of our history, and to share anecdotes of members of the 'international brigade' I worked with.

The period is post-1990 to April 1993, during the suspension of armed struggle following the Pretoria Minute in August 1990, the signing of the Peace Accord a year later and the start of constitutional negotiations at the end of 1991. Our war was raging against the Nationalist government and its proxies, Inkatha. I will tell the story in brief.

I'm the son of immigrant Egyptian Greek parents who arrived in Yeoville in 1963 with two suitcases and no money. My father worked as a carpenter for Roberts construction and my mother was a seamstress for Greek and Jewish ladies in Yeoville.

After going to school at Yeoville Boys and King Edward VII School and managing to get a rugby bursary for the first year at Wits, I completed a degree in construction management and as a result of a reluctance to go to the army I ended up in Botswana.

I started my journey with the ANC accidently, over a braai grid and a shared bottle of brandy with the late Marius Schoon in Kanye, Botswana, in 1981. I carried messages and boxes of *African Communist* and *Mayibuye* for him to South Africa several times between 1981 and 1983. I felt liberated, on the side of justice. My wife and I went to Zimbabwe early in 1986.

Soon after arriving, we met Muff and Cal through a mutual friend. It didn't take long for me to be recruited to work with MK's Ordnance department. I had no reservations. I wanted to fight the just fight and this brought me into real action.

I was trained in rules of secrecy and disguise, coding and securing communication, and the preparation of 'legends' and cover stories. I practised digging holes for weapons caches in the nearby game reserve. I received weapons training, including the use of limpet mines.

In Harare I worked for a British government NGO and that included a big house in the fancy suburb of Highlands with a deep basement we used to store 'material'. One day I came home to a wide-eyed domestic worker who told me that Jack, the gardener, had found a cache of weapons while retrieving something our young daughter had lost down the trap door in the floorboards. We frantically moved a big bakkie load of material out that night expecting the police any moment.

Besides storage of weapons, my work involved training and controlling a number of international operatives. These are some of the stories about luck, contingency and bravery, and making do under pressure.

I'd like to mention the most remarkable Canadian comrade, Martha Gordon, or Charlotte, her nom de guerre, whom I first met when I sent her off with her work partner Peter Craig or Hasani on a mission from Harare. Hasani was a gentle person. They made a good pair. With a legend that they were American missionaries, they set off in a benign, pale yellow VW golf bakkie with a deadly package of weapons in a small hidden compartment behind the seats. On top of all of this were bibles and crosses. The irony is that Martha ended up an Anglican priest and Hasani a Buddhist academic.

Six months later in South Africa in June 1990, because many of the South African MK comrades were still in exile, I took operational responsibility for a series of international comrades based internally under both Ordnance and Vula command who had been involved not only from Zimbabwe but also from Botswana.

The first was a Frenchman, clearly very strong and brimming with confidence. I've no idea who he was. He left a vacant house in

Rosettenville for me to mop up strewn with debris, smells and images that heightened my anxiety. Seemed he'd had an active and indiscreet love life in a conservative neighbourhood of tightly packed houses of a curious conservative Mozambique Portuguese community. He left a garage packed with forty 60-kilogram boxes of weapons that had been brought into the country by the Africa Hinterland vehicle.

I had arranged with a South African comrade Shelley Wells to temporarily move the boxes into her place. They ended up in Parkhurst in deep suburbia where Martha Gordon stayed. The Sunday night of the transfer turned out to be a wet one. We drove to the Rosettenville house and packed the bakkie under the curious eye of the old lady next door who peered occasionally from behind lace curtains wondering what was going on.

The boxes were too heavy for my comrade, so she kept watch while I packed. We drove across the CBD twice that night in the rain. Loading and offloading more than 2000 kilograms. The poor bakkie groaned slowly, its axles to the ground. That blue Bantam bakkie was a real stalwart though. My hands were cut and blistered, and my muscles ached. The next day I had an important meeting in Phola Park informal settlement, but I made it.

The next international comrade I met was Andrea Meeson, a Canadian. We relocated eight or ten boxes from the truck from her house in Mayfair to the safehouse in Parkhurst where Canadian Martha stayed. Then I was introduced to a wiry young Dutch man – Pierre Koster, who was without a passport. A senior comrade had promised to get him a renewed visa stamp from our networks in the Transkei government. It never arrived. We pushed Pierre under the fence wire at the Botswana border and left him to his own devices. We'd sent him off to wander on holiday until we could retrieve his passport. I went on a long weekend camping trip with friends to a site on the KZN coast and as we entered the campsite, who should we find but Pierre camping on his own. We ignored each other, naturally, but Luke, my three-year-old son, went to tell him all about our family.

Martha and I ran 20–30 operations to KZN and probably around 30 in Gauteng in three different vehicles in 1991–1992. Each vehicle has a story. I coordinated collection and safe storage of weapons, organised vehicles, moved weapons to operatives and managed communications with receivers of packages. Martha did not mind travelling the long route to KZN or driving on her own to Cape Town.

Sometimes as comrades we threw caution to the wind. One working morning Cal came to my house with an unusual request that I was not happy about given the efforts we'd gone to to stay safe until then, but these were desperate times, our people were being hammered. He left me with a list and a set of car keys and asked me to drop two duffle bags of weapons that morning in the boot of a silver BMW on the rooftop parking area of Eastgate shopping centre an hour later. I did just that. I drove to Eastgate with two duffle bags of weapons and popped them in the boot of the car with a security guard only 40 metres away. I sauntered off to find an espresso to calm my nerves before dropping off the car keys in a brown envelope marked Seeraj with the cashier at the CNA.

I said each car had a story. The blue Bantam daredevil never recovered from that night in Rosettenville. She leaked oil through her spark plug points for the rest of her tour of duty. We went back and forth to Durban with cans of oil in the back to regularly replenish her exhausted engine. Another car, a low-slung Rover, had been sent to the structures in KZN to use. I'd shown a senior ANC political figure, then working with Self Defence Units in KZN, how to operate the fancy vacuum-sealed compartment in the boot of the car but clearly the lesson was lost, or it was just too tedious a procedure for him to bother about. We found out in the *Citizen* newspaper months later that KZN comrades had been caught at the border of Swaziland, with a boot full of weapons. They hadn't closed the DLB properly.

Here's another vehicle incident. We had to pick up a vehicle with a load from Zimbabwe in a shopping centre car park opposite the Turfontein racecourse. However, the comrades had sent the weapons in the 'blue monster', a rusty old blue rattletrap double cab VW combi. The blue monster's radiator was screwed. It didn't start. Beeper messages whizzed about. Turned out there was a hidden cut-off switch under the dashboard we had not been told about. But all ended well. The Monster spluttered and finally started.

On another occasion the car was an old double cab VW with a huge compartment behind the seat filled to the brim. Martha called from a tickey box in Durban to my beeper. She had broken down outside Villiers 100 kilometres from Joburg on the way to Durban and two young Afrikaners towed her to the garage in Villiers for repair only to discover she'd run out of petrol. They saw nothing. Martha was back on track to make the drop in ten minutes.

What pride and relief I felt, though admittedly some trepidation, when with integration in 1994 the SADF trucks drove away, packed to the brim, with ten tonnes of weapons we'd assembled at Winston Harper and his wife Sandra Jacobson's house in Troyeville. I knew them as Henry and Millie. Winston was the unit's mechanic and builder of the hidden compartments in our vehicles and Millie also worked with Ordnance. I remember with pain in my heart when Millie went missing. We searched for her for days. Winston eventually found her in Hillbrow, sometime in late 1997. She had been murdered and dumped in the boot of her own car.

A special acknowledgement must go to my wife Louise Oppenheim for holding the fort while all this was going on. The struggle would be nothing without her!

JOHN SPYROPOULOS lives in Cape Town and works with local township builders and landowners to build low-income houses. He is also involved with government on informal settlement programmes and provides advisory services related to urban planning and community development.

21
Mtintso & Ngculu – The Botswana Front and Solidarity

WE BEGIN THIS ARTICLE with this statement by O.R. Tambo in Stockholm, 18 June 1968:

> We have asked the world to assist at two separate levels – the one is to withdraw assistance from apartheid. Instead, that assistance has been increased. The demand that no arms should be supplied, that there should be no trade with South Africa, that there should be economic sanctions against South Africa, was a demand for withdrawal of the assistance which makes apartheid so difficult to conquer... The other form was not of withdrawing assistance but giving assistance to us directly.[34]

International solidarity and support for the South African struggle is very broad with many countries, organisations and individuals involved. History will not absolve us if the story is not told. We will limit our contribution to the post-1976 era with special focus on our own experiences of solidarity and internationalism in the training camps in Angola and in the forward

---

34   Oliver Tambo in E.S. Reddy, ed., *Oliver Tambo: Apartheid and the International Community. Addresses to United Nations committees and conferences*, Kliptown Books, 1991.

areas, mainly Lesotho and Botswana.

To properly locate the role of internationalism and solidarity in the South African struggle we refer to the context under which such solidarity was sought and secured. Firstly, the liberation movement led by the ANC defined international solidarity as one of the 'four pillars of the struggle'.

Secondly, African countries and their people led by the Organisation of African Unity (OAU) played a critical role in the liberation of South Africa guided by Pan-Africanism. The OAU's primary objective was the complete decolonisation of Africa. The OAU and the progressive countries pressed for mandatory sanctions against apartheid South Africa, resulting in the UN declaring it a pariah and a crime against humanity in 1966.

Africa's support to the liberation movement was met with ruthless aggression of different forms by apartheid South Africa, including economic strangulation, cross border raids and massacres, assassination and abductions of activists and sponsoring of counter-revolutionary military forces to destabilise those countries.

The worst to meet the wrath of apartheid were the frontline states, Lesotho, Botswana, Swaziland, Mozambique, Tanzania, Zimbabwe and Zambia, into which the South African youth from especially the 1976 uprisings poured in search of education and military training.

Angola was subjected to a war by FNLA and UNITA, supported by apartheid South Africa, that lasted from 1975 till 1988 with the withdrawal following the Battle of Cuito Cuanavale. MK established camps and trained its combatants in Angola from 1976 and so did SWAPO. Expressing his unflinching support to the liberation movements operating from Angola, former President of MPLA, Agostinho Neto stated,

> Angola is and always will be, the firm trench of revolution in Africa, Africa seems like an inanimate body where each one comes to peck at his own piece. Ah, who compared Africa to a question mark whose point is Madagascar?... In Zimbabwe, Namibia and South Africa is the continuation of our struggle.[35]

In Lesotho, a coup d'état was engineered overthrowing Prime Minister Leabua Jonathan who supported the struggle against apartheid.

---

35   Agostinho Neto, Angola Press Agency, 2020.

Mozambique, facing massive destruction of its economy and counter insurgency of RENAMO supported by apartheid South Africa, was forced to sign the Nkomati Accord that saw the removal of MK from Mozambique to save the country from complete collapse and attempt to restore peace and security. However, as Professor Vladimir Shubin of the Soviet Union said, 'We never believed that South Africa would observe this Accord and that's what really happened'.[36]

Despite these atrocities, the African people and their governments continued to show the liberation movement ubuntu, supporting them through all the difficult times and being true to what Jose Marti affirmed that 'the best way to find yourself is to lose yourself in the service of others'. In appreciation of this support, Nelson Mandela declared:

> I would also like to thank the frontline states and the OAU ad hoc committee on southern Africa for the meticulous manner in which they respected our right to determine our own future, while fully combining with us in the common effort to liquidate the apartheid system and thus achieve the total liberation of our continent...'[37]

Forward areas were countries closest to South Africa where ANC structures – Regional Political Military Commands (RPMC) – were set up for underground work in 1983. Operating in these areas possessed its own perils as they were susceptible to cross-border raids by apartheid security forces. All cadres were underground and thus entirely dependent on both the nationals of those countries and expatriates for their operations such as transportation and storage of material, including weapons, venues for their meetings and training of operatives, transporting operatives from and to South Africa, producing propaganda material, acting as couriers into and carrying out reconnaissance in South Africa. They provided food, accommodation, rented houses for the ANC and MK. This was dangerous as they could either be deported if exposed or killed during the raids as some of them indeed were.

Pallo Jordan has stated: 'They were drawn from different backgrounds

---

36   Sue Onslow and Anna-Mart van Wyk, eds, *Southern Africa in the Cold War, Post-1974*, Wilson Centre, Philadelphia, 2013.

37   Nelson Mandela at the 26th Assembly of the OAU Head of States and Government, 9 July 1990.

and political formations on the left. What they shared was a readiness to risk life and limb in the struggle for another country ... these dedicated women and men helped the liberation movement to rebuild its capacity inside South Africa at a time when repression had all but extinguished the embers of resistance.'[38]

LESOTHO, THE 'ISLAND'

Lesotho, because of its location in the belly of South Africa, was a hub of politico-military activity in almost all its locations from Qacha's Nek mountains where internal operatives were trained, to Tele River and all the bordering towns where both operatives and materials moved. In each area there were locals who supported us whose names may not be remembered. The RPMC under Chris Hani and Lehlohonolo Moloi serviced the whole of the Western, Eastern and Northern Cape, Free State and part of the then Transvaal. Apartheid atrocities in Lesotho included but were not limited to:

- Parcel bomb explosion on 6 July 1979 maiming Father Osmers, Phyllis Naidoo and injuring five others.
- Abduction of Sizwe Kondile in June 1981. It emerged at the TRC hearings that he was tortured by the Special Branch, shot dead and set alight on the banks of the Komati River while his killers enjoyed a braai.
- The first Maseru massacre of 8 December 1982: of the 42 people killed, 12 were Basotho citizens.
- A second Maseru massacre on 20 December 1985 killed nine people.

A full roll call of those who paid with their lives still has to be done.

Of all internationalists in Lesotho, Father John Osmers stands out for the daring work he performed, as does Father Michael Lapsley. [Refer to Father Michael Lapsley's tribute in this book].

The 'Bare-footed Nuns of Masite' were a community of nuns in the mountains of that area who accommodated refugees, organised schooling and unquestioningly opened their doors to operatives who needed refuge.

Maggie Mdlankomo was a Mosotho national who gave support to operatives. Her husband Ligwa 'Zakes' Mdlankomo was killed in the 1982

---

38   Ken Keable, ed., *London Recruits: The secret war against apartheid*, Merlin Press, 2012.

Lesotho massacre in the evening of the birth of her daughter.

There were also stalwarts of the ANC, SACTU and SACP who had long settled in Lesotho such as Elizabeth Mafeking and Gilbert Hani, father to Chris Hani, both running a shop in Mafeteng used for storage of material and transit of operatives to and from South Africa; Kgalake Sello (a Lesotho national who had been active in Durban); Bob Matje; Seakale; and many others who supported the operatives. The Lesotho Communist Party rendered immense support to the ANC.

Research of all the internationalists in Lesotho still has to be done.

Botswana, called 'P'

Botswana under the RPMC, led by Comrade Lehlohonolo 'A' Moloi, after his expulsion from Lesotho, serviced the Western Transvaal and was very important as MK operatives could move from Zambia and Zimbabwe through Botswana into South Africa.

Apartheid atrocities in Botswana included but were not limited to:

- Assassination of Vernon Nkadimeng on 14 May 1985.
- Botswana Raid on 14 June 1985 killing 12 people including two Batswana, a six-year-old and a Somali-born Dutch national.
- 14 June 1986: A Boer attack on Anna Mabuza's house in Gaborone killing one Motswana woman, Mamatsela Polokelo, maiming Nthabiseng Mabuza and injuring others.
- Assassination of Jacob 'Biza' Molokwane on 13 January 1988.
- Another Gaborone raid on 28 March 1988 killing and burning the bodies of one South African, and three Batswana.
- Assassination of Sandile 'Naledi' Sehume and two Batswana women assassinated on 29 March 1988.

While there were many atrocities in Botswana this list only scrapes the surface, and a proper roll call needs to be done soon.

Gunvor Alida Endresen was a Norwegian working with NORAD in Botswana who risked all that she had in support of the operatives in Botswana. We used her house for debriefing and accommodating internal contacts and MK leaders such as Chris Hani, hiding material including weapons, creating false bases in cars to transport material into the country and transporting operatives. This not only jeopardised her career but was dangerous for her. Regrettably she passed away in 2017 without ever being recognised in any way by the ANC and the democratic government. Judy Seidman was a very active American who tells her own story elsewhere in this book.

Anna Mmatau Mabuza accommodated Cde Lehohonolo 'A' Moloi and other operatives in Gaborone and carried out underground work, especially storage of material and transportation of operatives and reconnaissance. Her house was attacked by the Boers on 14 June 1986 and her daughter Nthabiseng was left paralysed while her youngest daughter Nobantu has never recovered from the trauma. Anna passed away in 1995 without any acknowledgement from the ANC and the democratic government.

Clement Bogatsu, Botswana citizen, worked for the Gaborone City Council and was arrested several times for activities that included reconnaissance and infiltration of operatives into South Africa. He was sentenced to Robben Island around 1985 and released in 1992.

Lindi Kraai, a South African working for United Nations Development Programme (UNDP) in Gaborone, supported operatives with accommodation, transport and couriering.

Elaine Byrne, an Irish teacher at Maru a Pula High School in Gaborone, provided accommodation for operatives, carried out reconnaissance and provided 'cover' for operatives.

Mr Abel Mavandla and Mrs Eugenia Nontuthuzelo Ntwana, who ran a shop in Mochudi, accommodated operatives and stored material. Tat'Mbulawa in Gaborone and his son, Andile, allowed us to use his son's computer shop to produce 'work permits'.

Father John Osmers, after deportation from Lesotho, arrived in Botswana, supported and linked the operatives to Defence Force soldiers.

Father Chance of the Anglican church in Gaborone opened his parish for meetings of the RPMC and provided 'cover' for operatives. There were many more nationals and expatriates who assisted us in Botswana, but space only allows us to mention a few.

THE CAMPS: CUBAN AND SOVIET SUPPORT

The MK military camps in Angola were centres of both political and military training from outstanding stalwarts such as Jack Simons, Mark Shope, Ronnie Kasrils and Pallo Jordan, who in turn produced other layers of instructors and commissars. Politics was the fundamental basis for armed struggle. It is in these camps that young 'Krusants' (Russian for cadets) came to understand the significance of and practically witnessed international solidarity. The Cuban and Soviet Union instructors became the face of internationalism and, in reality, showed their comradeship and commitment to our struggle and freedom. During training we witnessed the selflessness and internationalism of the Cubans as instructors treating themselves in no different ways from ourselves. This measure of solidarity has remained embedded in our minds since then.

The Cubans, like all of us, used pseudo names for security reasons. One of these was comrade Faye, who was perhaps the only one who quickly grasped South African slang.[39]

We also interacted with the Soviet military advisors who, for many years, provided expert advice to the ANC and MK leadership and cadres. There were outstanding comrades such as Comrade Ivan (Vyacheslav Shiryaev), a decorated Soviet navy captain, Comrade George German Pimenov, a colonel and Comrade Viktor (Mikhail Konavalenko), also a colonel. Many MK comrades went to the GDR, Soviet Union, Cuba and other countries for further training.

Many MK songs were composed, such as 'Cuban/Soviet people, lovely people, here we are far from home, we shall need you, we shall love you for the things you have done for us'.

The Finnish group of advisors who came to impart technical skills to MK cadres in Angola are worthy of our recognition. They were allocated a piece of land called the 'Plot' where they trained many cadres in various skills such as agriculture, carpentry, bricklaying, etc. They also assisted MK medical officers with mathematics, physics, biology and chemistry in preparation for medical schools in various parts of the world.

In Angola, and elsewhere, we experienced the warm hands of internationalist solidarity through donations of food and civilians from the Anti-Apartheid Movement (AAM), socialist and Nordic countries. Every cadre looked forward to getting decent second-hand clothes and shoes through what we referred to as 'umphando'.[40] This included the most basic needs for 'umzana', women combatants – sanitary pads.

---

39   Interview with Clarence Kwinana (Patrick Makhaya [MK]).

40   Umphando (noun) or ukuphanda (verb) means to investigate or to rummage in Xhosa.

In his book, Tor Sellström states that 'In May 1969, the Swedish parliament endorsed a policy of direct official humanitarian assistance to the national liberation movements in South Africa and Guinea-Bissau'. Sweden, followed by others, became the first Western country to enter into a direct relationship with movements that in the Cold War periods elsewhere in the West were shunned as 'communist' or 'terrorist'.[41]

The international community also provided cultural and occupational games like Scrabble, chess sets, playing cards, soccer balls, volleyballs and books, which greatly contributed to recreational facilities in the camps. It is partly thanks to the international solidarity that cadres could mentally survive and maintain high morale and commitment.

The AAM also provided opportunities for the MK cultural group, Amandla, to perform internationally to expose the atrocities of apartheid as well as raise funds for the struggle.

It is important to constantly remind ourselves of the role and resilience of women in our struggle. Women played a critical role in the internationalism and solidarity detachment, thus disrupting the gender stereotypes. Women could more easily cross borders than men, do reconnaissance, accommodate men under the pretext that they were their 'partners' and could carry out military work without raising suspicion.

These heroines demonstrated nerves of steel under intense levels of stress. They faced their tasks with commitment and discipline at massive cost to their lives, comforts, careers and even arrests that led to some of them spending years in apartheid prisons. Mary Chamberlain, from England, who carried out clandestine work for the Movement, puts it eloquently in stating, 'I feel honoured that the ANC trusted us on that mission. It remains my proudest achievement.'[42]

The last clause of the Freedom Charter, 'There shall be peace and friendship', was the guiding principle in the struggle against the apartheid monster and these internationalists engaged to ensure the achievement of that peace and friendship.

These internationalists, many of whom have not been mentioned, must be celebrated. Are we as South Africans keeping the promise made by

---

41   Tor Sellström, ed., *Liberation in Southern Africa: Regional and Swedish Voices*, Nordic Africa Institute, 2002.

42   Ken Keable, ed., *London Recruits: The secret war against apartheid*. Merlin Press, 2012.

President Mandela at the OAU when he thanked Africa for its unwavering support:

> Our obligation to you and the millions of people you represent is to remain true to the vision of a free and prosperous Africa which inspires all of us, even as we battle to resolve the immediate problems that confront us. We make the solemn pledge that the ANC, its leadership and members, the rest of our democratic movement and the masses of our people will not fail you, because to do so would be a betrayal of everything which all progressive humanity holds dear.[43]

THENJIWE ETHEL MTINTSO post MK became South Africa's ambassador to Italy, Romania and Cuba. She was deputy secretary general of the ANC from 1998 to 2002 and is accredited as South Africa's ambassador to the Kingdom of Spain.

JAMES NGCULU post MK participated in the negotiations for democratic transition, was elected as an MP and chaired the Portfolio Committee on Health. He is the author of two books and currently serves on the ANC's Integrity Commission.

---

43   Nelson Mandela at the 26th Assembly of the OAU Head of State and Government, 9 July 1990.

22

Judy Seidman – From the 'Red Nest' in Connecticut to Botswana

I WAS BORN A MIDDLE-CLASS white female in 1951, the second of five children of left-wing American activists. My first ten years were in Village Creek, an inter-racial left-wing housing co-op in Connecticut (dubbed the 'Red's Nest' by *Life Magazine* in the late 1950s).

My parents left the US to lecture at universities in newly independent Africa, first in Ghana and Nigeria, later Tanzania, Zambia and Zimbabwe; interspersed with years in universities in the USA and running workshops on law and economics in the Soviet Union, Beijing, Indonesia, Ethiopia, (post-1990) South Africa, and other places.

Aged 11, I attended Achimota secondary school in Ghana, under Kwame Nkrumah. In Achimota I first learnt about South Africa's anti-apartheid movement. In the school library I read *Drum* magazine (West Africa edition) about the Rivonia Trial. I near-memorised Peter Abrahams *Tell Freedom,* a set book for the West African School Certificate.

One exalted night during school vacation, I danced with 5000 people to Miriam Makeba singing in Accra's Black Star Square. A different lesson at Achimota: I stood in shadows while the headmaster presided over a bonfire burning all books of Marx and Lenin from our school library, after the coup that toppled Kwame Nkrumah.

My family returned to the US after that coup. I graduated from the University of Wisconsin with a BA sociology and MFA fine art/painting, and extracurricular specialisation in political meetings and silk-screening posters against the war in Vietnam. I planned to live and paint in a loft in Chicago. Instead I went to visit my parents, then professors at the University of Zambia. And stayed. I married Neil Parsons, a historian writing on Botswana.

The first artwork I did for the ANC was a poster for the funeral of Boy Mvemve ('J.D.'), killed by a parcel bomb at the ANC's Lusaka office in February 1974. After that I drew occasional graphics for the ANC: posters, cards, cartoons, covers for publications, a series of portraits for Woman's Day, 9 August.

From 1975 to 1980, Neil worked at the Swaziland campus of the University of Botswana, Lesotho and Swaziland. I painted. We had our first child. We spent a year in the UK, moving to Botswana in late 1980. Our second child was born shortly after we arrived in Gaborone.

I joined Medu Art Ensemble, a collective that positioned arts and culture within South Africa's oppressed communities and the liberation movement. Medu debated and created resistance culture and brought 2000 cultural workers to the 1982 Culture and Resistance Conference in Gaborone. In Medu I made art as part of open, 'above-ground' mass mobilisation (although other Medu members worked with the underground and MK).

But in the front-line states, no links to the movement were safe. Joe Gqabi was killed in Harare on 31 July 1981, having recently left Gaborone. In April 1984, not far from my home in Gaborone, Rogers Nkadimeng died in a car bomb. On 28 June 1984, my close friend Jenny Curtis Schoon and her six-year-old daughter Katryn were killed by a parcel bomb in Angola, six months after they left Gaborone after a failed hit there.

My marriage could not survive the tensions. My husband and I separated. We agreed to live apart, and share childcare for our two daughters, in Gaborone.

On 14 June 1985 the SADF hit Botswana, killing 12 people, including Medu members Thami Mnyele, Mike Hamlyn and George and Lindi Phahle. My house was not attacked, most likely because I was a single white American woman with two small daughters, with no known links to the liberation struggle other than artwork. But Medu ceased to exist. Most surviving Medu members left for Lusaka or London. I stayed in Gaborone.

Post-raid, we needed to structure and regulate my involvement with the ANC. Barry Gilder (also from Medu) sat me down to discuss this – a clear chain of command, structured contacts, specific tasks and safety measures.

This formalised tasks I had done haphazardly before the raid. I would arrange places for cadres to stay in Botswana; provide a contact point and phone line (before cell phones); sometimes transport people; collect mail; pass on information that came up at my day job (as layout artist in Botswana's *Mmegi wa Digang* newspaper). I would monitor the press (which we received daily), collecting information on South African resistance and repression.

I now worked within a unit. I acquired an underground name, Wendy – since my nine-year-old daughter Annie was cast as Wendy in her school's production of *Peter Pan*, striding around the house in a white nightgown declaiming lines about caring for her boys. My comrades (mostly) respected my wish to keep weapons out of the house with kids living there. After my kids left for England in 1988, I got basic self-defence weapons training and kept hand grenades. Fortunately these were never needed.

I respected, trusted and depended upon my comrades' courage and commitment, training, grasp of strategy and tactics, humour and creativity under pressure. These comrades, among others, enabled me to function in my small ways, to even survive that time: Serge Phetla (Carlos/Brian/and many other names); Barry Gilder (Mfo); Thenji Mtintso (Elizabeth, Molly).

I worked with other internationalist activists based in 'P': Norwegian Gunvor Alida Endresen; American feminist, activist and academic Judith Van Allen; journalist and writer Gwen Ansell (also a Medu member and sub-editor at *Mmegi* – Gwen was deported from Gaborone in 1988, then managed the ANC's music ensemble Amandla in Lusaka and Harare); and my ex-husband Neil.

In 1986 the Botswana police detained me overnight for 'harbouring terrorists' (a comrade I knew as Zulu was arrested in a house I had rented). The US consulate intervened; I was released, and got a lecture from the US ambassador, warning me to cut ties with the liberation struggle, and to look under my car bonnet for bombs every morning.

SADF killings in Botswana continued. On 6 December 1988, my ex-husband's house was petrol-bombed. Neil was at a conference in Sweden; our daughters were staying with me. We don't know why apartheid forces petrol bombed Neil's flat. They burned out the kids' bedroom, burning beds, clothes and Barbie dolls. If our kids were sleeping there they would not have survived.

Perhaps they intended to terrorise supporters of the struggle. If so, they succeeded. Neil took the kids to live in London. I stayed on in Gaborone but moved for the fifth time since the 1985 raid.

In late 1989, while visiting my parents in Beijing, the Botswana police raided my house, arrested a comrade and found weapons. The police said I could leave Botswana willingly or be deported. I moved to Harare and commuted every month to Gaborone.

But this was 1990: Mandela was released from prison. Comrades were returning, legally and illegally. In July 1990 I relocated to Johannesburg. And remained. My kids grew up; I have two grandchildren. I still paint, still make posters, still confront current iterations of race, class and gender to end oppression and exploitation.

I still believe that the on-going struggle in South Africa remains key to fighting global race, gender and class oppressions. I am humbled, and proud, to be part of this.

JUDY SEIDMAN works in Johannesburg as a visual artist, arts educator and cultural activist.

23

Ramila Patel – From Anti-Nazi League Britain to Botswana

MY FATHER WORKED AS A carpenter at a sawmill in rural Masindi, Uganda, during the 1950s, where I was born. I have vivid memories of watching the Ugandan Independence Day parade in October 1962 with my pregnant mother and remember her discussing the events surrounding the Zanzibar revolution with neighbours in fluent Swahili. She heard rumours of the approaching storm, which hit in 1972 when Idi Amin expelled the entire Asian community.

The early warning enabled us to leave in 1966 and avoid the horrendous expulsion. We settled in Bolton, in Lancashire, where both my parents worked in the textile mills. Our home was a gardenless double-storey terraced house among a multitude of identical streets, a typical L.S. Lowry industrial landscape with tall factory chimneys belching smoke. Bolton was 'a dour northern town' as author Alan Gibbons described it, and my home for 20 years.

My father, as a young man, was on the Salt March with Mahatma Gandhi. In Bolton he was in the Labour Party and, aged 18, I joined the local International Socialist (IS) group after meeting them during a picket against the closure of my art school. I attended weekly meetings, sold *Socialist Worker*, leafleted outside supermarkets which sold South

African products, joined picket lines and attended large anti-apartheid demonstrations in London. The Grunwick strike of Asian women fighting for union recognition led by Mrs Desai was particularly significant and attracted national support from the left. We regularly took the Sunday night bus from Manchester to London to join thousands on the morning picket.

This was Thatcher's Britain and, with the rise of neo-Nazis such as the National Front (NF) and the British Movement (BM), black communities lived in fear of violence. Many unemployed Asian youth looked for a channel to vent their frustrations. Inspired and encouraged by the images of the courageous Soweto youth fighting in South Africa, we organised counter demonstrations every time the NF or the BM marched in black areas. Soweto 1976 had a profound effect on us.

An elderly member of IS who had served in the International Brigade in Spain introduced me to the ideas of internationalism and international solidarity.

As more Asian youth joined IS, we formed an Asian Youth Organisation, inspired by the black youth involved in riots in Toxteth, Brixton and Southall.

IS became the Socialist Workers Party (SWP) in 1977. The NF and BM were gaining support among the unemployed white youth and reached a turning point when the NF faced a major defeat at the 'Battle of Lewisham' when thousands of anti-fascists and local black youth broke up the NF march.

An NF march in Hyde in October 1977 was banned but with the assistance of the Greater Manchester chief constable, the NF leader, Martin Webster, was allowed a one-man march accompanied by 2000 police. The SWP response was a lone marcher opposing Webster. I accepted without hesitation. I jumped out with my placard and walked in front of the Nazi. I was terrified but felt a sense of triumph on behalf of all the anti-fascists.

Subsequently, the formation of the Anti-Nazi League (ANL) gave us a platform to fight back openly to oppose the neo-Nazis. 'Never Again' became our slogan. When the NF put up a candidate in the local elections, we saturated Bolton with a mass door-to-door leafleting campaign leading to a considerable decline in their vote.

A grassroots campaign, Rock Against Racism (RAR), was formed in early 1978 to counter right-wing hatred through music prompted by racist slurs by Eric Clapton and David Bowie. RAR demonstrated it was possible to use pop culture to highlight political causes.

Parallel to racist events unfolding on the streets, Strangeways Prison in Manchester had a notorious reputation for employing NF prison wardens. On 15 July 1978, I addressed a rally of 15 000 gathered outside Strangeways Prison for the Manchester, Northern Carnival against Racism; it was an emotional moment, and I felt an acute sense of solidarity with the crowd. Being in the SWP during the Thatcher years was a way to fight back against her destruction of the British labour movement.

As undergrad students in 1980s Manchester we abandoned classes to attend a rally addressed by a member of ZANU-PF. Newly independent Zimbabwe offered us a glimpse of what could be achieved. The atmosphere was electric, with everyone chanting 'Pamberi ne Chimurenga' (Forward with the Revolution).

The mid-1980s was a period of heightened sanctions in South Africa. In July 1986, Ronnie Kasrils (Frank to us) approached my partner and me, to run a 'safe house'. Our profile was different from his other white 'London Recruits' though I was unaware of it at the time. Frank wanted us to be based in Botswana following the June 1985 SADF raid. We were to run a safe house that would be almost exclusively for Frank. Our brief was to establish a stable home and to operate legally without raising suspicion. We arrived in Gaborone via Lusaka where we were briefed for three days in 'tradecraft', a term coined by Frank's favourite writer – John Le Carré – on the need for secrecy, operating without attracting attention, surveillance and counter-surveillance.

I secured a teaching job within two days of my arrival in Gaborone at an international school and once a week I taught art to prisoners at the Gaborone Central prison. Each day was challenging and demanding, as in any new teaching job, in a new school, a new city, a new country, but I settled in with ease. However, in my other life, secrecy became the essence of my existence.

I would collect Frank from the airport wearing a blue jacket as a signal it was safe to join me. Perhaps I was trying to blend in with the Avis workers dressed in blue. Frank called in advance, chatted and indicated through certain phrases his arrival time at the airport. My inventive dress code became the norm for airport pick-ups, with Frank saying, 'You looked lovely the last time I saw you', which was an indication to wear the same outfit.

During journeys to South Africa, we investigated back routes to Johannesburg and made observations during the border crossings. The gate passes with numbers circled to identify race fascinated me. Number 1 represented a white person, number 2 Indian, 3 coloured, 4 black and 5 other. I was identified as 2, 3 and once even 5. Having British passports meant swift border crossing.

The security forces in both countries were on high alert due to the height of the state of emergency. We passed through many army roadblocks with ease as we were not in possession of anything illegal. We drove along the border fence with a video camera on the Botswana side to look out for possible crossing points to pass on to Frank, who found new safe routes for jumping the border.

At the end of 1989, the need for a safe house diminished as the political situation in South Africa was changing rapidly. In 2012, long after I had left Botswana, I discovered that the work I had done was part of a much larger network.

I stayed on in southern Africa, built my career and made my home in an international community. I spearheaded and supervised a community service project to teach art to inmates from a correctional facility. I have been fully immersed in African art, having based my MA research on Swazi material culture. The need for international solidarity is greater than ever and working with young people engaging with and questioning global issues in their formative years continues to provide a challenge in my teaching.

RAMILA PATEL teaches visual arts at Waterford Kamhlaba, United World College of Southern Africa in Eswatini (formerly Swaziland).

24

Damian de Lange – African Internationalists in the Frontline Underground

THE SWAZI INTERNATIONALISTS, if we wish to use that term, were the water in which the MK swam like fish. We were at home. They, for all intents and purposes, were our comrades. Some died fighting together with us. Others lost their possessions or suffered sanction from the conservative Swazi government system. Twenty years into democracy in South Africa and most of us probably no longer cast our minds back to the days when the apartheid regime hunted down its opponents like dogs in the veld. Among the hunted were those who chose to support and serve as comrades-in-arms. These were the internationalists without whom the South African road to liberation would have been much more difficult.

By the 1980s MK had grown to become a more organised and commanded force with several formal military training camps in Angola and informal training areas in the frontline states. MK's command structure sat in Lusaka, Zambia, with regional structures in the frontline states and clearly defined operational structures in the forward areas that were linked to operations inside South Africa. In 1985 Swaziland was in the frontline of the battle against the apartheid South African regime.

This battle was a battle of life and death which claimed lives and limbs, destroyed homes and families in South Africa and in the neighbouring states. Swaziland, a forward area and trapped between South Africa and Mozambique, is one of Africa's smallest countries, a former British protectorate and one of the remaining monarchies in Africa.

In 1985 Swaziland was nominally ruled by the Queen Mother Ntombi Tfwala and driven by a council of men who seemed to have moved away from the late King Sobhuza's attempt to steer a middle road between the demands of the resource-rich apartheid South Africa and the wider African nationalist agenda of the rest of Africa. This swing enabled greater collaboration between the South African security forces and elements of the Swazi security establishment.

In the mid-1980s the Nkomati Accord cut operational support for military and political operations through Swaziland into the central and eastern parts of South Africa. The apartheid government made great use of the tactical space for manoeuvre they had created through the Nkomati Accord, increasing their operations into Swaziland to hunt down, kill and capture members of the African National Congress, its soldiers of MK and any supporters. With their hallmark arrogance, the Pretoria regime trampled on international norms, raiding homes at will and killing anyone they believed to be an enemy of the state, knowing that the West would issue a statement of concern at best. This was the Swaziland I travelled to in late 1985.

I had never been to Swaziland before and through work and everyday life I got to see the country's beauty and I got to meet and know many Swazi nationals. And I got to work with Swazi nationals who supported our cause, lived with our hopes and dreams, and often sacrificed much to provide us with support, friendship, love and, in a way, a glimpse of a normal life.

Deployed as a soldier of Umkhonto we Sizwe, or MK as it was more fondly known, I would work in Swaziland for a little over a year. This was a very short time compared to others who worked in similar areas and compared to the nationals who called Swaziland home and provided support for the ANC and MK. During my short time in Swaziland, countless cross-border raids were conducted by Pretoria. MK members were killed or taken back across the border to be tortured and, if lucky, to be put on trial and jailed. Houses that the Boers believed were being used by the ANC or MK or supporters were raided and destroyed. Often the wrong houses were raided and innocent people, generally Swazis, were killed, maimed or captured. When working underground MK operatives often had a legend. The legend was a critical part of the camouflage of an underground operative.

Life for me was a weird contradiction. I was Mike Lang, a Zambian national working legally as a freelance photographer and at the same time participating in illegal military operations. This meant long hours working during the day and then again at night. Our 'underground' work involved moving people and equipment to the border with South Africa, meeting people from South Africa who brought news, or important information or who had come out to collect material for operations in South Africa. We slept armed. I was often scared, and fear became a kind of speed that kept me going, constantly moving and constantly working.

Through the political teachings in the camps of Angola I had learnt about internationalists who were people not of your country who were prepared to fight for your cause out of principle and conviction. In Angola I met Finns, Brits and Portuguese who had found their homes in Angola supporting the liberation movement. They supported us through their understanding and opposition to colonialism and the ills of tribalism and racism that colonialism brings. There were the Russians and Cubans and East Germans in Angola who were carrying out their internationalist duty. And, in Tanzania, there were Brits, Swedes, Danes, Dutch, Irish and Finns who worked alongside and together with ANC members.

In Angola and Tanzania the local ANC leadership would regularly go to great lengths to praise the internationalists and call on us to emulate the kind of sacrifice they had made. I am sure that from time to time the same local leadership also offered thanks to the nationals of the country where we were living but had it not been for the time I spent in Swaziland I would probably remain with the perception that internationalists (other than the Cubans) were Europeans and white in colour. In Swaziland I learnt to work, and live, with Swazis who saw themselves as Swazis, were proud of their nationality, at times apologetic for the undemocratic system in Swaziland and committed to the liberation struggle of South Africans out of a deep understanding about the unfairness of apartheid and possibly out of a hope that freedom in South Africa might bring about a better life for Swazis in future. Using the terminology democratic South Africa uses today, these Swazis were black, coloured and white. Some were from the middle class or even the wealthy. Others were tradespeople, students and lecturers. And some were ordinary people who tended their cattle and fowl in rural areas. The Swazis who supported the ANC cause in Swaziland were ordinary people who had families and homes, who wished for a better education for their children or greater chances in the economic life of Swaziland or the region. Some of the black Swazis had worked in South Africa and experienced the naked racial brutality of the apartheid system. Some of the coloureds were descendants of mixed marriages between Swazis and former colonialists. Some of the whites were the descendants of Europeans or white South Africans who had settled in Swaziland and made it their home. A further addition in Swaziland were the South Africans, black, coloured and white, who had fled South Africa for political, social or economic reasons. These South Africans often provided a bridge or connection with Swazis and life in Swaziland.

It would not be true to argue that all Swazis of whatever shade or colour supported the ANC or the anti-apartheid cause. Many Swazis, black, coloured and white, saw the ANC and MK as a problem and some actively worked against the ANC and worked with the security forces of the Pretoria regime.

Some Swazis became so notorious in their drive to do the dirty work of Pretoria that some of us wanted to carry out acts of retribution against them. The same can be said of the white Rhodesians who had fled a liberated Zimbabwe and settled in Swaziland. This group of people were known for their open support for Pretoria and were unashamedly racist. We had identified some of their houses as safe houses of the South African security forces and wanted to carry out our own form of pre-emptive strike. It was only the clear thinking of our commanders and political direction that forced us to focus on what we were in Swaziland to do: support operations inside South Africa.

When the South African security forces carried out raids on our safe houses, we moved into the homes of Swazis. Accommodating us in their homes carried a real and serious danger. More than once, South African security forces raided a Swazi home long after it had been used by us. They left the dead behind and on occasion took the living for interrogation in South Africa.

On the borders of Swaziland lived Swazis who lent their donkeys to carry heavier equipment across the border. This activity can be likened to the support locals gave to partisans in the Second World War and carried the same kind of danger.

At the university, lecturers found space for MK operatives to live and to pretend to be students. The operatives often used the opportunity to recruit students who would then travel legally into South Africa carrying messages, political material or military equipment. Upon their return, these Swazis would provide reports and information necessary for the conduct of further military or political operations in South Africa. The Swazis provided us with the materials to forge drivers' licences and passports. This they could do by virtue of where they worked; and the risk they knowingly took was that if an MK person broke under interrogation they could be exposed, leading to sanction at work and a South African security force raid at home. I know that ANC and MK operatives in Lesotho, Botswana, Zimbabwe, Mozambique and many more countries have had similar experiences to my own in Swaziland. They too found nationals of those countries who supported them and others who fought alongside them as comrades-in-arms. And there were those brave people from the northern hemisphere who became our comrades-in-arms smuggling in weapons and money, crossing borders with information and material and taking the same kind of risk we took for a cause that they supported out of principle.

However, being an African by birth and from my experiences in Angola, Tanzania, Zambia, Botswana and Swaziland I tend to look to Africa first.

And, when I look back today, almost 20 years after our democracy, it is with some sadness and cynicism. It seems that now we have our freedom, democracy and our own government we have become focused narrowly on improving our own individual lives and we, as a nation and as individuals, have forgotten some of the people who walked with us on the long and hard road to liberation. I do not discount the value of the odd political speech in Parliament or over a tombstone in one of the neighbouring countries. Neither do I wish to cast any disrespect on the efforts of a few individuals who have tried to establish ways to recognise the contributions of African internationalists. But I do not see real and substantive recognition for the role of African internationalists in our liberation struggle. My children are not taught about this contribution at school, there is no dedicated state system to provide support for those internationalists who lost a father, mother, brother or sister in the liberation struggle. The populist xenophobic outbursts that we see in South Africa today are not countermanded strongly enough and a great deal more needs to be done to educate our people about the role that other nationals played in achieving our democracy.

If you were a Swazi and your son had been cut down by South African security force bullets while he stood side by side with an MK commander, would you not wonder today for what and why he died?

I do not believe that we, as a nation, can repay all that has been lost or suffered by our internationalist friends and comrades, but I do think that our government, which came to power with the support of internationalists, could set up dedicated programmes to recognise the role that African and global internationalists have played. For me, the Swazis we worked with in those difficult and dangerous days of 1985–1987 made me learn and understand the real value of those who are prepared to fight for another's cause.

DAMIAN DE LANGE is a retired military officer who has served in three armies and now manages defence industry companies and is a part-time lecturer. He lives in Johannesburg with his wife Susan, whom he met and recruited into the struggle when underground in Swaziland.

Extracted and edited from *The Thinker*, Vol 58, 2013.

25

Ivan Pillay – Stalwarts of Swaziland

MAZIBUKO AND MHLONGO

I CROSSED THE FENCE into Swaziland with my brother Joe Pillay in the winter of 1977. We were part of a clandestine ANC structure. As arranged, we contacted Comrade Lukele, who ran the Swazi Handicraft store. We soon came to realise that we needed local nationals to assist us in our clandestine work.

During our onward journey by bus we overheard an animated conversation by a few middle-aged men about a national teachers' strike. They were members of the Swaziland National Association of Teachers. After we alighted at the terminus, we approached one of the men, and introduced ourselves as South African refugees. His name was Mazibuko. He invited us to visit his home in Manzini.

We became good friends and learnt that his wife was related to a member of the ANC, Reggie Mhlongo. Reggie, we guessed, probably went into exile in the early 1960s. We arranged for an introduction. Those initial contacts proved very useful. Mazibuko was promoted to a senior position at the faculty of agriculture of the University of Swaziland. The family moved to a house on the campus with a one-bedroomed servant's quarters at the back; ideal as a safe hideaway to accommodate people and resources. Many cadres from South Africa stayed there and many debriefing meetings were held there.

Reggie Mhlongo had become as valuable as the Mazibuko family. He was the manager of Manzini Motors, and he bought and sold second-hand vehicles. On occasion, we borrowed vehicles from his garage. These premises also became one of the contact points for cadres from South Africa.

David Manyatsi

A few months later my brother Joe, a teacher, moved to a school at Mzimpofu. It was part of a Catholic mission on the outskirts of Manzini. Father Ciccone was in charge of the mission. He welcomed us and supported us throughout the years. The Swazi teaching staff were just as warm. We grew especially close to Fr Ciccone, Hleziphe Nkosi and Dudu Dlamini. David became our courier and allowed us to accommodate cadres in his house.

My brother was kidnapped by South African agents in January 1981. I had been tipped off by the late Nzima (Petros Msomi)[44] that we were on a list of persons to be kidnapped. Although alerted, Joe felt that since he was a full-time teacher and no longer directly involved in MK, he was no threat to the apartheid regime. One evening, hearing a knock at the door, Joe opened it to see strangers on his doorstep. They asked for Joe. He directed them to David's house, so that there would be witnesses. When David opened the door, they [the kidnappers] realised that Joe had fooled them. They overpowered him and bundled him into the boot of a car and drove off. At least there was a witness to the kidnapping – and one of the kidnappers had dropped his identity document. This gave substance to the campaign to demand Joe's return.

There was a stroke of luck that probably could only happen in a small place like Manzini. David was walking down a street and recognised one of the kidnappers. He was an exile from Mozambique, a member of RENAMO. The kidnapping was led by members of the South African security forces supported by members of RENAMO. David informed friendly members of the Swazi security establishment of his suspicions. The suspect was put

---

44   On 4 June 1982, Petrus 'Nzima' Nyawose, ANC deputy chief representative and his wife, SACTU representative Jabulile Nyawose, were killed in a car bomb explosion outside their flat in Matsapha near Manzini, Swaziland. The bomb was planted by South African agents.

under surveillance and arrested. A few weeks later, Joe was returned to Swaziland and the RENAMO suspects released to South Africa.[45]

David was an internationalist. He was a great supporter and a participant in our struggle.

The Khumalo family
The Khumalo family lived in an area bordering South Africa. Their home was just a few metres from the fence separating the two countries. MK operative Totsi Memela used their house to move cadres across those borders. The family would give her an account of the movement of security forces. Just before departure, members of the family would conduct a final check. Mac Maharaj and Simphiwe Nyanda entered South Africa with the blessings of the Khumalos.

Michael and June Stephen
From Scotland and the USA, this couple came to reside in Swaziland to help the ANC underground, while working as teachers. They assisted us in many ways, which June describes elsewhere in this book.

Lucia Raadschelders
Lucia was a member of the AABN [Dutch Anti-Apartheid Movement]. She had initially been deployed to assist the ANC in Swaziland and was withdrawn when her security had been compromised, and then deployed to Lusaka. There she worked for Operation Vula. Besides general support, her main duty was to manage our computerised communications system between Vula cadres in South Africa and ANC headquarters. Later, Ineke Vos and a comrade named Links were deployed to assist Lucia to deal with the increasing flow of communications. Committed to South Africa, Lucia made it her home after the unbanning of the ANC. She worked at the Nelson Mandela Foundation until her untimely death.

Others
There were a number of others I will mention briefly: Mariejie Riele, Marianne and Fred Lubben, Rens and Barbara Trimp, Alice Armstrong

---

45   Evelyn Groenink, *The Unlikely Mr Rogue, A life with Ivan Pillay*, Jacana Media, 2021, p. 98.

and Ann Saunders. The first three are Dutch citizens. Alice is an American and Ann is British. All worked in the education sector in Swaziland. They provided general support, including accommodation, and served as couriers and much more in the period 1980–1985.

Jaap Geldof, a Dutch citizen and a builder by trade, was sent to Swaziland. He found a job as a teacher/instructor in a trade school. He was followed by Andre Ravesloot who worked as a chef in a restaurant. Andre played a support role in Operation Vula. Andre and Kieran Meeke, an Irish citizen, participated in the infiltration of Mac Maharaj and Simphiwe Nyanda into South Africa.

Baba Nsibande

In 1977 my commander in Swaziland, the late Judson Khuzwayo, introduced me to Baba Nsibande. Round faced with a stubble beard, Baba was of average height and dark in complexion, then in his late forties. A large man, he had a lame right leg. He had four children. The eldest, Paulus, owned a mini-bus taxi. The two younger children were at school. The second oldest son was in prison for theft. I never met his wife. Baba was a typical backyard mechanic. His house was in a state of disrepair that matched the surrounding cannibalised vehicles. The house did not have electricity, nor did it have running water. The cars he drove reinforced the stereotype: a good mechanic does not need a faultless vehicle. Baba wanted to be involved in our struggle. He felt it was his struggle too. We matched his strengths with our needs and managed our interactions with him securely.

Ruled by a monarchy, Swaziland had a population of about half a million at the time. King Sobhuza II claimed membership of the ANC[46] and allowed the ANC to have a 'chief representative' in Swaziland. He was Stanley Mabizela, a teacher at Salesian High School in Manzini. During his long reign, the king always managed to maintain good relations with the ANC without alienating the South African government. However, some members of the Swazi special branch did South Africa's bidding.

In the first few years, we used Baba very carefully to take people in and out of South Africa. On some occasions he took messages and ANC

---

46   The aged Swazi monarch had indeed been a member of the ANC when it was founded in 1912.

publications to our operatives.

Stephen Lee, an MK member who escaped from Pretoria Prison, needed help to get to Swaziland. Judson Khuzwayo and I briefed Baba and Paulus on the mission to extract Lee. We went through a rigorous planning exercise to manage all risks. As the talk went on and on, Baba and his son told us in frustration, 'You are politicians! We know how to do this. Leave it to us!' And indeed two days later they delivered Stephen to us.

On his last trip to South Africa Baba noticed he was under surveillance. When he thought that he had shaken off his pursuers, he ditched anything that would incriminate him, hired a breakdown truck, drove his kombi onto the truck and travelled back to Swaziland sitting in the cab of the truck.

That was the last occasion on which he travelled to South Africa for the ANC. Since he was 'blown' we began to fully utilise Baba inside Swaziland. We provided him with an allowance and rations like any other ANC member. We moved him and the family to a brick and mortar home with a sewage system, water and electricity. As a self-taught mechanic he was naturally curious and creative. He knew many people who could help us, as well as people who lived near the border.

When the king died in August 1982, the ANC feared the worst without its historical ally. King Maswati III was under age, so his mother was made queen regent. Battle for power within the Swazi royal family intensified. Prince Mfanasibile was reportedly the real power behind the queen. Yet, according to rumour, the prince was a republican. He ensured that his ally Commissioner Majaji was appointed to head the Swazi police force. The struggle for power and influence in Swaziland occurred within an environment where South African security forces had already killed and maimed dozens of freedom fighters in what we called frontline states.

When FRELIMO unexpectedly succumbed to the growing pressure by South Africa, and signed the Nkomati Accord on 16 March 1984, the pressure on the ANC increased. Many MK members slipped out of Mozambique into Swaziland.

It was inevitable that this large number would be noticed by Swazi police and South African agents. Sporadic firefights erupted. It was a time of shootings and kidnappings, blood and death. Swazi security forces detained scores of ANC members in an old army camp. Swazi Special

Branch allowed South African security force members to interrogate detainees.

Then, a notorious high-ranking Swazi policeman, Colonel Hlubi, who also worked for the South African security forces, was assassinated by an MK cadre. While there was an immediate, harsh retaliation from the Swazi Police, the death of Hlubi drove home a truth: those who collaborated with the racist regime in South Africa were vulnerable. Many Swazi policemen approached us individually to ensure their safety. It was the right time to talk to the Swazi authorities. Baba Nsibande knew the new commissioner of police, Majaji. Early one Sunday, Baba and I drove to his house. We gave him no prior notice and surprised him with a knock at the door.

The commissioner was in his dressing gown. He was visibly trembling. I knew then that we had made our point. He too was vulnerable. He quickly ushered us in. I told him that our fight was not with the Swazis, and that MK and the Swazi police needed to reach an understanding. We agreed that despite any provocations we would both hold back our forces. Baba would be our go-between.

The whole discussion took less than an hour. When we departed, he begged me to not give his address to our cadres. We did not rule out that his forces might pursue us. We drove away calmly until we were out of sight, then floored the accelerator.

In the main street in Mbabane the car spluttered and came to a standstill.

I, an illegal person, needed to disappear as soon as possible.

I picked up my bag, put on my cap, took off my glasses and walked away briskly.

Swaziland was considered too hot for me, and the leadership deployed me to Zambia to be the 'project manager' of Operation Vula. I returned to Swaziland frequently until 1991 for work on Operation Vula. The stalwart Baba continued to provide invaluable support for the infiltration of cadres and weapons into a country he worked to liberate, out of his keen sense of solidarity.

IVAN PILLAY retired after a life of dedicated service to the ANC and government. He was a casualty of 'state capture' and vindicated.

26

June Stephen – Out of New York to Swaziland

BORN IN NEW YORK IN 1953, I grew up during the civil rights years of the 1960s. As a student at the City University I studied anthropology and learnt about many cultures.

I moved to England in 1973 and met Michael Stephen at Southampton University, where we were both studying archaeology. We married in 1976, and soon after that he was introduced to Ronnie Kasrils by a mutual friend in the Communist Party. Michael was recruited to work for the ANC (we were already supporters). We started off by working in Mozambique. Little did I know when we went off to southern Africa in 1977 that we would be playing a small part in the undercover activities of the ANC.

In Mozambique, we worked in the archaeology department of Eduardo Mondlane University, Michael teaching history, and me working in the library. I then worked in the Centre of African Studies under Ruth First, studying the impact on Mozambican miners of working away from home in South Africa for ten months of the year in the gold mines.

Michael was sent north to Niassa province to work on an archive project during this time, so we were not together.

We waited for the ANC to contact us, but the message never got through from Ronnie to comrades in Mozambique that we were in the country and available to do things. However, through our friendship with Albie Sachs we were approached by an ANC member Bobby Pillay (real name Sonny Singh), working with the underground. When he needed our flat for meetings, we would go out for dinner, to leave him and his friends on their own.

Our daughter Monica was born in Maputo in 1979. When Ronnie (whom she eventually came to know as Uncle Frank) finally arrived in Maputo, we were about to return to the UK. But he convinced us to move to Swaziland (now eSwatini), where we could be of more help.

During our five years in Swaziland we crossed the border into South Africa almost 50 times, doing tasks for the ANC. I was editing a book for the University of Swaziland, so I was lent a golf-ball typewriter. This became a crucial piece of equipment on which I produced leaflets for the ANC and SACP. I would type an original copy, and then multiple copies would be printed for insertion into leaflet bombs and dead letter boxes (DLBs).

We also travelled into South Africa to check the locations of roadblocks and draw up plans of strategic locations that could be attacked, such as power stations and military bases. We wrote extensive reports after our trips, accompanied by maps and plans. We often travelled to Johannesburg, where we planted DLBs with material. We were rarely challenged, perhaps because we were a family of three and therefore not apparently suspect; but we always had to have our stories worked out in case we were questioned.

One stormy night I had to collect Ronnie from a bus stop outside the University of Swaziland. He was absolutely soaked through and relieved to see me. We would take him on family picnics near the border with Mozambique. Michael would escort Ronnie up to the border fence, where he would re-enter Mozambique. In 1981 Michael and I smuggled thousands of leaflets to an area of wasteland near Soweto, where he dug a DLB while Monica and I drove around to give him time to do the digging and cover the cache with ground pepper and broken glass to keep dogs away from it.

The Nkomati Accord was signed in March 1984 (Mozambique renouncing support for the ANC and South Africa renouncing support for RENAMO). I drove Ronnie to the airport in Swaziland for a flight to Maputo but, on landing, the immigration authorities (knowing he was now prohibited to be in Mozambique) put him straight back on the plane to Swaziland. He made his own way to our house, where on returning from work I found him and Michael in the sitting room with a bottle of Scotch on the table. He spent the next six months in hiding with us, and sometimes with other comrades.

In the early 1980s Ronnie introduced us to Ivan and Rae Pillay, full time in the underground. They dropped by regularly to give us news and collect ANC funds stashed in a hiding place in our kitchen.

We helped to smuggle Ebrahim Ismael Ebrahim (Ebe) out of South Africa With Monica in our camper van we crossed the Swazi border, checking for roadblocks as we drove for two or three hours to the town of Piet Retief, where we found Ebe disguised as an Asian woman in a sari and shawl. We drove him to the southern Swazi border and met up with a young African woman, Busi 'Totsie' Memela, who took him over the fence at a safe crossing point. He made his way to our house, where I had to cut his grey hair and dye it black. He was taken by Rae and Ivan to a rented house where he lived and worked with other ANC comrades.

We left Swaziland in November 1985 and settled in Britain, where I worked for Oxfam. In 1996 the three of us returned to Mozambique, Swaziland and South Africa. In Cape Town we had lunch with Ebe, by now a member of Parliament, along with other ANC members, including Ronnie, who by that time was a government minister. Ebe showed us round the Parliament building. It was an empowering experience for us.

JUNE STEPHEN, former information services manager, Oxfam headquarters, is now retired and living in England near her daughter Monica who grew up in Swaziland.

27

Conny Braam – The Dutch Connection

THIS IS A PERSONAL STORY, but also the story of hundreds, thousands and ultimately tens of thousands of Dutch people who have committed themselves to the fight against apartheid in South Africa.

The shadow of the Second World War hangs over the early days of the anti-apartheid movement. We, the activists from the very beginning, belonged to the first post-war generation with mostly traumatised parents who wanted nothing more than to forget the violence of war, the horrific consequences of fascism and racism as quickly as possible. A new life had to be built and the West soon found itself in another war, the Cold War with the Soviet Union – the main ally in the fight against Hitler.

There was little interest in what was going on in South Africa, the country of Jan van Riebeeck, the country of blood relatives, where many Dutch people had an uncle or an aunt. The war against the Nazis had been won, so the institutionalised racism in South Africa did not fit the image of reconstruction and the slogan 'never again fascism'.

But the Sharpeville massacre and the trial of Nelson Mandela and his fellow combatants were certainly noticed by the post-war generation. And Dutch people started asking questions about how the horror of fascism and racism during the war years could be reconciled with the tolerance of a similar system in South Africa.

I was born in 1948 and belong to that generation that started asking questions of parents, politicians and church leaders. The answers we received were unsatisfactory and the lack of interest was perceived as shocking. It was surprising and relieving when, in the second half of the 1960s, it turned out that these feelings of discontent were shared by countless young people around the world. In the Netherlands, as in many other countries, students and learners, supported by workers, revolted en masse. I too took part in the heated discussions and first demonstrations.

We understood that there was a connection between the war in Vietnam, the fascist regime in Spain and Greece, apartheid in South Africa and the politics of our own country. In this way, international solidarity became a concept that we interpreted in our own way.

In 1970 the Anti-Apartheid Movement Netherlands (AABN) arose. I remember how tough the early years were. I regularly travelled to all corners of the country lecturing about the oppression and exploitation of the black population in South Africa. I encountered a lot of ignorance and opposition. For the first time, I had to experience the prejudices I aroused by standing up for the black population in South Africa as a young woman in her early twenties.

In order to establish a connection with the Second World War, we sought cooperation with the Anne Frank House in Amsterdam, even then an international symbol of the persecution of the Jews. An exhibition was set up in which similarities between Nazi Germany and apartheid South Africa were pointed out. There, one Sunday, my first encounter with white South Africans took place. Emotional about the fate of Anne Frank, they could not tolerate the comparison with South Africa. It became clear to me how violent South African society could be when I was dragged through the exhibition space by my hair.

The AABN's support quickly expanded and we increasingly collaborated with trade unions, women's organisations, student movements, artists and churches, so we grew from a wild activist group who wanted to chase away South African water polo players in a swimming pool into a broad solidarity movement.

With the support of the municipality of Amsterdam, we were able to move into a large building on the Lauriergracht where dozens and eventually hundreds of volunteers supported our work. It was the time of barricades and countless heated discussions, of idiosyncratic people who not only met endlessly, but also very creatively and in collaboration with other AAMs in the world set up boycott actions and cultural activities. And of course, we sought a confrontation with the Dutch government for its scandalous South Africa policy and the multinational companies for their equally reprehensible pursuit of profit.

One day we stood in the pouring rain for hours protesting the imminent execution of a political prisoner; the next day we ran laughing behind an ANC man we wanted to teach to cycle. We felt not so much that we were fighting an apartheid system, but rather that we were providing support to people who were engaged in a stubborn and bitter struggle for a decent existence – people we often knew personally, because, over the years, many AABN employees worked with hundreds of ANC activists. As a result, there was always optimism and admiration for the endurance of the leaders, but also for the enthusiasm of the many choir members, dance groups, speakers, poets and writers.

Halfway through 1986 I took the next step, which seemed logical. ANC leader Mac Maharaj asked me for support for the covert Operation Vula. ANC leaders would be smuggled into South Africa to support domestic resistance underground.

Practical problems arose in this regard. Many operatives were well known to the South African police and secret services and had to be disguised. Thanks to the many cultural activities of the AABN, I had a large network of theatre and film people, whom I could now deploy with the utmost care: wig makers, make-up artists, actors, dentists and costume designers. During a week-long stay in Amsterdam, the operatives underwent a metamorphosis so that they could work safely with their new appearance.

In addition, I looked for Dutch people who were willing to settle semi-permanently in the frontline states or in South Africa – to look for a job there and build a social life like any other emigrant but, in reality, offer a safehouse to one or more operatives.

The entire Dutch Vula team, some 75 men and women, who had been helpful in one way or another – from the dentist who made false dentures to the computer specialist who helped set up a communication system

– were all motivated by a deep-felt abhorrence of the apartheid system, but many were especially inspired by the men and women who had been in the resistance against Nazism during the war or who had fought as internationalists in the brigades against fascism in Spain.

How massive the anti-apartheid movement in the Netherlands had grown became apparent on 10 February 1990, when Nelson Mandela walked out of prison. The cries of joy from all those activists thundered through the country and when Mandela visited the Netherlands not long after, the spacious Leidseplein in Amsterdam was packed with the Dutch who in one way or another contributed to the largest solidarity movement that the Netherlands has known. I hope future generations will be inspired by it.

CONNY BRAAM, founder of Dutch Anti-Apartheid Movement (Anti-Apartheidsbeweging Nederland – AABN) is a prolific author of note.

28

Janet Love – Internationalists and Operation Vula

A CHILD OF A HOLOCAUST survivor and decorated soldier who was involved as a Wits student on and off campus, including working with the Industrial Aid Society, I was drawn into ANC work in 1975 by one of the trade union organisers involved in the Metal and Allied Workers Union.

While in exile, for ten years from 1978, I worked for the South African Congress of Trade Unions (SACTU) and with the ANC political machinery. I spent periods in Amsterdam, London, Lusaka, Angola, Cuba and Moscow. I met with comrades from inside South Africa in Swaziland and Maseru; I transported messages, military equipment, leaflets and money from one frontline state to another; and, in the midst of trade union training programmes with the ILO in Zambia and Zimbabwe, I briefed and debriefed comrades who were part and parcel of the democratic forces that were growing ever stronger inside our country. I also received political and military training and was prepared for underground work with specialist courses including communications, disguise and other skills, including lock-picking!

I returned to South Africa in 1987 under an assumed identity as one of the comrades involved in the setting up of infrastructure for Operation Vula, particularly its communications, and remained working underground until June 1991.

Operation Vula was a response to the heightened momentum of our struggle against the regime. In 1985, the Kabwe conference endorsed the need to relocate members of the ANC from exile to be based inside South Africa to provide the immediate leadership needed within the country. Under the command of Comrade O.R. Tambo and Joe Slovo, Operation Vula's mandate included the need to work with internal leaders, to build more effective communications between those inside and outside South Africa (including in prison), to enable greater coordination of underground political and military activity, to enhance mass mobilisation, to build the infrastructure and stockpile equipment necessary for the war against the regime. Although Operation Vula had a specific role and identity, over time there were overlaps with comrades involved in other operations. Some of these connections, such as with Operation Bible, were planned and intentional.

The ANC alliance benefited from some already told, and many more untold, acts of commitment and generosity of so many internationalists from around the world: and Operation Vula's experience epitomised this. The character of our organisation – the ANC, SACP and SACTU – was informed by the assertion of the primacy of politics over warfare and the emphasis on the universalism of our struggle. The reality of exile, in particular, was infused with evidence of huge international support. International solidarity was always emphasised as a cornerstone of our strategy: it saw us learning from others and taking positions to support their struggles. The contributions of people from both our neighbouring countries and the global North were critical.

I did not encounter directly many of those comrades whose actions made Operation Vula possible, but the transportation of arms across our borders in the quantities we dealt with clearly involved the willingness, inventiveness and abilities of Mozambicans – like Pedro who used to fix our vehicles and Adolfo the waiter whose restaurant storage room was used to store our materials. So often, when comrades moved from Mozambique via Namaacha and Lomahasha to Oshoek or Piet Retief, they were saved from last-minute crises by comrades from Swaziland (today's eSwatini) who rallied round to provide accommodation, fix our cars, devise new concealments in suitcases, parcels or vehicles, and to help with communications to make sure that the unexpected was relayed to those who needed to know.

There were comrades – some expats from the North who had settled in neighbouring countries and others who travelled directly from North America and Europe – who brought in various materials, including the packages that concealed the updated versions of the Vula coding programme disk. Others made sure that some of the computer equipment we used was safely received.

Inside the country, I worked with comrades who maintained our safe houses, including Susan Grabek and Maria Kint. There was also invaluable support from comrades like Pierre Koster who invented the most creative DLBs and criss-crossed the country doing whatever they could. Theirs was often a very tough life – maintaining a show of normality in the most abnormal situation. I had experienced the dislocation of exile: but these comrades had to embed themselves in a society that was not only away from their homes but, more often than not, they also had to ensure that they avoided socialising with those with whom they had most in common in order not to draw attention to themselves. Their discipline, commitment, trust and loyalty was awesome and deserves much recognition and thanks.

In the months following the Vula arrests at the Knoll safe house in Durban, most of these comrades were unceremoniously required to leave the country, being left to deal with the tension and insecurity of their time inside South Africa with little contact or support.

JANET LOVE has postgraduate degrees in public sector management and finance. She is currently the vice-chairperson of the Electoral Commission, South Africa.

29

Douglas & Douglas – A Canadian Safe House for Operation Vula

WE WERE RECRUITED IN Canada in early 1987. Rob had been active in anti-apartheid solidarity work since 1976 and we had approached the ANC rep in Toronto, Jojo Saloojee, about the possibility of volunteering at Solomon Mahlangu Freedom College in Tanzania.

A few weeks later, Rob was asked to go to Toronto, where he met with Jojo and Mac Maharaj. If we were willing to risk going to a frontline state, they said, there was something else we could do that would be dangerous but more useful for the struggle. Given the crackdown in South Africa, they needed white internationals to go in as immigrants, to get work and establish a presence to provide cover for underground activists. Would we go?

We immediately dropped out of contact with friends and told our families that we were travelling in Africa, maybe to South Africa. Rob was able to leave at the end of April and started setting up in Johannesburg. Helen arranged things in Vancouver and joined Rob in mid-June.

It was exciting but also a shock to land in South Africa, which we knew so well from a distance. This was just after a magistrate's court bombing, so we quickly had to come to terms with being part of an armed struggle ourselves.

As we had been instructed, Rob bought a second-hand car and rented a flat near Yeoville as our 'official' residence and a house in Orange Grove to serve as the safe house. He found work teaching science at a private multiracial tutorial college in town. Helen became a bookseller at Exclusive Books in Hyde Park. We maintained our personas as apolitical tourists, never expressing our opinions or going near any political activity. It's interesting how much you learn about others when you stop talking about yourself. We made good friends at work but we were always lying to them about who we were.

We had moved quickly because we thought the safe house activities would start up as soon as we were in place but by the time our six-month return flights were about to expire, we still had no contact. Helen thought that maybe Jojo and Mac had lost touch with us and that we were sitting in apartheid South Africa for no reason, paying taxes and wasting our time. Rob was certain that someone would come. We agreed to give it another six months. After a year, still no contact. We agreed to give it another six months.

By September 1988, we ran out of money. We gave notice on the flat and moved into the house, where we had actually been living for months. Within a week, there was a message on the phone and Rob – with a shock – recognised Mac's voice. We rushed back to the flat and sat there until he arrived the next night. It was the first time Helen met him. He stayed long enough to find out how we were and arrange to meet at the house. We were beside ourselves with excitement. Now it was all happening! And what on earth was Mac doing in the country?

In the next few days, he told us about Operation Vula (although not by name) and that our house would be a base for him in Johannesburg. Siphiwe Nyanda ('Joe') also came to meet us around then. We had become friendly with the African family who lived in the servants' room behind the house: we hadn't expected that rental accommodation 'came with' people to clean and garden, but Rob didn't have the heart to make them leave. Now the Orange Grove house wasn't suitable, and we scrambled to find a new safe house, landing up in an Afrikaans neighbourhood in Northcliff that wasn't suitable either, but the best we could find. Finally, in April 1989, we found the perfect house in Parktown North. It was a small three-bedroom bungalow surrounded by a wall, with a pool and a small cottage in the back garden. We put out an ad for a tenant for the cottage, setting up the legend that Mac was our tenant, and installed an automatic garage door so that he could come and go discreetly.

Mac and Siphiwe were travelling a lot but would join us for supper when they could. Mac especially understood the stress of our double lives and made a point of keeping us informed about the state of the struggle, treating us as comrades and friends, always teaching and telling stories. Rob wanted to be more active, hating that others were taking risks that we weren't asked to. We considered whether Rob could access chemicals from his school or if we should buy weapons and learn to use them, but always came back to the importance of maintaining our cover for the safe house. Helen didn't mind as she was finding the whole business stressful enough.

We did take on some communications tasks, sending out and receiving encrypted reports via public phones. Helen also assisted in setting up a meeting between Mac and Govan Mbeki in Port Elizabeth. Those were our only real James Bond moments. We didn't know all that was going on with Vula, but it was ramping up. Janet Love came in to take over some of the communications work. Ronnie Kasrils also arrived later. Mostly only Mac stayed with us, but it was a workplace for all of them.

Then came February 1990 and De Klerk's sudden unbanning of organisations and the release of the Rivonia leaders. Such joy, excitement, promise and confusion everywhere. Mac went out of the country in order to return legally under indemnity. Then, in July, Siphiwe and other comrades fell into the hands of the security police in Durban. Mac arrived very late on a Friday night to say that we might be compromised. He sat with us for more than an hour, coaching us on our cover story. The police and soldiers arrived en masse and heavily armed on the Monday. Maybe they were expecting to find MK's High Command, but it was just Rob. The first man through the door was a former student of Rob's, just out of high school. He greeted him in surprise: 'Hello, sir!' Various men in suits questioned Rob for two hours, but he kept to his story. They searched the house and left, promising to return. We patched together an escape plan and flew out of the country on the Thursday morning. A few days later, we were in London with Tim Jenkin when we heard that Mac and others had been arrested. And then we went home.

Back in Vancouver, Helen basically fell apart. She continued as a bookseller, reading widely to understand what we had undergone. There is very little written about the kind of underground support we provided, but she found three clues. One shell-shock study from the First World War described the trauma of non-combatant frontline soldiers having to endure attacks with no possibility of either fighting or flighting. One book on guerrilla warfare highlighted the importance of a thorough political understanding to safeguard the sanity of freedom fighters. Another book on women in political detention stressed the question of identity in clandestine resistance, astutely noting that 'bourgeois notions' of subjectivity and relationship are entirely inadequate to account for dedicating one's life in solidarity with oppressed people.

In 1995, we decided to come back to South Africa, but first we finished our undergraduate degrees so that we might contribute to the new democratic order. Rob studied mathematics and Helen took humanities and philosophy courses, deepening her understanding of our experience and what it all meant. We moved to Cape Town in 1997, ten years after our first arrival.

ROB AND HELEN DOUGLAS ran a safe house in Johannesburg as part of Operation Vula from 1987 to 1990. They now live in Cape Town. Rob has taught maths for 22 years at Fish Hoek High School. He developed service/outreach programmes that took FHHS learners out to preschools in the various communities, and weekly maths workshops for matric students from the area's high schools. Helen received an MA in Philosophy from Stellenbosch University in 2002 and worked with Ben Turok's Institute for African Alternatives. Since then, she has developed a philosophical counselling practice that offers a meaningful alternative to psychotherapy (https://philosophy-practice.co.za).

30

Susan Grabek – A Patient Canadian

IN THE 1970S AND 1980S, I participated in a range of anti-apartheid activities which led to my being approached by the ANC, in the fall of 1987, to go to South Africa to support the liberation struggle against apartheid.

Everything in my background led me to agree. As a young child, my parents took me to protests against racial segregation in the United States. As a teenager in the late 1960s I met exiled South African activists in Toronto and participated with them in anti-apartheid activities.

In 1975 I was working at Radio Havana Cuba when newly independent Angola was invaded by South Africa. Cuba responded to the MPLA's call, sending troops to help defend the country, while the Cuban people as a whole regarded Angola's struggle as their own.

I arrived in Johannesburg in July 1988 and become part of what I later learnt was Operation Vula. I knew no one in the country. I found a place to live and was given instructions to send a coded message abroad indicating where this was. I also had to look for a job. I had only the little money I had brought with me to survive on until I made contact. I knew that I needed to be careful around spending. So, when I first got to Johannesburg, I lived in Hillbrow.

My communication instructions from Canada were not clear and this led to me having to travel to Zimbabwe at Christmas to attend a prearranged meeting: 'Be at Hotel X, on this day at this time, dressed in black, wearing sunglasses, a newspaper on the table.' It felt like something out of a John Le Carré novel. There I passed on my information, which enabled contact within the country.

I managed to find a job at Redhill School in Sandton. Mac Maharaj contacted me there. After meeting Mac, it was clear that I had to find more suitable accommodation for use as a safe house. The first two houses I rented did not work out. Finally, I came across an advert for a house on 12th Street in Parkhurst, a quiet, upscale neighbourhood.

During this period, I felt some of the strangeness that came with my role – the inability to be sociable and mix easily for fear of attracting unwanted attention to yourself, your movements and the comings and goings of the underground operatives for whom you needed to provide a safe space. This was the essence of my mission. I had to find a way to appear to be living a normal, unobtrusive, 'white' suburban life while keeping a 'safe house' for whatever purposes were needed.

I had a driving licence from Canada, for an automatic. Mac organised a car for me to use and I parked it in an underground garage near the place I was staying at the time. Days later the car was stolen – car theft was not uncommon. It felt crazy having to deal with police, but it was unavoidable. The police caught the thief trying to drive it over the border and contacted the Durban dealership from which it had been bought – supposedly by me – and where it was still registered. It turned out that someone working at the dealership was connected to Operation Vula. I did not know who the comrade was, but I had a sense of being connected to a wide network.

I went to the police station to claim the car, but the colour and license plate numbers didn't match those on the car's paperwork. I fumbled through somehow blaming the thief, shrugging and looking for excuses until I was eventually escorted to the car. But I was unnerved and crowned the whole thing by immediately backing into another vehicle as I was trying to leave. Racism and sexism worked hand-in-hand to save the day. I was white and played ditsy. The cop, rather than becoming suspicious, drove me – the 'damsel in distress' – to a panel beater to repair the car.

When I took up the house, I was aware of the interest that Vula comrades showed in the existence of a trap door in the floor of one of the bedrooms. It led to a large open cellar space for arms storage. Visits from Vula comrades were sporadic and very brief. At work I was friendly but guarded every word I said. I had no other interactions with people. Constant lying was hard. It was lonely. I made a point of not looking where I didn't need to look, not asking questions I didn't need to ask. Of not knowing more than I needed to know. But certainly I could see what was happening around me, as Vula comrades were brought in. They stayed in the house, working throughout the day in the room, covering the area with wall-to-wall carpet each night. I never went down into that space, though I slept above it every night.

One night, comrades had a large stash of guns that had been buried and were covered in soil and I stayed up through the night helping to clean them so they could be properly stored in the cellar; then I showered and dressed to go to work.

I was working at Centurion College in Braamfontein where I taught English to teenagers from the townships. I shared, silently, in their joy as they danced in the school's halls on Nelson Mandela's release from prison.

In June 1990 I returned to Canada for a few weeks to deal with personal matters. Two weeks after I returned, the South African government detained members of Vula and I had to flee the country.

Susan Grabek has remained active in friendship and solidarity work with Cuba and Latin America. She is now retired and living in Toronto.

31

Clarence Kwinana – Helping Hands for Radio Freedom

FOLLOWING THE BANNING OF the ANC and the PAC in 1960, leaders and activists were arrested, detained without trial, banned and banished. Some went into exile while others went underground in Rivonia. Leaders could no longer reach out to their constituencies through mass meetings or offices. No free political activity could possibly take place under the iron-handed rule of the Pretoria regime.

A progressive engineer from the Congress of Democrats took the initiative to assemble a transmitter, to enable the underground leadership of the ANC to broadcast to the masses of the people.

Walter Sisulu, assisted by Ahmed Kathrada, prepared a message to the people of South Africa from the Rivonia underground. The message was pre-recorded on a tape recorder to be played on a chosen date, at an appropriate time. On the evening of 26 June 1963, the tape recorder was inside the assembled transmitter, which was mounted on high ground in Parktown, Johannesburg. The broadcast broke through the frequencies of the South African Broadcasting Corporation and interrupted normal programming. Walter Sisulu's voice, on behalf of the underground leadership in Rivonia, went on air:

Sons and Daughters of Africa

I speak to you from somewhere in South Africa

I have not left the country

I do not plan to leave

Many of our leaders of the African National Congress have gone underground. This is to keep the organisation in action; to preserve the leadership; to keep the freedom fight going. Never has the country, and our people, needed leadership as they do now, in this hour of crisis. Our house is on fire...

The broadcast went on for about 15 minutes.

What had been introduced as Radio Liberation was meant to continue the broadcasts beyond that first day. Unfortunately, the police swooped in on Rivonia on 11 July 1963, arresting the entire ANC leadership. They went on trial from 30 October 1963 before they were all sentenced to life imprisonment in June 1964. The leadership in exile had no immediate means of communicating to the people inside the country.

From then, many developments took place inside the country and internationally in pursuit of the struggle in underground conditions.

These included the military training of cadres of the Luthuli Detachment abroad and their engagement with the joint forces of Ian Smith and John Vorster in the hills and valleys of Zimbabwe from 1967. These cadres were on their way back to South Africa but were intercepted by enemy forces.

When the campaign was called off in January 1969, new strategies were developed at the Morogoro conference, Tanzania, in April 1969 to pursue the struggle. One of the decisions that emerged was the creation of a broadcasting division within the ANC to enable the movement to reach out to the people in South Africa. This was a follow-on to the vision of the leadership in Rivonia to run broadcasting from the underground six years earlier.

Thus, the first Radio Freedom (RF) unit went on air over the External Service of Radio Tanzania Dar es Salaam (RTD) in July 1969. The second to come on stream was RF Lusaka, over the External Service of Radio Zambia in May 1973. The third RF unit went on air on 16 June 1977 over Radio Nacional de Angola in Luanda. The beginning of 1979 saw the creation of the fourth RF unit in Tananarive that went on air over the

External Service of Radio Madagascar. The last to come on stream was the RF unit that was broadcasting from Addis Ababa, Ethiopia from October 1981. These RF units went on air in the evening, using transmitters of the host stations, at different times and frequencies, on Short Wave. The broadcasts could be received in South Africa with varying degrees of clarity as the regime had a dedicated service to jam them. It was also illegal to listen to the broadcasts of a banned organisation as that could attract a maximum sentence of eight years. RF units operated under the umbrella of the ANC's Department of Information and Publicity (DIP).

The named African countries provided support by beaming Radio Freedom programmes over their short-wave antennas, but European countries also played a great role by providing the necessary training in broadcasting.

While the original radio announcers relied on 'on-the-job training', the ones who came after them were trained at various centres in Europe. In 1976, ten would-be operatives of Radio Freedom were trained at the Institute of Social Studies in Moscow. Others were trained at the International Institute for Journalism in Berlin, in the then German Democratic Republic. The Dutch programme came on stream when yours truly became the first Radio Freedom operative to be trained at Radio Nederland Training Centre in Hilversum, in 1983. The Dutch went further to equip all Radio Freedom units wherever they broadcast from in Africa, with their own studio equipment, in their residences, so that they did not solely rely on studios of the host countries. Through programme genres such as news bulletins, commentaries, features, documentaries, interviews and music, Radio Freedom was able to mobilise the masses to make the country ungovernable and apartheid unworkable and amplify the role that was played by the international community in the South African struggle.

CLARENCE KWINANA was a member of the 'June 16' Detachment of MK and a former operative of Radio Freedom. He was trained at Radio Nederland Training Centre, Hilversum, as a professional broadcaster. Today, he is a town planner based in Centurion, Pretoria.

Electric power pylons, dynamited by MK, New Age, 8 November 1962. The weekly newspaper was banned later that year.

Nelson Mandela, with Robert Resha at left, who became the ANC representative to an independent Algeria, visits military facilities of Algerian National Liberation Front (NLF) in Morocco, 1962

Julius Nyerere, Tanzanian president, with Sam Nujoma, SWAPO, and Oliver Tambo, ANC. Undated picture.

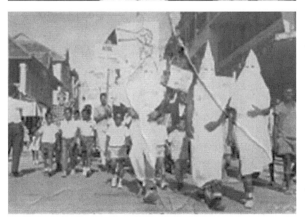

ANC solidarity march, Dar Es Salaam, 26 June 1965. The hooded figures depict the unholy alliance of Verwoerd (South Africa), Ian Smith (Rhodesia), Salazar (Portugal). Ronnie Kasrils in check shirt 2nd at left, James Hadebe, ANC chief representative Tanzania, at centre.

Oliver Tambo with E.S. Reddy, secretary of United Nations Committee Against Apartheid, New York. Undated picture.

Campaign poster, Belgium: Don't Buy Cape Fruit. ABVV – Algemeen Belgisch Vakverbond – General Belgian Trade Union , central organ of trade unions operating as an arm of the Belgian Labour Party.

German Democratic Republic (DDR) solidarity poster. Literature was published gratis for liberation movements.

Tambo with Olof Palme, Prime Minister of Sweden and Lindiwe Mabuza, ANC chief representative in Sweden at Swedish People's Parliament Against Apartheid, Stockholm, 21 February 1986.

Ant-Apartheid rally London demanding freedom for South Africa and Namibia: At centre: Abdul Minty, Thabo Mbeki, Trevor Huddleston. Third from left: Mike Terry, secretary AAM, at right Shapua Kaukungua (SWAPO) and Joan Lestor, MP, June 1986.

Anti-Apartheid rally, Amsterdam: At right Pallo Jordan and Connie Braam; Allan Boesak 3rd from left and on his right, Jeroen Krabbe, Dutch film star.

Anti-Apartheid march, New York, protesting US corporate investment in South Africa, organised by Pan African Students Organization in the Americas and Youth Against War and Fascism (YAWF). One of the targets was Chase Manhattan Bank. Southern Africa Magazine, January–February 1978, Private collection – George Cohen.

Anti-apartheid march, Reggio Emilia, Soncini Ganapini Archives, Panizzi Library, Italy.

Alex and Marie-Jose Moumbaris, campaigning in Paris shortly after his dramatic escape from Pretoria prison, 1979.

Joe Modise, MK commander at right; Oliver Tambo third from left, Cuban representative centre; MK passing out parade, June 16th Detachment, Nova Catengue, Angola 1977.

MK combatants, Angola, ready to confront the enemy, circa 1985.

Belgian Anti-Apartheid Coalition, protesting their country's banking ties with racist South Africa. Stock Exchange, Brussels, 1987.
© Jan Vanheukelom

Soviet military instructors at MK base, Kakulama, Angola, 1987. Colonel Mikhail Konovalenko and Major Boris Dovbnya, in conversation with MK commander 'Vusi'.

Left *Sweden: solidarity in the snow with African liberation movements. Lena Johansson of Africa Groups. Undated photo.*

Right *Oliver Tambo welcomed by Mayor Ugo Benassi and Giuseppe Soncini, Reggio Emilia, Italy, National Solidarity Conference, 1978. Soncini Ganapini Archives, Panizzi Library*

Funeral in Paris of Dulcie September, ANC's chief representative, 9 April 1988. Photo Lily Franey

ANC's monthly journal, featuring Kabwe Conference, June 1985. Top frame: Tambo addressing conference. Sechaba, was one of the many publications printed free of charge by the GDR.

Maputo 1983: Guido Van Hecken, Helene Passtoors, Joe Slovo. Photo Van Hecken family collection

Klaas De Jonge, liberated after a prisoner exchange, welcomed in Brussels by Godfrey Motsepe, ANC chief rep, following his release in August 1987.

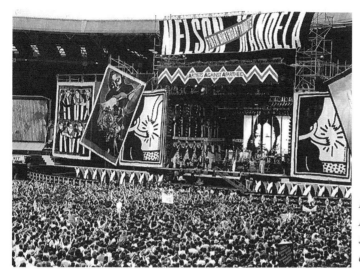

Free Nelson Mandela! Wembley Stadium, London, concert June 1988.

Nelson Mandela and Fidel Castro, Havana, Cuba, July 1991.

Blue Plaque, listing Liverpool seamen who assisted ANC (see Aventura Episode), alongside roll of honour commemorating the city's members of the International Brigade who fell in the struggle for Spanish democracy 1936–38. Liverpool HQ, Unite trade union, Jack Jones House. Photo Lawrence Harris

32

Albertini – French Arms Smuggler in Custody had Mitterand Fuming

PIERRE ANDRÉ ALBERTINI explains to anybody who wants to listen how normal he found it to work for the ANC and MK.

'I served as courier, relayed messages, transported arms and nothing of this seemed to me as exceptional. In fact, I would like to think that most French of my generation would have done the same', he has gone on record as saying.

Having arrived to teach French at the University of Fort Hare in the independent Ciskei Bantustan, he quickly discovered the realities of South Africa. Without going into too much history or theory he explained to several interviewers the problems facing the university, focusing on the authoritarian behaviour of the authorities there as well as the repeated and violent interventions of the police. Bit by bit, Albertini said, he dismantled the cogs and methods of repression in his own mind.

Once caught by the Ciskeian authorities for his MK work, Albertini refused to testify in a terrorism trial against a former fellow lecturer, the Rev. Makhenkesi Arnold Stofile and four others, after turning state witness. His reason for his stance was that upon return to France he would be ostracised by the people.

His parents, who were close to the Communist Party, started a campaign for his release after his four-year conviction by the Ciskeian authorities. The South African government decided to act as an intermediary, claiming that the Ciskei was an independent state with its own laws and government.

The furious French President François Mitterrand decided not to accept the credentials of South Africa's ambassador designate, Mr Hennie Geldenhuys. A French ad-hoc ambassador sent to South Africa by Jean Chirac was requested to intervene in a dossier intended to organise an exchange of prisoners.

Albertini was included among those prisoners swapped in Maputo in August 1987, jointly with Klaas de Jonge and Cuban soldiers, in exchange for the bodies of fallen South African soldiers in Angola and a major Wynand du Toit.

The end of 11 months' detention and his return to France was the raison d'être for a massive Fête de l'Humanité in Évreux (Eure) on 9 December 1987 with more than five thousand jolly participants. Without claiming honours, Albertini explained, I'm not a communist, for me it was an internal revolution.

FURTHER READING

Pierre André Albertini, Un Français en Apartheid, Gallimard, Paris, 1988.

Stéphane Dupont, 'Review of Pierre-André Albertini's Un Français en Apartheid', Politique étrangère, Number 3, 1988, p. 758. https://www.persee.fr/doc/polit_0032-342x_1988_num_53_3_3805_t1_0758_0000_2. Retrieved 29 July 2021.

OM

33

Michael Lapsley – Tribute to Fellow New Zealander Reverend John Osmers

SINCE THE NEWS FIRST BROKE of John's passing on 16 June many of us have been going down memory lane recalling the innumerable ways Fr John touched our lives. More than anything he ever said, as valuable as that was, John's actions were much louder than his words.

It was Isitwalandwe[47] Trevor Huddleston's writing that first confronted John Osmers with the evil of apartheid in faraway Aotearoa, New Zealand.

In 1958, when I was nine years old and many of us were not yet born, John came by boat to South Africa and spent six weeks travelling across South Africa on a motorbike. From that time, South Africa and her people were in his blood.

John studied Sesotho in London and trained for the priesthood with Fr Huddleston's religious congregation. Then, on advice from Fr Huddleston, he came to Lesotho to work as a priest. Like many of us, he became a southern African.

John was involved with the progressive University Christian Movement which helped shape and form a generation of young Christian social justice activists in South Africa and Lesotho.

---

47   Isitwalandwe is the highest award given by the ANC.

As far back as 1970, Fr John was banned from entering South Africa.

Many of us can bear witness to the key role Fr John played in their lives following the Soweto uprising. It was against this backdrop that we witnessed John's faith displayed in his practical solidarity with the refugee community.

John realised that the time had come to throw in his lot with the liberation movement. So he applied to join the ANC, which nearly cost him his life, unlike more recent times when some have joined to feed their greed.

1979 was another defining moment. A parcel filled with copies of *Sechaba* was intercepted and turned into a bomb injuring Fr John, [Solomon] Soks Sokupa, Wandile Kalipa, Phyllis Naidoo, Vuyisile Madaka and Siphiwe Sithole. It is worth noting that those present were five black people including Phyllis Naidoo, a black South African of Indian descent, and a white internationalist. I say this in the context of the increasing number of unchallenged racist attacks on Indian South Africans that seek to destroy our nation.

At the memorial in New Zealand on Monday, John's sister Elizabeth recalled the conversation with the doctor: 'I am sorry, Father, you have lost your right hand.'

John replied, 'It's fine, I am left-handed.'

The doctor continued: 'I am sorry Father; you have also lost a testicle.' Father John responded, 'It's fine, I am a celibate priest.'

When I was chaplain to the National University of Lesotho, I had a large poster on my glass front door of Sam Nujoma after the Cassinga Massacre holding two babies in his arms with the caption: Babies of a colonial war. A wealthy, although compassionate, white Lesotho resident went to my bishop to complain about the poster. The bishop called a meeting of his senior priests which included Fr John to decide what to do with this political priest. Fr John said he didn't see any problem with the poster and 'by the way,' he said, 'I gave it to him.'

I tell the story to illustrate John's view that charity was not enough, it was necessary to advocate for and work for liberation, whilst feeding the hungry and clothing the naked.

In time, the apartheid regime leaned on Lesotho to make Bishop John a persona non grata.

In the run-up to the 1981 Springbok tour of New Zealand, Fr John played a key role in mobilising people across New Zealand to oppose the tour, waving the stump of his missing hand to emphasise his points.

In 2012, Fr John was presented with an ANC Centennial Award for his outstanding contribution to the international campaign against apartheid.

When Fr John became a parish priest in Molepolole in Botswana he was able to provide a discreet safe house for MK soldiers being infiltrated back into South Africa.

Once more Fr John became a target of the apartheid death squads. He was tipped off by the Botswana security and had to leave Botswana at a moment's notice.

Strikingly, the attempts by the apartheid regime only served to deepen his faith and commitment and never to intimidate.

For a number of years Fr John served as chaplain to the ANC in Lusaka whilst being very active in the Anglican Church in Zambia.

When it was time to come home to South Africa, Fr John chose to stay in Zambia. He was elected unopposed as the first bishop of a new diocese in north-eastern Zambia where his ashes will be buried.

Back in 2007, the New Zealand government appointed him as a Companion of the New Zealand Order of Merit for his services to the Anglican Church. Along with Desmond Tutu, and President Kaunda, in 2016, Archbishop Thabo Makgoba conferred on Bishop Osmers his Peace with Justice Award.

Several years ago, Bishop Osmers went blind, but it did not deter him.

Until his last breath he remained committed to the rights and welfare of refugees in Zambia from a number of African countries, especially Rwandese.

Just a week before his death, Bishop John, still recovering from pneumonia, was driven for eight hours back to his old diocese. The occasion was the opening of a new centre named after him. However, his motivation for going there was to meet the prime minister to hand over a letter and advocate for the plight of Rwandese refugees in Zambia who, for reasons of realpolitik, are denied refugee status.

And then Bishop John got Covid and died a few days later.

Bishop John had tried to get a South African pension but failed. It was not to spend on himself but to help with the support of refugees.

My prayer is that the ANC would propose to the government that we give Bishop John a posthumous national award.

Fr John was a man of deep faith. We all have much to learn from him.

He was a freedom fighter. He was also a saint. While he related with people of all faiths, and those with no religious faith, for many, over the last 60 years he spent on our Mother continent, he was the face of Christ.

Bishop John was a victim of Covid. Now that he is in heaven, I am sure he is praying that we all get vaccinated.

Bishop John has left us during one of the most momentous weeks in our history as the country waits and watches to see if our last democratically elected president will accept as he told us he would, his bitter pill of going to prison yet again.

As Nelson Mandela said at the inauguration of the Constitutional Court: 'Today I rise not as an accused, but on behalf of the people of South Africa, to inaugurate a court South Africa has never had, a court on which hinges the future of our democracy.'

I am sure Bishop John is sad that former president Jacob Zuma is going to prison as a consequence of his own actions. I am equally sure he is delighted that the rule of law is triumphing and that the wheels of justice are beginning to hold the corrupt to account.

Bishop John Osmers did not give 60 years of his life to bless looting on an industrial scale. I have no doubt it pained him to see some of his erstwhile comrades betraying the country because of greed. What would pain John particularly is to hear that there are political parties and some politicians fanning the fires of xenophobia.

Now that John is in heaven, when he is not chatting with O.R. and Albertina, and Helen Joseph and Phyllis Naidoo, I am certain he has God's ear, I am sure that he is telling God that the new saints of our time are whistle-blowers, some investigative journalists, members of the SIU, judges like Sisi Khampepe and politicians of different parties who still have a conscience who fight alongside the poor and the oppressed as John did throughout his 86 years.

As Bertold Brecht told us: 'There are those who struggle for a day, and they are good. There are those who struggle for a year, and they are better. There are those who struggle for many years, and they are better still. But there are those who struggle all their lives. These are the indispensable ones.'

Bishop John was such an indispensable one

As for us, Judith February reminded us, in a quote from Coretta Scott King, 'Freedom is never really won. You earn it and win it in every generation.'

LETTER TO BISHOP JOHN OSMERS

Dear John

It is just a few days since you left us to join the ancestors.

To me you were always an older brother ... as we often say in our part of the world, a brother from another mother.

When we first met, you were already the priest at Masite parish in Lesotho and beginning to receive the Soweto generation of young people, fleeing apartheid violence.

When I was expelled from South Africa as part of the class of 1976, you were there to meet me.

We were kindred spirits, both of us New Zealand born, both Anglican priests, both members of the ANC with a lifelong commitment to South Africa's liberation struggle and to the welfare and rights of refugees everywhere. Both of us survivors of attempted assassination.

I only discovered since your passing, that like me, your conviction that apartheid was evil and should be ended, came from reading Trevor Huddleston's *Naught For Your Comfort.*

Our voices were important also for the anti-apartheid struggle in New Zealand, as two kiwis, immersed in black communities in southern Africa.

All of us were in awe of how you responded when you were grievously injured by the parcel bomb attack in 1979. Your indomitable spirit and even humour, in the face of that act of state terror, inspired and gave courage to many.

Throughout your ministry, you have embodied the relationship between faith, compassion, kindness and transformative justice. Across southern Africa, you were a comforter, a confidant and an advocate for countless freedom fighters and refugees.

When you had to leave Botswana under further threat of assassination, I was honoured to receive you in Zimbabwe. You never wavered in your belief in the justice of our cause as something noble and godly.

Your ministry from Lesotho to Botswana to Zambia touched the lives of thousands, inside and outside the church. Indeed all those who love peace and justice were your companions.

Even as we considered you to be part of our families, we have rejoiced that your birth family, Elizabeth and Derry, John, Susannah, Margaret and Charlotte and their children, were by your side in every way possible, over the decades.

Even blindness did not deter you from your advocacy and support for Rwandese refugees in Zambia. Only John Osmers could commute between Christchurch and Lusaka not for selfish ends, but to get the resources to support and educate your extended Rwandese family.

My dear John, your life is both an inspiration and challenge to each of us to continue as you did, until God says, your time is up. We consider you to be a hero. We wish more bishops and leaders of faith communities were like you. Across the world, we will tell Father John Osmers stories even as we carry you in our hearts.

Rest well, good and faithful servant ... your work is over, your battle won.

Edited excerpt from Michael Lapsley's eulogy to John Osmers who passed away on 16 June 2021. Father Lapsley resides in Cape Town. For more about him see page 342.

34

Roger Allingham – From English Farmer to SA Navy Commander Via MK

I WAS BORN IN 1945 in rural Hertfordshire in England. My father was a sheet metal worker who was never politically active. My mother was the daughter of a Swiss farmer who settled in England just prior to the Second World War and was apolitical.

My first political activities were with the youth section of the Labour Party, but I became disillusioned with them, and helped form a Young Communist League (YCL) branch in 1964.

I spent three years at Teacher Training College as a mature student at the height of the student uprisings in Europe. I was very active in student politics, forming a Marxist group and later broadening the base to a Socialist Society.

I gained a Bachelor of Education degree at university, and spent three years teaching, then moved to Wales, in a young people's holiday adventure camp. Then, eight years working for the London Borough of Hillingdon as a youth and community worker.

In 1985 I met Ronnie and Eleanor Kasrils through a mutual friend. The upshot of discussions was that I agreed to move to southern Africa to undertake underground work for the ANC.

I was trained in underground work that stressed no one should know of my activities.

I resigned from my job, telling everyone I was taking a sabbatical to visit Botswana. I organised transport for my beloved small flock of sheep to a local market where they were auctioned.

On arrival at Jan Smuts Airport I was nervous but cleared custom and immigration without incident. I reconnoitred the café where my first meeting with my contact Susan was to take place.

We met up the following day. She had bought a VW Kombi and rented a three-bedroomed house in Henley-on-Klip, south of Johannesburg, in a spot with empty adjacent plots. We furnished the house with cheap second-hand furniture and bought curtains for the many windows.

Susan departed and I was on my own, with the legend that I was a writer and collector of Africana books, while I reconnoitred the military bases in the vicinity of Pretoria, Johannesburg and the Vaal Triangle.

The 'safe house' in Henley-on-Klip was primarily to be used for a planned attack on a South African military base (code named 'Uncle Barney') on the Golden Highway south of Johannesburg and next to Soweto. The Doornkop Military Base was the home of the 21 South African Infantry Battalion. For the planned attack on 'Uncle Barney' I carried out surveillance and gave information back to the ANC.

The crossing of borders always involved border formalities and inspection by soldiers in camouflage accompanied by sniffer dogs. It could be nerve-racking, but any small arms we carried were hidden away in secret compartments and were packed in a sterile way that prevented the dogs picking up explosives.

For short communications from South Africa I used the system of book coding to send secret messages, hidden inside greeting cards, to neutral addresses in England. These were duly passed on to Eleanor Kasrils to pass on again to Ronnie in Africa.

When I next saw him, he explained a plan to infiltrate a special unit into the country. I soon met the group in Botswana, commanded by Damian de Lange. We agreed on an exact date, time and place that I would rendezvous with them on the border.

Everything went like clockwork. I picked up the group and drove them to Johannesburg. They settled into the cottage on a farm, and I went back to a new residence in a flat in Rosettenville.

On return to my first-floor apartment I saw someone jumping over the wall of a neighbouring garden. I wondered if it was a burglar or if I was under surveillance.

The very next morning when I left, I indeed came under surveillance. At first everything seemed OK but then I noticed an old model grey Peugeot 505 with black occupants. I was clearly being followed.

Now the cat and mouse game started. I took my dirty laundry to a launderette for washing. When I left, I detected my tail. I led them around various places during the day and then retired to my apartment in Rosettenville. The next day I was expecting a tail, but not as heavy as it turned out to be – that day I counted five different cars following me around Johannesburg, with mostly white occupants, as I continued with a normal day of shopping and visiting the bank. One couple even followed me into the bank.

They froze at following me into the underground car park of Carlton Centre, a shopping centre in downtown Johannesburg, and were confused. Realising that I was not being tailed I quickly left the mall on foot and walked around Johannesburg. When I returned and left with my vehicle the tails were back.

The next day I tried the same trick using the underground car park, but they had reorganised and picked me up on foot straight away. The following day was the first of the prearranged meetings with the Damian unit if we had trouble.

The meeting was in a bookshop in downtown Johannesburg. I browsed around for some time, but my comrades did not show up. As I went down the stairs, I bumped into one of my 'tails' coming up the stairs. He stopped and very self-consciously looked at a picture on the wall as I walked away.

The next day I went to the fall-back rendezvous meeting place. During the next half hour I saw the surveillance team traipsing round and my comrade observing them. The tails were being tailed by my comrades. I left the restaurant and walked into the connected Carlton Hotel to take the lift down to the car park. As I stepped in, I was surprised when Damian de Lange suddenly jumped into the lift with me.

He reported that surveillance on me was very heavy, and I should immediately prepare to leave the country.

The next day I approached the British Consul. I claimed I was looking to set up a business and was being followed. He looked at my passport and asked why I kept visiting Botswana. I said I had a girlfriend there, and he replied, 'Please don't take this amiss, but if she is black, this is probably the reason you are being followed.' He asked: 'What do you want me do?' I explained I wanted to leave the country, but I feared that I would be prevented from doing so. He said, 'Make a booking for your flight and advise me of the details.'

He gave me his personal home phone number and told me to phone him from the departure lounge when I left, explaining that if I did not make the call they would follow up with South African authorities on my whereabouts.

I had a few days to kill before my flight, so I entertained my tails by taking them to places of interest. I went to Johannesburg Zoo. It was hilarious walking around looking at animals and observing tails all over the place watching my every move.

On the day of departure, they followed me, but I flew off without problems. Back in London, Eleanor Kasrils debriefed me. She told me the unit had not been detected. Damian's unit survived for a number of years. They carried out several attacks before being given away by a member of the cell while living on a smallholding at Broederstroom near Pretoria. Quite why I had been under surveillance remains a mystery.

After a few months the ANC gave me a new British passport in the name of Simon Cottle. I joined a new safe house in Gaborone, Botswana with Peter Smith, a veteran recruit of Ronnie's from London.[48]

On the border fence we met up with comrades from South Africa many times to supply them with arms and ammunition, by literally handing the stuff over the fence – including a Strela which could be used to bring down low-altitude aircraft.

Back in Gaborone, Ronnie discussed a plan to open up a sea route involving the smuggling of arms and ammunition into the country. Knowing I had been a keen yachtsman in Britain, he wanted me train in Cuba to captain an ocean-going vessel.

Beforehand, I carried out a reconnaissance trip of the coastline,

---

48   See Ken Keable, ed., *London Recruits: The secret war against apartheid*, Merlin Press, 2012.

reconnoitring suitable locations for landings.

I flew to Cuba via Shannon Airport in west Ireland. I was accommodated in a Havana house in a quiet neighbourhood. My instructor was Alberto, a giant of a man with a wonderful sense of humour, who taught navigation and seamanship in relation to small motor vessels.

Back in a changing South Africa, following Nelson Mandela's release, and with the ANC still vigilant, expecting possible setbacks, I enrolled at the Seaman's Training College in Cape Town harbour and qualified as a master of a fishing vessel.

I was redeployed into Ordnance, and Rashid became my handler. I worked in the Johannesburg office of the African Hinterland project smuggling weapons.

When the project was folded in 1993 it was decided I should join the navy. My integration was going smoothly until it was discovered I was a UK citizen. The integration agreement stipulated that only South African nationals could integrate. I contacted Ronnie Kasrils, who was by then the Deputy Minister of Defence. He fixed things. The following day, I was summoned to the Department of Home Affairs to meet with the director general and sworn in by him as a South African citizen.

I met, for the first time, ten fellow MK comrades who had trained in the Soviet Union and were also integrating into the SA navy.

The ranks of naval officers integrating from MK was a contentious issue. In 1993 the integration of the SADF and non-statutory forces was guided by a Joint Military Command Council (JMCC). The 'white' SADF tended to dominate discussions. MK, as largely a land army, had little say over the air force and navy. The SADF navy contingent tried to force non-commissioned ranks on the MK officers instead of commission ranks. In my own case I was given the commissioned rank by MK of Captain (Temp) Commander (Substantive).

Once the enlistment process for Navy MK officers was completed in Pretoria, we were bussed down to SA Naval College at Gordon's Bay in the Cape. We were kitted out with naval uniforms and underwent a three-month orientation programme.

In 1995 I completed my combat officers course and began service.

In 1997 when I was appointed as the executive officer (second in command) of SA Naval College, several hundred Naval recruits from MK who trained as seaman at SAS Saldanha appealed against their ranks and appeared before appeal boards that looked at their educational qualifications, military courses completed, and leadership positions they held in MK. The overwhelming majority were re-ranked to one or two higher positions.

In 1999 I was promoted to captain (SA Navy), and I assumed command of the SA Naval College, Gordons Bay. I then served as senior staff officer for maritime strategy; and in 2005 ended my naval career as senior staff officer for fleet planning, Simonstown naval base.

I set up home with my wife Stella and family in Gordon's Bay.

ROGER ALLINGHAM now has a small sailing boat moored in Gordon's Bay harbour and looks forward to more time on the water.

PART TWO

Solidarity Across the Globe

35

Christabel Gurney – The Role of the AAM Internationally

'YOU ARE THE FRIENDS from five continents who kept hope alive,' Nelson Mandela told comrades from around the world at a conference in Tanzania in 1993. 'You took the plight of our people, our hopes, our dreams and our struggle to your hearts and made it your own. You refused to let the world ignore the tragedy wreaked by apartheid.'

The 1980s saw an extraordinary upsurge in global action to end apartheid in South Africa. From the frontline states of southern Africa, which stood firm in spite of the wrecking of their own people's aspirations to freedom by civil wars fomented by South Africa, to Sweden, which supplied the ANC with funds to run its administration and look after its members in exile, and from the Soviet Union, which trained MK fighters, to the USA, where grassroots campaigners pressured Congress into overriding the presidential veto on economic sanctions – the movement spiralled.

In Britain, the Anti-Apartheid Movement mobilised hundreds of thousands of people to call for sanctions against apartheid and to support the liberation movement. Unlike earlier international campaigns, like that against the slave trade or forced labour in the Congo, the global Anti-Apartheid Movement was not paternalist, an operation where outsiders told those living under apartheid what to do, but a movement of solidarity which responded to the needs of the liberation movements. And in the decade of Thatcher and Reagan, it was a people's movement: where governments did act, largely because of pressure from below.

The decade was dominated by neoliberal economics, the privatisation of public services and abandonment of state regulation. This generated strikes and racial unrest. In Britain, race riots in London, Liverpool, Leeds and Manchester in 1981 were followed by a national miners' strike in 1984–85. Society was polarised and young people were radicalised in response to the rise of the right and authoritarian governments. They created a new counterculture of design, rock music and alternative comedy. Solidarity with those fighting to end apartheid in South Africa became part of their repertoire of resistance.

The young women and men whose stories are told in this book were part of this ferment. They looked for new ways of taking a stand against right-wing ideologies. Against a background of mass campaigns for boycott and sanctions against apartheid, they volunteered to join the ANC's armed struggle, putting their lives and liberty on the line.

The solidarity movement with the people of South Africa was as old as apartheid itself. In 1947, the year before the National Party came to power, British students protested against the royal tour of South Africa. The British Boycott Movement was set up in 1959 and the following year, after the Sharpeville massacre, it transformed itself into the Anti-Apartheid Movement. Through the 1960s and 1970s the AAM was a small but determined pressure group, never giving up, but with only occasional successes, like the cancellation of the Springbok cricket tour in 1970. In other countries, such as Sweden and the Netherlands, which were later pillars of support for the ANC, action on southern Africa in the 1970s focused on the liberation movements in the Portuguese colonies of Mozambique and Angola, rather than on South Africa.

The explosion of solidarity in the 1980s was above all a response to the growth of resistance within South Africa. The formation of the United Democratic Front (UDF) in 1983 and the insurrection in the townships in 1984–86 changed the potential for anti-apartheid action in the international community. Anti-apartheid campaigners forged new links with those struggling inside South Africa and the ANC gained new authority as its own best international advocate. In the 1960s and 1970s, leaders of the ANC in exile had close personal links with solidarity movement activists, especially in Britain and the Nordic countries. But the international movement had few contacts with anyone who was able to travel to and from South Africa. The liberation movements had been forced underground and opponents of apartheid who left the country came on one-way exit permits. Overseas citizens who had spoken out against apartheid were forced to apply for visas, which were always refused. In the 1980s there was a sea-change and the British AAM and other national groups established close working relationships with the UDF and other above-ground South African organisations. UDF leaders like Valli Moosa and Murphy Morobe travelled overseas. In 1984 a delegation visited London in an attempt to get Prime Minister Thatcher to intervene on behalf of six UDF leaders who had taken refuge in Britain's Durban consulate.

The ANC became more public-facing, developing new publicity skills in Western capitals and a media-friendly image. In 1987 it convened a solidarity conference in Arusha, Tanzania, at which a wide range of international delegates, such as community activists from London's Broadwater Farm estate,[49] met ANC leaders.

In the 1970s, the mainstream media in Britain had reflected white South African attitudes and gave little coverage to anti-apartheid campaigns or the southern African liberation movements. But in the mid-1980s reporting changed. In September 1985 a *Times* correspondent wrote: 'It is hard to envisage an eventual settlement in South Africa that does not involve the ANC.'

From 1984, the apartheid government unleashed a wave of vicious reprisals against the township insurrection. For a few months in 1985 British television showed troops attacking unarmed protesters in South African townships on almost every news bulletin. During the States of Emergency declared in South Africa in July 1985 and June 1986 the authorities detained and often tortured children and young people. Young

---

49 An uprising that began in Tottenham, London, following the police shooting of a black woman, Dorothy Groce, and later death under suspicious circumstances of the mother of another police suspect. For an account of the Broadwater Estate uprising see, https://turbulentlondon.com/2016/10/06/on-this-day-the-broadwater-farm-riots-6th-october-1985/comment-page-1/. Retrieved 10 August 2021.

MK guerrilla fighters were sentenced to death, and some, like poet Benjamin Moloise in October 1985, were hanged. Even unarmed bystanders like the Sharpeville Six and Upington 14 were sentenced to hang. The British AAM and the International Defence and Aid Fund (IDAF), also based in London, led campaigns to publicise the apartheid government's descent into wholesale repression. This sparked condemnation from ever wider sectors of public opinion and gave a whole new impetus to the call for the total isolation of apartheid.

In 1985 in the UN General Assembly, some Western governments joined with African states to pass a resolution asking member states to take unilateral measures against South Africa, including a ban on new investment and loans and an end to trade promotion. The UN Security Council passed a resolution proposed by Denmark and France calling on UN members to impose a wide range of sanctions. Only the USA and the UK abstained.

Meanwhile the Commonwealth, at its heads of government meeting in the Bahamas in October 1985, wrestled over how far it would go in imposing sanctions. The majority of members, including the white majority dominions of Canada, Australia and New Zealand, wanted to impose a wholesale ban on trade and investment in the apartheid economy. Only British Prime Minister Margaret Thatcher held out against a ban.

At a press conference, she talked down the limited measures that were eventually agreed and she exacted as the price of her formal acquiescence an agreement to send a Commonwealth mission to South Africa. The following year, the mission reported that the South African government was intransigent and that there was no prospect of holding meaningful negotiations to end apartheid. The rest of the Commonwealth went ahead with banning the import of South African agricultural products, new investment and air links. But Britain refused to take part, only imposing voluntary bans on new investment and tourism, which it never enforced.

Similarly, attempts by the Netherlands, Ireland and Denmark to impose meaningful sanctions by the European Economic Community were thwarted by Britain and West Germany. In 1986 the EEC banned the import of South African iron and steel products, but with so many exceptions that the ban only applied to an estimated 2% of total EEC imports from South Africa. It took no measures to stop imports of coal, the export commodity that really mattered to the apartheid economy.

Paradoxically, it was the hostility of the Thatcher and Reagan governments to economic sanctions that transformed anti-apartheid action in Britain and the USA into mass movements. Although the Conservative Party won three successive general elections, Thatcher was a divisive figure, loathed by wide sections of the British public. Anti-apartheid campaigning became an integral part of the opposition to Thatcher, supported by Labour-led local authorities, trade unions, anti-racist organisations and very many otherwise apolitical people. The flipside was that Thatcher's intransigence made it more difficult for the movement to achieve its aims through conventional political channels.

In 1985–86, in response to Thatcher's refusal to compromise, the AAM mounted its biggest ever campaign for sanctions. Its strategy was three-pronged: to lobby the government and put pressure on MPs; to mobilise mass demonstrations; and to create broad alliances within communities to boycott all links with South Africa.

In autumn 1985, activists presented a 200 000-signature petition to parliament. In June 1986 it organised the biggest ever lobby of parliament on an international issue, backed by the British Council of Churches, the Trades Union Congress and the National Union of Students. At the same time, hundreds of thousands of people took to the streets. On 2 November 1985 in London, marchers from the east, west and south of the city converged on Trafalgar Square to hear ANC President Oliver Tambo, SWAPO leader Shapua Kaukungua and US civil rights leader Jesse Jackson call for sanctions. And in June 1986, after the collapse of the Commonwealth mission to South Africa, a quarter of a million people gathered on Clapham Common for the Artists Against Apartheid's Festival for Freedom in Namibia and South Africa. In the Welsh capital Cardiff, thousands marched demanding sanctions against apartheid.

At the grassroots, in towns and villages countrywide, local anti-apartheid groups held motorcades and demonstrations outside supermarkets. In March 1986 they distributed 750 000 leaflets – including a multilingual one for ethnic minority communities – calling for a boycott of South African products. The month ended in a day of action with around 1000 pickets and demonstrations in shopping centres all over Britain.

During the campaign there were pockets of spontaneous trade union action. Passport office workers rejected applications from South Africans entitled to dual citizenship and clerical workers at the British Library refused to process records from South African libraries. Portsmouth health workers kept up a long-running dispute with the local health authority to persuade it to boycott South African medical supplies, with the support of their trade union. A mass meeting of workers at the Ford car plant at Dagenham in east London voted to refuse to work on components to be exported to South Africa.

After the Conservative government was re-elected in 1987, the AAM mounted a new campaign for people's sanctions. It had always asked individual shoppers to boycott South African goods. Now it called for mass action to stop supermarkets from stocking apartheid products. Tesco and Sainsbury's were subjected to regular days of action when activists handed out leaflets warning 'Every bite buys a bullet' or piled South African fruit into trolleys and refused to pay. In two areas with big Afro-Caribbean communities, Brixton in London and St Paul's in Bristol, Tesco agreed to take South African goods off the shelves.

The campaign found new targets – gold, coal and tourism. A coalition of groups set up the World Gold Commission to research gold sanctions. The AAM linked up with the National Union of Mineworkers to plan an embargo against South African coal imports. In Swansea in South Wales, dockers refused to unload a shipment of South African coal. Activists picketed travel agents telling their customers 'Apartheid is no holiday'.

The campaign met with a remarkable response. In June 1986 a public opinion poll found that 27% of British shoppers boycotted South African products. Just over 50% were in favour of some form of sanctions against South Africa. Fruit and vegetable imports from South Africa fell by 8.5% in 1986; between 1983 and 1986 imports of South African textiles dropped from £14 million to £9 million, a fall of over 35%. The South African Canned Fruit Export Board said: 'Although there are no official sanctions against South Africa, there seems to be a reluctance of buyers to take the risk of stocking South African products.'

At last, partly in response to fears about instability inside South Africa and partly in response to campaigns in their home countries, British and US companies pre-empted government action and started pulling out of South Africa. In November 1986, Barclays Bank, the target of a 16-year campaign by students and community organisations, announced that it would withdraw. It admitted: 'Our customer base was beginning to be adversely affected.' Altogether 55 British and 114 US companies disposed of their South African subsidiaries.

As Britain and the USA continued to veto mandatory economic sanctions at the UN, in 1988 the international movement stepped up its call for the release of Nelson Mandela. On his 60th birthday, in 1978, Labour Prime Minister James Callaghan had sent birthday greetings from the British Parliament. Now, on Mandela's 70th birthday, the British AAM launched its biggest ever campaign 'Nelson Mandela: Freedom at 70'. Rock musicians had campaigned against apartheid from the early 1980s, when Jerry Dammers's song 'Free Nelson Mandela' was high on the charts. Fundraising for the AAM became part of the repertoire of bands like The Smiths and UB40, and in April 1987 Artists Against Apartheid filled London's Albert Hall with an all-star line-up. The centrepiece of the 'Freedom at 70' campaign was the concert at Wembley Stadium on 11 June 1988 which sold out to a capacity audience. The concert was broadcast by the BBC, which made it available to television stations worldwide, so that it had a potential audience of a billion people in 63 countries – a record number for a live event. The concert was followed by a five-week 'Freedom March' from Glasgow to London by 25 marchers, one for each year of Mandela's imprisonment. On 17 July, the eve of Mandela's birthday, the marchers reached London welcomed by a crowd of 250 000 in Hyde Park. The campaign had a huge international impact. It projected Mandela, not just as the world's most famous political prisoner, but as the future leader of a non-racial South Africa.

All over the world solidarity action was spreading. In the USA, starting in the universities in the late 1960s, grassroots campaigns for disinvestment mushroomed, until by the early 1980s they had become a national movement. Led by black student and community groups, the movement for divestment was decentralised and focused on individual universities, institutions and local and state governments.

By 1986 popular pressure enabled Afro-American Congressmen to introduce and pilot through Congress a bill for sanctions, the Comprehensive Anti-Apartheid Act (CAAA), and to override Reagan's presidential veto. Perhaps even more important, in July 1985, Chase

Manhattan Bank refused to roll over a major loan to South Africa, forcing the apartheid government to announce a moratorium on the repayment of its foreign debts and the temporary closure of the foreign exchange markets and the Johannesburg Stock Exchange. By 1991, 28 US states and 92 cities had imposed some form of economic sanctions against South Africa.

Unlike in Britain and the USA, the Netherlands government gave funding to the southern African liberation movements and to Dutch anti-apartheid organisations. Feeling against apartheid was strong, especially among young people. A coalition of groups campaigned for a global oil embargo, focusing on the oil multinational Shell. Starting with an international conference on the oil embargo organised in cooperation with the UN Special Committee Against Apartheid in 1980, they set up the Shipping Research Bureau to unravel South Africa's secret worldwide oil trade. The leading Dutch anti-apartheid organisations, the Dutch Anti-Apartheid Movement (AABN), the South Africa Committee (KZA) and the church-based Kairos were committed to nonviolent action. But starting in 1985, other unidentified groups bombed and burnt down installations belonging to oil companies which had dealings with South Africa, including several Shell petrol stations.

The other focus of Dutch anti-apartheid action was the celebration of South African music and culture. The Netherlands had a formal cultural agreement signed with the Afrikaner-dominated apartheid government in 1951. Thirty years later this was finally cancelled. The Dutch Anti-Apartheid Movement responded by organising a conference to strengthen cultural ties between the Netherlands and the ANC. A second two-week celebration and conference on the way ahead for South African culture was held in 1987, attended by some 300 South African performers and activists, some exiles and some based in South Africa.[50]

The frontline states of southern Africa stood firm in the face of armed raids and the fomenting of civil war by South Africa's armed forces. Cuba played a crucial role in supporting MPLA resistance to South African aggression in Angola and its war against the Namibian liberation movement SWAPO. The Soviet Union gave military training to MK; the countries of eastern Europe, especially the German Democratic Republic,

---

50   Culture in Another South Africa, held in December 1987 in Amsterdam.

supplied assistance in kind and training for anti-apartheid exiles. Sweden and the other Nordic countries gave vital financial support to the ANC. Importantly, where governments acted, it was with support from their citizens, 'a compact formed between civil society and their state/ government', as one former activist described the assistance sent from the Nordic countries.

By the end of the decade it was clear that apartheid could not continue in the same old way. A combination of internal resistance and external boycott and sanctions forced the South African government to look for compromise with anti-apartheid forces.

In February 1990 President de Klerk announced the lifting of bans on the South African liberation movements and released Nelson Mandela. For the next four years the regime ducked and dived in an attempt to forestall a constitution that guaranteed one person one vote in a unitary South Africa. Its aim was to bring about a compromise so that South Africa was accepted in the international community, but that would privilege the white minority.

After the highs of the 1980s solidarity campaign, this was a difficult period for the international Anti-Apartheid Movement and for the activists who had joined MK undercover. The movement continued to press for sanctions and undercover activists took part in Operation Vula.

The achievement of one person one vote elections in April 1994 and the election of Nelson Mandela as president owed much to the hundreds of thousands of activists all over the world who took time off from their daily routines to campaign against apartheid. It was also a triumph for the small band of activists who risked their personal freedom, and sometimes their lives, to fight alongside their South African comrades.

CHRISTABEL GURNEY, activist and historian, was involved in the Anti-Apartheid Movement from 1969 to 1994. London-based, she continues to research and write, and is the curator of anti-apartheid archives, documentation and history.

36

Abdul Minty – Birth of AAM, UN, Commonwealth, Huddleston, Luthuli

THE ANTI-APARTHEID MOVEMENT (AAM) grew out of the boycott movement established on 26 June 1959 in London in response to an appeal by ANC President Chief Albert Luthuli and other South African leaders. The boycott appeal was endorsed by Father Trevor Huddleston, Julius Nyerere and other anti-apartheid leaders. June 26 was South Africa Freedom Day emanating from the adoption of the Freedom Charter on that date and it was celebrated as Solidarity Day annually until the liberation of South Africa.

Some of the AAM key leaders included Father Trevor Huddleston, Barbara Castle, Ros Ainslie, David Steel, Bob Hughes, Bishop Ambrose Reeves, Canon Collins, Fenner Brockway, Ethel de Keyser, Mike Terry, Ruth First and many others. But the one person who worked in a bureaucratic position at the UN in New York and perhaps did most to internationalise the work of the AAM was probably Enuga Sreenivasulu Reddy. He effectively inspired and coordinated all the anti-apartheid organisatons across the world.

For a UN civil servant to function as an African freedom fighter is a huge transformation and he managed this role with great distinction. It was in effect a self-managed role because it was extremely difficult to work as an international civil servant and a great supporter of all types of anti-apartheid institutions in various countries. On 27 April 2013 he received the Order of the Companions of O.R. Tambo (silver) and also other tributes for his remarkable work for southern Africa at the UN and elsewhere.

E.S. Reddy, Secretary of the UN's Special Committee Against Apartheid, met Vella Pillay and me to establish a comprehensive relationship with the AAM that continued until the end of apartheid in South Africa. Prior to this meeting, O.R. Tambo met me and conveyed to me the importance of developing a close working relationship with E.S. Reddy and the UN.

At the time of the 1961 Commonwealth Conference in London, Barbara Castle organised an AAM 72-hour picket demonstration with prominent participants calling for the exclusion of South Africa from the Commonwealth. There was such great opposition to apartheid South Africa, both within and outside the Commonwealth because of the Sharpeville massacre of children, that it led the regime to decide not to proceed with its application as a republic. South Africa was thus effectively excluded from the Commonwealth.

In 1962 Ros Ainslie had to retire as AAM honorary secretary and Oliver Tambo approached me to stand for this post. It was a difficult decision since I was a full-time student but, in the end, I agreed to do so since Barbara Castle would only accept the position of president of AAM if I was available as the honorary secretary.

As a result of our campaigns we got to know several Commonwealth leaders personally. Canon Collins of St Paul's Cathedral was an early active supporter of the South African liberation struggle and when the regime decided to initiate the major Treason Trial against Congress leaders, he raised funds for the defence and aid of those who were charged. It was undoubtedly due to the legal assistance that was provided for the accused that they were eventually discharged. Many experts believe that had it not been for the legal assistance provided via Canon Collins some of those charged could have been sentenced to death. Later, at the time of the Rivonia Trial, Canon Collins was able to establish a much larger International Defence and Aid Fund with support from several governments and individuals. This was a long trial with major campaigns in a large number of countries for the release of all detainees and the prosecution at the end of its case only asked for life imprisonment. In a sense it was a major victory against the apartheid regime, but it also led us to initiate world international campaigns for the release of these leaders.

Much earlier, in 1959–60, I was at Leeds University for a year and worked to obtain the Nobel Peace Prize for Chief Albert Luthuli. I discovered that professors of law and philosophy at universities could nominate individuals for the Nobel Peace Prize. I went to see the chancellor, who also put me in touch with the respective departments whose heads could nominate the Peace Prize candidates. I supplied biographical and other information about Chief Luthuli, and he was nominated and awarded the Nobel Peace Prize of 1960 in 1961. This was a great victory, and the regime was forced to provide him with a passport to travel to Oslo for the ceremony. Oliver Tambo and other senior leaders also went to Oslo. The Norwegian public was very sympathetic and so began the development of one of the most reliable, though small, solidarity movements in Europe. In Britain and other countries a large number of parliamentarians were also lobbied to nominate Chief Luthuli, and Richard Crossman in London asked to see me a couple of times about the nomination.

Another venue for active lobbying was the Commonwealth because of its large Afro-Asian membership – though later Margaret Thatcher acted as a reliable ally of the apartheid regime. Before each summit we had meetings with the secretariat officials and the secretary general in London and presented them with documents on various subjects to be raised at the summit.

In 1969 I wrote a short study entitled 'South Africa's Defence Strategy' based on detailed research carried out while at University College London. In addition to detailed facts about South Africa's strategy there was one official ministerial statement reproduced in the booklet: 'We must not look at only the peaceful uses of nuclear energy.'

It was clear from much of the evidence that South Africa was developing a nuclear device. On the eve of the second OAU/UN international conference for action against apartheid in Lagos in 1977, we heard that Western satellites had picked up evidence of a secret South African test site. There was an international outcry, but prior to that the AAM had approached all the major Western countries about their nuclear collaboration with the apartheid regime. All of them without exception said that their nuclear cooperation was for peaceful purposes only; yet their leaders were now calling upon the apartheid regime not to detonate a nuclear device. So we asked how they could detonate what they did not have.

The chairperson of the UN Special Committee Against Apartheid Olof Palme of Sweden, David Steel of Britain and many other personalities and leaders of the liberation movements were at the conference, as was the Norwegian prime minister who kindly agreed to attend personally although no other Western head of government did. The Norwegian prime minister informed the UN that if I came to Oslo then, since Norway expected to be on the Security Council, they could take up issues related to the arms embargo. With the assistance of Abdul Reddy, the UN Special Committee against Apartheid decided to propose to the AAM that it should open a special office in Oslo called the World Campaign against Military and Nuclear Collaboration with South Africa. The AAM agreed to this and, although I was expected to resign from AAM, I was told that the officials had decided against it and that I should keep both posts.

Although the UN Security Council had set up special committees and other structures to monitor UN sanctions against the illegal regime in Rhodesia, it instituted virtually no effective machinery for the arms embargo against South Africa. All that existed was a Security Council committee to monitor the arms embargo against South Africa under Ambassador Bishara of Kuwait, who did his best and used much of the evidence presented. In effect I was the only person presenting evidence to the committee since virtually no country wanted to give evidence about another country that had violated the arms embargo.

In June 1984 the Botha regime calculated that it would be able to make major inroads into international sanctions and the isolation that the apartheid regime experienced as a result of the Nkomati Accord, which could give it additional legitimacy. Botha arranged an international trip with a major stop in Britain to gain international respectability, but it resulted in massive hostile demonstrations in London.

The AAM asked to see Margaret Thatcher before she met Botha and Trevor Huddleston, and I had an important meeting with her when she made a statement re-affirming the arms embargo as well as the Gleneagles Agreement. She also agreed to look into reports about South Africa breaching British laws and violating the arms embargo. It was certainly not a successful summit and Botha had the same cold treatment in other countries.

As the internal resistance in South Africa increased and Namibia became independent, the Pretoria regime was isolated even further and its armed and security forces could not manage to impose its authority and power for very much longer. It had experienced severe punishment during its military engagements in Namibia, including with Cuban forces. Thus it had to prepare to give up political power by redressing whatever authority and control it could. In the end it had to listen to advice from the major Western countries that the white power system was not sustainable and if concessions were not made it could be swept from power by a hot revolution.

Abdul Minty was appointed honorary secretary of the Anti-Apartheid Movement 1961–1995. He was Director General of Foreign Affairs until 2004, Ambassador to the UN in Geneva till 2015 and is now retired.

37
E.S. Reddy – A Giant at the United Nations

E.S. REDDY WAS THE secretary of the UN Committee Against Apartheid from 1963 and made this institution an indispensable resource for the anti-apartheid movement.

Coming to the United States from India in 1946, E.S. Reddy was both a witness to and an important participant in the international struggle to end apartheid in South Africa. He went to work for the United Nations Secretariat in 1949 and served there for 35 years. From 1963 to 1984 he was the UN official in charge of action against apartheid, first as principal secretary of the Special Committee Against Apartheid and then as director of the Centre Against Apartheid.

United Nations action both legitimated and was influenced by the momentum of popular mobilisation against apartheid. Reddy was probably the most consistent and influential of the UN officials working behind the scenes, ensuring that the United Nations not only represented governments but also helped build bridges between liberation movements and their supporters in the United States and other countries.

Inspired by his own country's struggle for independence, he first connected to Africa through the Council on African Affairs in New York. Later, when African countries gained influence at the United Nations, he was able to use his position in the Secretariat to work closely with the American Committee on Africa and Episcopal Churchmen for South Africa in New York, and with other groups around the United States and around the world.

E.S. Reddy spoke with Lisa Brock in New York City on 20 July 2004:

I was already interested in the anti-apartheid movement in the 1940s, when the struggle in South Africa took on new forms and Indians and Africans were cooperating in the struggle. During the Second World War, the United States and Britain talked about four freedoms in the Atlantic Charter, but those freedoms didn't apply to India or South Africa. As Indians we were very much interested in South Africa, because a lot of Indians were there, and they were treated as second-class citizens or worse. And of course, Nehru was talking about South Africa, Gandhi was talking about South Africa and so on.

I arrived in New York in 1946, shortly before the Indian passive resistance and the African mine labour strike in South Africa. I learnt from a friend that there was a Council on African Affairs in New York with a library that got newspapers from South Africa. So, I began to go to the council almost every week and look at the newspapers. That is how I met Dr Alphaeus Hunton, a very fine man. He was head of research at the council at that time, later executive director. We became good friends.

In June 1946, India complained to the United Nations about racial discrimination against Indians in South Africa and the matter was discussed in November and December of that year. A delegation led by Dr A.B. Xuma, president-general of the African National Congress, came from South Africa to advise the Indian delegation and lobby the United Nations. Paul Robeson, who was chairman of the Council on African Affairs, hosted a reception for them and I met the delegation. The council organised a demonstration in front of the South African consulate in New York. I was in contact with the council and took a group of Indian students to join the demonstration.

When the Indian delegation came to the United Nations in '46 for the first time – the free Indian delegation – they said the main issues in the world for us were colonialism and racism. They were not interested in the Cold War. India felt very strongly about discrimination in South Africa, and also took up the question of South-West Africa [Namibia]. It not only tried to get support from other countries, but tried to build up support from the public, especially in Britain and the United States.

All those who supported India's freedom now began to support African freedom, because solidarity can easily be transferred when the basic issue is freedom. The people who were in the solidarity movement for South Africa in those early days were mostly the people who were in the solidarity movement with India.

In 1952, after the African National Congress decided on the Defiance Campaign, India and some Asian and African countries got together and asked the United Nations to discuss the whole question of apartheid. By that time, I was working in the UN Secretariat, and my boss called me in for a chat. He said, 'Don't you think it's illegal to bring that up? It's an internal problem.' So, I said, 'No, I don't think so. I think it's a matter of how you interpret the charter.' Because you know when the UN charter was signed, the real India was not there. And we had a different attitude towards the charter than some of the Western countries; it's a psychological thing. He didn't like that at all. He said I was prejudiced, not objective. Supposedly UN staff should be objective, neutral and all that sort of thing. So he moved me from research on South Africa to the Middle East.

The atmosphere in the UN was terrible for many years, until the sixties. It changed after many African countries became independent and joined the United Nations. Third World countries became a majority. So, the situation was much better when the Special Committee Against Apartheid was established and I was appointed secretary.

The Western countries refused to join the Special Committee. As a result, all the members and I thought alike. Not only were we against apartheid, but we supported the liberation struggle and opposed Western collaboration with South Africa. The members of the committee, who were delegates of governments, and I could work together as one team. That could not happen in other committees where the members were divided, and the Secretariat was supposed to be neutral.

Coming from India, with the influence of Gandhi and Nehru, I felt that we had a duty not only to get India's freedom, but to make sure that India's freedom would be the beginning of the end of colonialism. Rightly or wrongly, I had a feeling that I had not made enough sacrifice for India's freedom, so I should compensate by doing what I could for the rest of the colonies. That feeling was in the back of my mind.

The real opportunity came when I was appointed secretary of the Committee Against Apartheid in 1963. Other officials were not interested, as they felt the committee was worthless. I wanted to give the best I could, and I did for more than 20 years.

Soon after the committee was formed, we had a private meeting of the officers. I explained to them what I knew of the situation in South Africa and what I thought the committee and the United Nations could do. The chairman was Diallo Telli from Guinea, who later became secretary general of the Organisation of African Unity. He liked my presentation, and said, 'Look, Mr. Reddy, we are small delegations, we are terribly busy with so many things, so many issues, documents and meetings and so on. We don't have the time or the staff to do research. So you study the situation, you propose to us what we should do, and we'll say yes or no.'

So our relationship developed into tremendous confidence. Most of the resolutions were written by me. Reports were written by me. Even speeches were written by me for many years. But I can't claim too much credit because nothing would have happened unless the chairman and other members took the responsibility and made the necessary decisions.

And I told them, 'Look, I'm a very junior official in the UN, so there is a limit to what I can do. I will get into trouble if it gets known that I did this or that. You have to take the responsibility for everything.' That they very loyally did. And of course, they obtained credit for all that I quietly and often secretly helped them in doing. So, with their protection I was able, for instance, to discuss with the liberation movements about their needs and the possibilities in the United Nations, contact anti-apartheid groups, seek their advice, and help, and propose initiatives for the Special Committee. I was very lucky that I had a job doing something I believed in; it has given me a lot of satisfaction. In the course of my work, I was able not only to help the liberation movements, but to develop closest cooperation with anti-apartheid groups because their activities in promoting public opinion and public action against apartheid were crucial for the effectiveness of the United Nations.

It could have been an extremely frustrating job because whatever we did, repression was getting worse in South Africa year after year and people were suffering. But I was not frustrated.

Once a proposal I suggested did not get enough support and I was depressed. Robert Resha, a leader of the African National Congress, was with me. He said, 'E.S., why are you frustrated? We are not frustrated. It's none of your business to be frustrated. We are going to win.' So, I kept that in mind.

We were able to win small victories and help people. For instance, we set up a fund for scholarships; we set up a fund to help the political prisoners and their families. And they developed into big things. Thousands of South Africans got scholarships. The fund for the prisoners was my idea. And millions of dollars started coming in after a while. Every day we could see that this fund was helping a prisoner or his family, financing defence in a trial and so on. We could derive some satisfaction from what we could do. So, we had faith that we were going to win, and that faith never left me.

E.S. REDDY, an Indian-born supporter of Gandhi, campaigned for boycotts, divestments and other protests against the South African government. Reddy oversaw the UN's efforts against apartheid first as principal secretary of the Special Committee Against Apartheid and then as director of the Centre Against Apartheid. He is a recipient of the Order of the Companions of O.R. Tambo

Reprinted from Lisa Brooke, *E.S. Reddy: Behind the Scenes at the United Nations* pages 63-66 in Minter, William et al (Richmond Hill, NY: D.K. Hunton, 1986). This article was reproduced with kind permission from William Minter, Hovey Gail and Cobb Charles Jr. (eds), *E.S. Reddy: Behind the Scenes at the United Nations* in 'No Easy Victories: African Liberation and American Activists Over a Half Century, 1950–2000' Published by Africa World Press, 2007. The book is available from: http://www.noeasyvictories.org/select/02_reddy.php.

38

Horst Kleinschmidt – International Defence and Aid Fund's Silent Solidarity

THE INTERNATIONAL DEFENCE and Aid Fund (IDAF) was one of the earliest anti-apartheid solidarity organisations proving, over 35 years, to be perhaps the most effective in terms of its reach of support, cost effectiveness and the numbers of volunteers who provided that solidarity.

It was launched in 1956 in the basement of the home of Canon John Collins of St Paul's Cathedral in London in response to an appeal by then ANC president, Chief Albert Luthuli, for legal aid assistance in the notorious Treason Trial of 156 anti-apartheid activists. The following Sunday's collection at St Paul's was sent to defray the initial legal costs.

That trial lasted for four years and, as resistance to apartheid grew, more activists were arrested, and more trials ensued. The demand for legal aid increased, as did the call to help the families of arrested and jailed activists.

Collins soon found himself raising funds from supporters in Sweden and elsewhere. Such solidarity was anathema to the apartheid regime, since it made the legalistic persecution of activists far more difficult while lessening the pressure the state could exert on their families. IDAF was banned in South Africa in 1965 and it became a criminal offence to receive funds or assistance from the organisation.

'The Canon', as he was fondly called by those who knew him, was not deterred. He found secret ways to finance legal defence. With the help of South African exiles in London, money was channelled to a go-between law firm in London to create anonymity. This firm, in turn, instructed other law firms in Britain, who then instructed South African lawyers to act on their behalf. The legal costs in South Africa, it was said, were covered by prominent British citizens keen to see that due legal process was assured. The instructing law firm in Britain felt satisfied that the 'legend' they spun to the benefactors was ethically justified.

IDAF provided defence costs without regard to the political affiliation of those charged, nor did it question if the accused were charged with the violent overthrow of apartheid. Anyone who stood up against apartheid was deserving of a defence, the Canon maintained, despite himself being a pacifist.

And there were still the families of those detained, on trial or imprisoned. The Canon set about establishing a global network of correspondents who sent letters of support and financial aid to these victims of apartheid. The selected correspondents were not told who funded the regular postal orders they sent but knew that the letters of acknowledgement they received from South Africa served as a receipt and had to be sent on 'to an address in London'.

Such family-to-family aid was often maintained for two decades and longer. On average six letters passed to-and-fro each year between the solidarity supporter and the South African family. Lasting friendships developed.

IDAF kept records of this correspondence and, when apartheid ended, IDAF sent, in two shipping containers, the letters and all other records to be archived at the University of the Western Cape. Some of the most powerful in this collection are the letters from struggling, mostly indigent and generally women, who comment on everyday life in this racially oppressed and politically persecuted period.

The Canon set himself a further task, to 'keep the conscience of the world alive'. To this end he had published, in all the world's major languages, books, pamphlets and posters, the detailed evidence that

IDAF had secured from within the apartheid state and from the supporting entities across South Africa's borders. This served as the bedrock of factual information for the global anti-apartheid movement. The Canon explained to the UN Special Committee on Apartheid, that IDAF 'builds and sustains the morale of the people in the face of a policy that aims to break their spirit'. After his death in 1981, aged 77, the work he had set in train continued. A new board was chaired by retired Archbishop Trevor Huddleston. During this last decade of apartheid, IDAF had to adjust and grow rapidly to respond to the increasing conflagration that finally broke the yoke of apartheid. In 1990 IDAF was formally 'unbanned' and in 1992 the organisation was shut down – it was no longer needed with first democratic elections two years away.

That the apartheid state realised the importance of IDAF can be seen in the attempts to compromise and infiltrate the organisation. Bureau of State Security spy Gordon Winter admitted to rummaging through Canon Collins's dustbins. Nearly a decade later, another spy, Craig Williamson, who later became notorious as a letter bomb killer, tried to gain evidence that would compromise IDAFs operations. He admitted to the TRC that the one anti-apartheid organisation the Special Branch had failed to infiltrate was IDAF. The IDAF hallmark of anonymity and secrecy was never breached.

With hindsight, the sheer scale of IDAF's work is extraordinary. During its existence, IDAF transferred more than £200 million in legal aid and in solidarity assistance to the families of jailed, detained, banned and executed anti-apartheid activists. This money came from no less than 56 governments around the world, the bulk of it coming from Scandinavian countries. Their act of consistent solidarity was not least built on IDAF throughout producing clean accounts.

IDAF was outlawed in South Africa for 25 years of its 34-year history. Despite this it grew and by the 1980s some 180 attorneys and 70 senior counsel in South Africa were receiving IDAF funds to fight for the rights of countless thousands put on trial by the apartheid state. And, at any one time during this period, some 2000 families of activists were supported financially and emotionally by 'supporter families'.

HORST KLEINSCHMIDT, after IDAF, worked for Lawyers for Human Rights, was director of the Kagiso and Mvula trusts, and was appointed head of the fisheries department in government. Horst now lives in Cape Town where he writes and continues his activism for equality and justice.

39

Victoria Brittain – African Continental Solidarity Defied the Cold War

FOR ANYONE WHO DID NOT live the hopeful, febrile, political life in and around the African liberation movements of the 1960s, 1970s and 1980s, it may be hard to imagine their power over imaginations and political and social aspirations far beyond their own continent – including in Europe and in the US – and the magic of a handful of their leaders. Among them were the southern African leaders Oliver Tambo, Nelson Mandela and Amilcar Cabral of Guinea-Bissau.

Algeria's independence war from 1954 to 1962, which forced France out of their country, and Vietnam's routing of first the French, at Dien Bien Phu in 1954, and then the Americans in 1975, were the lodestars which promised Africans they too would end colonialism. This was especially the case for South Africa's majority, crushed in the social, political and economic tentacles of the apartheid system's laws, and for Portugal's African colonies, which had to take a military route for independence.

Already, in 1961 before Algerian independence, several dozen Angolans were being trained in Maghnia in the north-west of the country by Algeria's National Liberation Front (FLN) guerrilla army. At the same time FLN refugees in Morocco and Tunisia, and wounded fighters, were being given aid from the revolutionary government in Cuba. A key solidarity nexus was formed.

In Nelson Mandela's 1962 secret visits across Africa, he was welcomed in Algeria and the first links between the ANC and Algeria's FLN were cemented. Financial and logistic support from Algiers to the ANC began then and continued through the decades of Mandela's imprisonment.[51]

The TriContinental conference of 1966, held in Havana after the original host, Ahmed Ben Bella leader of newly independent Algeria, was overthrown in a coup, was a marker of African and global South solidarity for the defeat of the apartheid regime, among other commitments to a more just world economic, social and political order. Another marker was the attempt to derail the TriContinental by the kidnap and murder of the brilliant intellectual conference chairman, Moroccan opposition leader Mohammed Ben Barka. He was assassinated in France by French and Moroccan officials.[52] Cabral and Chile's Salvador Allende too would later be among leaders of the TriContinental who paid with violent ends to their lives for Western fears of their political threat to the West's interests.

The Non-Aligned Movement was led by Cuba and Algeria in keeping an unwelcome public focus on apartheid South Africa – in 1964 in New York Che Guevara called for the country's expulsion from the UN. Over the years from 1975 Cuba's extraordinarily generous military and other material support to both Angola and the African National Congress changed their linked history as Héctor Igarza Cabrera details in his chapter.

The Cold War, which divided the continent, threw a long shadow over some African countries' solidarity with South Africa's majority in these decades. For some governments, it was a shadow of fear – fear of displeasing their powerful patrons, business partners and former colonisers in the West. Ronald Reagan and his firm friend Margaret Thatcher in the UK unashamedly continued support for the apartheid government as it ravaged the southern African region with targeted assassinations, invasions, bombing raids, infrastructure destruction and hundreds of thousands of deaths tallied by UN agencies.

---

51 *El Watan*, Sunday 22 August 2021 reveals details of Algeria's Colonel Mokhtar Kerkeb's discrete role in these links in an essay by his daughter, Djazia Kerkeb, based on the archive records she has.

52 Mehdi Ben Barka en Heritage, *De la TriContinental a l'Altermondialism. Syllepse*, 2007.

Before instant communications, and with Western media treating the apartheid regime as normal, and largely disregarding death and destruction in remote unknown places, it was easy for these realities to be ignored.

Reagan, Kissinger and Thatcher will be remembered for framing their apartheid support as staving off communism in Africa. Across the continent nationalist politicians were falsely tagged as communists. Angola's leaders Agostino Neto and Lucio Lara were key targets of these myths, along with ANC leaders. The Western goal was to prevent the MPLA (Popular Movement for the Liberation of Angola) from becoming the ruling party on 11 November 1975 when the colonial government of Portugal withdrew. The West had their own well-funded protégés: Jonas Savimbi's UNITA, and the FNLA headed by Holden Roberto, and based in Mobuto's Zaire. Multi-pronged invasions of Angola by apartheid South Africa from the south, Mobutu's units from the north, and British and American mercenaries were all involved in this ambitious and expensive CIA programme to ensure independent Angola would have a government friendly to the West, and to the apartheid regime.[53]

Cuba's Operation Carlota, headed by the ship *El Vietnam Heroica*, and an unprecedented complex military airlift from Havana, brought in 30 000 troops and supplies from the other side of the world and defeated that plan.

For the first decade of independence, Angola, supported by Cuba and with Soviet weapons, was in the eye of the Cold War storm in Africa. At the very moment of building new economic and social development, the country was ravaged by South Africa's military assaults and the CIA backing of UNITA on the military and diplomatic and propaganda fronts.

Nevertheless, Angola hosted crucial ANC military training camps with Cuban and Soviet instructors, and supported the Namibian liberation movement SWAPO, including refugee camps for hundreds of Namibian civilians who fled South Africa's brutal military occupation. In 1978 a South African bombing raid and ground troops attacked the Cassinga camp in southern Angola killing 600 people and wounding scores more. Within weeks 600 Namibian children were flown from Angola to Cuba's schools on the Island of Youth where the next generations of the African liberation movements were being educated.

---

53   John Stockwell, *In Search of Enemies: A CIA story*, W.W. Norton, 1978.

The other six African frontline states of Tanzania, Zimbabwe, Mozambique, Zambia, Botswana and Lesotho provided safe houses, logistics and more, despite the toll of South Africa's murderous destruction and deaths. Zambia hosted the ANC external headquarters. Zimbabwe laid on a narrative-changing conference in the mid-1980s. This brought together the ANC leadership in exile for decades, with the new generation of school children resisters who fell victim to South African police brutality, with their mothers and lawyers. For decades Tanzania hosted ANC offices in Dar es Salaam and a major inland facility, including a school, as well as offices for the Lusophone liberation movements, all of which were enmeshed with the struggle for the end of apartheid. Mozambique, vulnerable with its proximity to South Africa, was home base for ANC's fighters of Umkhonto we Sizwe, though not to the same extent as Angola. Later Uganda became a new home. And Libya was a generous donor.

The 1969 assassination by a parcel bomb (the work of colonial Portugal's agents) of the Mozambican independence leader Eduardo Mondlane in Dar es Salaam was the precedent for dozens of such acts by the apartheid regime across all the frontline states in the next two decades. However, the toll of lost lives and lost development, as incursions and bombing raids terrorised the region, did not dent the principled solidarity of the region. The unwavering support in the darkest of times was indelibly associated for more than a decade with the eloquence and moral leadership of Tanzania's Julius Nyerere.

Solidarity in these years was not only these principled state projects. It was individuals who made honourable choices, many of whom have written in this book. Damian de Lange's chapter spells out the brave and selfless role of solidarity activists in hostile Swaziland so close to the apartheid regime, while Vumile 'James' Ngculu and Thenjiwe Mtinso salute many heroes of consistent risk-taking across the frontline states.

I want to remember here so many others, such as the young Cuban doctors with dark shadowed eyes working round the clock in the desperately crowded, under-equipped Huambo hospital in the long months of the city's 1984 virtual siege by UNITA forces. Those doctors often requested a second or third assignment, fiercely attached to their patients, a never-ending tide of agonised land mine victims – poor peasant men, women and children from the countryside who would never get their old lives back. Others were the smiling Cuban soldier with pink hair clips describing how happily she and her husband had left their two-year-old child with her mother in Havana for the two years they had volunteered to fight in Angola; or the glamorous Cuban head teacher in Malange, an agricultural province, also under increasing UNITA attacks, who rose from the simple dinner made for the visit of top Angolan official Lucio Lara and smiling led him in a slow waltz around the room.

Like the tens of thousands of unknown people across the world described in Christabel Gurney's 'Global Solidarity', these individuals' principled life choices will always be remembered as how Solidarity changed the world in southern Africa.

VICTORIA BRITTAIN is a British journalist who has lived and worked in Saigon, Nairobi and Algiers as well as London and Washington. For more than 20 years she worked for *The Guardian* and several French publications. She is author or co-author of eight books and plays.

FURTHER READING
Piero Gleijeses, *Conflicting Missions,* University of North Carolina Press, 2003.

40

Oscar Monteiro – African Internationalism, a Mozambique Perspective

AFRICAN NATIONALISM AND international solidarity have a long, deep history. Workers and militants crossed borders, forged links and shared the lessons of oppression and the tactics and strategy of popular mobilisation and resistance. A generation of borderless leaders emerged with help from the African diaspora in Europe, the Americas and the Caribbean Isles and inspiration from Marcus Garvey and Padmore onward through Aimé Césaire and Frantz Fanon.

We had allies and could fight and win. Even some international churches and missionaries – enlightened by their work within slave communities in the diaspora – helped to spread the ideas of nationalism; and within the Catholic Church, despite its tight alliance with the colonial powers, some priests and nuns sided with and aided African militants. In Africa and worldwide, liberation support groups and progressive political parties sent aid and lobbied their governments to assist us. Indeed, we were not alone.

Like people, nations can live nearby and, despite having similar problems, remain isolated and weak. To forge a joint vision and common goals require a convergence of moments, perceptions and leaders united by the desire for peace and freedom and the vision of a more just, national and international socioeconomic order.

To mould the notion of Africa as an entity despite distances and poor communication took the vision of Kwame Nkrumah, the great movements for independence in the English and French colonies, the Arab emancipation and nationalism of the Free Officers led by Gamal Abdel Nasser, the anti-imperialistic nationalisation of the Suez Canal, the return of Mohamed V from exile in Madagascar, the fiery movement led by Sekou Touré for complete independence from France, and the logistical support by Modibo Keita's Mali for Algeria's independence. Thus arose an idea strong enough to overcome centuries of distrust and the relations of domination which still subsist.

The founding conference of the Organisation of African Unity on 25 May 1963 culminated those momentous – till then unrelated – events as an expression of a dream for a common goal, the complete liberation of the continent. But few realised how long it would take. For some, a powerful African army with or without a united African government would swiftly do the trick. Gradually, experience and knowledge of the real situation led to more sober views: in settler colonies, decolonisation would not be as easy as in Burkina Fasso or large countries like Nigeria. Thus, in *Struggle for Mozambique*, Mondlane referred to the role of independent Africa in supporting materially and diplomatically to be 'fought from within' with popular support and guerrilla tactics. Toward that end, the Organisation for African Unity's Liberation Committee worked out of Dar es Salaam and became highly effective in providing logistical support for the liberation movements.

Still, for years, African support was done by states. Support from political organisations, parties and youth movements was lacking. One could call it a 'state' syndrome. Even at OAU meetings, independent states – often with inadequate experience and knowledge of matters on the ground – took life-and-death decisions about the struggle while the liberation movements' representatives had to wait in the lounge. This belittling we could not countenance, especially from our African brothers. It was counterproductive and had to change ... and did. We gained full representation.

No one could have forecast that to accomplish the goal – even partly –

would take 40 years. Still, few organisations in the world have pursued so consistently one goal with internal and external support ... and succeeded.

Towards this end, nearly all African countries were active diplomatically at every conference, be it at the United Nations, where a Decolonisation Committee was created, or at the specialised UN agencies like the International Labour Organization (ILO), the United Nations Educational, Scientific and Cultural Organization (UNESCO), and the Food and Agriculture Organization (FAO).

The countries neighbouring the liberation struggles had decisive roles. For Guinea-Bissau, both Guinea and Senegal helped; for Angola, Congo Brazzaville faithfully supported the People's Movement for the Liberation of Angola (MPLA), though, in Congo Leopoldville, many brave Angolan fighters, including four valiant Angolan young women from my generation, died in the notorious Kinkuzu camp. Tanzania proved to be a bastion for many struggles, and it paid a price: Portuguese operatives sabotaged the bridge to Oyster Bay. The Portuguese also invaded Guinea; and other raids targeted Zambia. The ferocious raid on MK in Matola culminated South Africa's long campaign to destabilise Mozambique to undermine its support for the ANC and the anti-apartheid movement.

Having joined the North Atlantic Treaty Organisation (NATO), the Portuguese kept their colonies under a veil of silence. Information was crucial. Liberation movements had offices in Cairo and Algeria. In Cairo, with support from the Ministry of African Affairs, they produced material in Arabic; and FRELIMO Algiers issued a bulletin in French. Pro-liberation radio programmes run by the liberation movements were broadcast from Cairo, Lusaka and Dar es Salaam.

Pioneered by the ANC, the solidarity movement in Europe was replicated in Britain by MAGIC (Mozambique, Angola and Guinea Information Centre); in Holland, by the Angola Komité; and in Sweden, the Afrika Gruppen.

From 1970 onwards, Italy played a significant role. There, a wide political front of numerous political parties organised the first solidarity conference in a Western country in support of the liberation movements in the Portuguese colonies. Cabral, Neto and Marcelino dos Santos attended and even had a historic audience with Pope Montini. In popular admiration, Reggio Emilia, a progressive and prosperous region in

Italy, became a household name in southern Africa. These unexpected, yet vibrant, associations with the advanced sectors of European society strengthened the international nature of the southern African wave of nationalism and its resolve as a just cause, a nationalism not based on hatred, colour or race, now being tested in trying times.

OSCAR MONTEIRO was born in 1941 in Maputo and organised Frelimo as an underground organisation in Portugal, participated in the independence negotiations leading to the Lusaka agreement and was a member of the Mozambican government until 1991. Until recently was Professor of Constitutional Law (Mondlane University) and Public Management (Wits).

41

Peter Hain – Stop the Sports Tours

PEOPLE FORGET THAT THE international anti-apartheid struggle was bitterly hard-fought and, for most of the near-four decades involved, we were in a minority. Country by country voted in the United Nations to condemn apartheid but then traded with and armed the white state, ruling elites in predominantly white Commonwealth nations like Britain, Australia and New Zealand forcibly opposing campaigns to defeat it. Nowhere was that more evident than over campaigns to secure an international boycott of sports teams from South Africa.

From the mid-1950s in Britain, demands increased to shun whites-only South African sports tours. In New Zealand, the issue had greater saliency because of collaboration with white South African objections to competing against Māori rugby players, a shabby story going back years before.[54]

Meanwhile inside South Africa, campaigns for non-racial sport gained momentum as part of the resistance, leading to the launch of SANROC, the South African Non-Racial Olympic Committee. Such was SANROC's impact that its leaders were banned and harassed to an extent that, like the ANC, it was unable to operate legally inside the country and forced

---

54   Trevor Richards, *Dancing on Our Bones: New Zealand, South Africa, rugby and racism*, Bridget Williams Books, 1999.

into exile in London. Following a term in prison, its chairman, Dennis Brutus settled in London.[55]

Then, in 1969–70, came a game-changer. On the back of rising student militancy and worker strikes across Europe, sport might have appeared a quixotic choice for militant political protest. If so, that misunderstood the whole white South African psyche. They were sports mad, Afrikaners, especially fanatical about rugby. International sport also granted them the legitimacy they increasingly craved as the evil reality of apartheid began to be exposed, notably by the 1960 Sharpeville massacre. Whilst the United Nations passed motions of condemnation, the Springboks were fêted in London, Sydney and Auckland. It was also easier to achieve success through protest against sports links than it was to take on the might of either international capital or military alliances, both of which underpinned the white supremacist state.

From the late 1950s the British Anti-Apartheid Movement (AAM) organised protests outside sports venues hosting visiting white South African teams. But these 'symbolic' protests were patronisingly ignored by sports elites impervious to moral appeals, pickets, letters and delegations.

Then the South African government in September 1968 vetoed a planned England cricket tour because the team included Basil D'Oliveira, a coloured (mixed race) South African from Cape Town who had become a top England player after being barred from reaching those heights in his own country.[56] Nevertheless, the English cricket authorities brazenly announced in January 1969 that they would proceed with the scheduled 1970 cricket tour by a white South African team. There was uproar. In May 1969 SANROC held a public meeting in London and I pressed from the floor for militant action to stop the tour, with Dennis Brutus in the chair very supportive. Such direct action, I felt, could not be ignored in the way previous protests and lobbying had been. Because it was novel, it was also highly newsworthy, the product of that unique late 1960s era of student sit-ins, anti-Vietnam War protests, the Paris 1968 revolt, the American anti-war and civil rights movements. I and others merely applied similar direct

---

55 Brutus's successor as SANROC chair in South Africa, John Harris, was executed on the Pretoria gallows for his role in a bomb explosion.

56 For a comprehensive account of the sports apartheid struggle, see Peter Hain and André Odendaal, *Pitch Battles: Sport, racism and resistance*, Rowman and Littlefield, 2020; and Peter Hain, *Don't Play with Apartheid*, Allen & Unwin, 1971.

action techniques to the sports apartheid struggle.

In July 1969 I led a small group of protestors onto the pitch in Basildon, Essex, to disrupt an all-white South African cricket match sponsored by a wealthy businessman, Wilf Isaacs. The same month, a Davis Cup tennis match in Bristol between South Africa and Britain was disrupted when three activists and I ran onto the court in front of live television coverage. The publicity for each direct action protest encouraged others and, with the active encouragement of SANROC leaders Dennis Brutus and Chris de Broglio, the Stop The Seventy Tour Committee (STST) was launched at a press conference in September 1969. It had broad support from the AAM and National Union of Students, Christian groups, Young Liberals, Young Communists and the International Socialists.

Finding myself propelled aged 19 into being its national chair and spokesperson, I pledged mass demonstrations and disruptions throughout the 1970 tour; and demonstrations against the Springbok rugby tour which, rather belatedly, we had realised was due to start in six weeks' time and had determined would be a dummy run for stopping the cricket tour.

A mass movement soon emerged, locally based, spontaneous, independently organised, usually focused on university student unions, though involving trade unions, local AAM groups, socialists, communists, Marxists, liberals, independents and the churches. It was predominantly, though by no means exclusively, young and soon took the Springbok rugby tour by storm.

The opening match against Oxford University was switched after strong opposition from both the college authorities and student activists who sprayed weedkiller on the ground and threatened to wreck it. But the last-minute announcement that it would be played instead at Twickenham attracted morning front-page lead stories and set the scene for the remaining games of the 25-match tour.

I joined others leaping over the fence around the Twickenham pitch to run on and disrupt that match – though by then well-known, I was immediately grabbed by police. Local organisers suddenly realised they were part of a mass national movement, and each of the matches saw disruptions and demonstrations of varying sizes.

The white South African establishment was apoplectic, the government-supporting *Die Beeld* newspaper stating: 'it is degrading to see how a nation can allow itself to be dictated to by this bunch of left-wing, work shy, refugee, long hairs.'

In Britain police tactics became increasingly aggressive, the STST campaign was infiltrated by the Special Branch and my home telephone tapped, a familiar experience to my parents from their Pretoria activist days.

So an inner Special Action Group of trusted activists was established. It booked a young woman into the Springbok team's London hotel on the eve of the international against England at Twickenham. She gummed up the players' bedroom door locks with a solidifying agent. In the morning an STST activist, respectably dressed in a most un-protester-like suit, told the team's waiting coach driver he was wanted by Springbok managers inside the hotel, chained himself to the steering wheel, drove it away and crashed it. Others evaded the heavy police cordon at Twickenham and chained themselves to the goalposts. Orange smoke pellets were thrown among the players, which as well as interrupting play, produced dramatic television and newspaper pictures. Wherever it went, the team was under siege, resting, training or playing.

The tour finally staggered to an end, with the players bitter and unsettled. For the vice-captain, Tommy Bedford, it proved a cathartic experience. Within a year he publicly stated I should be listened to, not vilified in local media as South Africa's 'Public Enemy Number One'.

After their release two decades later, both Nelson Mandela and Govan Mbeki told me that on Robben Island news of the demonstrations leaked through the news ban imposed on the Islanders via their furious warders – Springbok fanatics to a man – and gave them an enormous morale boost. The Springbok tour had provided our militant movement with a perfect springboard from which to stop the much more vulnerable cricket tour, due in May 1970. However, the police had started getting the upper hand, seeming better organised, filling the space between spectators and players, making it harder to penetrate onto the pitches and disrupt the Springboks from playing.

So, with an eye on the original objective – stopping the cricket tour – late in the night of 19 January 1970, Stop the Tour demonstrators simultaneously raided 14 of the 17 county cricket club grounds, daubing all with paint slogans. A small patch in the outfield of Glamorgan's

Cardiff ground was dug up and weed killer was sprayed on Warwickshire's Birmingham ground.

Pre-planned telephone reports from each tight group poured in throughout the night to the Press Association news agency and to my home, the protests dominating the morning radio bulletins, followed by screaming headlines with photos in the evening papers and blanket coverage in television programmes and the following day's newspapers. Within weeks, 300 reels of barbed wire arrived at Lords and most county grounds introduced guard dogs and security. There was speculation that African, Asian and Caribbean countries would withdraw from the multi-racial Commonwealth Games to be staged that July in Scotland. A range of public bodies came out against the tour. Some trade unions threatened industrial action. Labour MPs, including the AAM's vice-chair, Peter Jackson, said they would join sit-down pitch invasions. The chair of the government-sponsored Community Relations Commission, Frank Cousins, told the home secretary that the tour would do untold damage to race relations.

On 12 February 1970, the governing body, the Cricket Council, met at Lords on a snowy night, the pitch eerily surrounded by barbed wire, silhouetted against the whiteness: a concentration camp image, symbolising the torment which had torn asunder the cricket world steeped in conservatism and colonialism. The tour was more than halved to 12 matches from its original schedule of 28, to be played on just eight grounds instead of the original 22. Artificial all-weather pitches would be installed as an additional security precaution.

The Conservative shadow attorney general, Sir Peter Rawlinson, attacked the Labour home secretary, James Callaghan, for remaining 'neutral' and thereby 'acknowledging the licence to riot'. Rawlinson also called for me to be prosecuted for conspiracy. And, after Labour Cabinet documents were made public 30 years later (ironically, when I was a serving Labour government minister), it was also revealed that ministers had discussed whether or not to prosecute me, with James Callaghan in favour and Tony Benn against.

Meanwhile our STST campaign grew and grew to around 100 000 activists. Committees and action groups to complement those established during the Springbok tour sprang up throughout the country.

Labour Prime Minister Harold Wilson said that people should feel free to demonstrate; though he specifically criticised disruptive protests. The British Council of Churches also called for peaceful demonstrations. The queen announced that neither she nor any member of the royal family would make the traditional visit to the Lords Test match, and the South Africans would not receive the traditional invitation to Buckingham Palace. The churches, led by the former England cricket captain and the bishop of Woolwich, David Sheppard, urged cancellation.

Then the Supreme Council for Sport in Africa – itself a challenge to the white- and Western-dominated elites from an imperialist age still running international sport – announced that 13 African countries would definitely boycott the Commonwealth Games if the tour went ahead; Asian and Caribbean countries soon followed, raising the prospect of a whites-only Games running alongside a whites-only cricket tour. Sparked off by nationally led but locally delivered militant action, the campaign had provoked an international diplomatic and political furore.

An Anti-Apartheid Movement campaign poster caught the public imagination. Under the caption 'If you could see their national sport, you might be less keen to see their cricket', it showed a policeman beating defenceless black residents in Cato Manor township outside Durban. There was an ideal spectrum of protest from the lobbying activity of the David Sheppard's Fair Cricket Campaign with its links into establishment opinion, through SANROC with its expert international contacts and the AAM's links to the labour movement. Although STST's direct militant strategy powered the whole campaign, it could have been isolated without that hinterland of broader support.

Meanwhile plans went ahead to blockade the team at Heathrow Airport. Thousands of tickets were bought up by local groups (the games had been made all-ticket). But, although such activity was coordinated by STST from the centre, local groups operated quite independently.

Finally, extremely reluctantly, and under huge pressure from the government, the Cricket Council met in emergency session and cancelled the tour in late May 1970, a few weeks before its start. A campaign conceived by a handful of people became one of the very few British protest groups ever to have achieved its objectives completely.[57]

---

57   For a fuller account see Peter Hain, *A Pretoria Boy: The story of South Africa's 'Public Enemy Number One'*. Jonathan Ball, 2021.

I announced STST would be wound up and encouraged all its supporters to join the AAM whose membership trebled. Activists blooded in militant sports protests went on to drive Barclays Bank off university campuses and thereafter out of apartheid South Africa. For the first time in ten long bitter years since the Sharpeville massacre black South Africans and whites involved in the resistance had something to cheer about. Moses Garoëb, a leading fighter in the South West African People's Organisation (SWAPO), told me in 1970 that STST had been an inspiration to SWAPO cadres in the African bush as they heard the news on their radios. But the apartheid state sought revenge. I was sent a letter bomb in June 1972 of the kind which, amongst others, later assassinated ANC activist Ruth First and student leader Abram Tiro; fortunately for me a fault in the trigger mechanism prevented mine from exploding. I also landed up in the Old Bailey for a four-week trial in August 1972, prosecuted for conspiracy, only narrowly escaping imprisonment; funding for the privately initiated prosecution came mainly from South Africa and the British far right.[58] Then in October 1975 I experienced a Kafkaesque arrest for a bank theft half a mile from my London home which I knew nothing about, revealed subsequently to have been committed by a South African agent looking rather like me. I was finally acquitted after a two-week Old Bailey trial.[59] But the pledge by South African Rugby president Dannie Craven during the militant anti-Springbok protests of 1969–70 – 'There will be a black Springbok over my dead body' – was of course emphatically buried when Springbok captain Siya Kolisi lifted the Rugby World Cup in 2019.

PETER HAIN, brought up in South Africa and the son of anti-apartheid activists, is formerly a British anti-apartheid leader, Labour MP and cabinet minister and presently a Labour peer.

---

58   Derek Humphry, ed., *The Cricket Conspiracy*, London National Council for Civil Liberties, 1973.

59   Peter Hain, *A Putney Plot?*, Spokesman, 1987.

42

Protests on the Pitch – The Failed 1981 New Zealand Springbok Rugby Tour

NEW ZEALAND IN 1981 saw the most astonishing protests ever witnessed in rugby's long history. This was the infamous tour of that rugby-loving country by the apartheid-era's Springbok team.

Match after match was disrupted by thousands of demonstrators in scenes that were reminiscent of a civil war. The army was called out in support of the police to enable matches to be played. Yet in such previous tours the Springboks had been greeted like film stars from the smallest of villages and towns to the biggest cities.

By the 1980s the international situation was markedly different, and New Zealand was no exception. Here anti-apartheid sentiment was rife, along with condemnation of the way the country treated its indigenous Māori population, as witnessed from their de-selection in the All Blacks teams (what an ironic term) that toured South Africa.

Not for the first time around the world did opposition to South Africa's apartheid practices give rise to the awareness of racism prevalent in countries such as Britain, France, Australia and New Zealand. After all, international solidarity is a two-way street, and this was seen as many of

New Zealand's indigenous Māori population joined in the protests.

The country was on tenterhooks, as were people in South Africa, at the opening game of the tour in the town of Hamilton in New Zealand. Bedlam erupted with the direct action of determined protesters. The match was cancelled after 350 protesters invaded the pitch, while thousands more cheered them on, despite violence from the obdurate rugby fans.

In Wellington protesters wore helmets when police attacked marchers – leading to the radicalisation of the protests. The pitch looked like a concentration camp with razor wire and ship containers placed around it to avoid pitch invasions.

The biggest protests followed in cities such as Christchurch and Auckland, where a low-flying plane dropped flour and smoke bombs on the rugby field, to the roars of approval from the thousands kept at bay beyond the police and military cordon.

So intense and successful were these mass protests that no Springbok team toured New Zealand again until after the demise of apartheid.

FURTHER READING

Politics and sport, 1981 Springbok tour. New Zealand history online, www.nzhistory.net.nz. 24 February 2009. Retrieved 26 July 2021.

Tour diary, 1981 Springbok tour. New Zealand history online, www.nzhistory.net.nz/. Retrieved 26 July 2021.

Steve Watters, 'A long tradition of rugby rivalry'. www.nzhistory.net.nz. Retrieved 26 July 2021.

Steve Watters, 'Politics and sport don't mix'. nzhistory.net.nz. /. Retrieved 26 July 2021.

OM

43

Magnus Walan – Sweden and Olof Palme to the Fore

SOUTH AFRICAN PRESIDENT Nelson Mandela spoke from the heart in the Swedish parliament in March 1999, before stepping down as president:

> We have come to once more thank Sweden from the bottom of our hearts for what you did: the labour movement, NGOs, churches and others, and the millions of ordinary Swedish men and women who insisted that the rights they enjoyed should be enjoyed by all people everywhere. Their passionate commitment was reflected in the resolute and remarkable support we had from the Swedish government.[60]

In the years 1972–1994 Sweden is estimated to have financed the liberation struggle in South Africa with around 4 billion SEK (Swedish crowns) or R6.7 billion in today's value. Sweden was the single largest donor to the ANC's non-military activities and similarly the largest donor to the UDF (United Democratic Front) during the 1980s and to the trade union federation COSATU (Congress of South African Trade Unions).

Why? How come a small country in northern Europe with seven million

---

60 Nelson Mandela's speech in Swedish parliament 1999. https://www.thelocal. se/20131206/nelson-mandela-1999-speech-in-swedens-riksdag/.

people during the 1970s and with 9837 kilometres between them made this political decision? There are many answers to that question, but here are some pieces to the puzzle.

Since 1874 the Swedish evangelical Lutheran church had sent missionaries to South Africa and built strong links to the South African Christian and Lutheran evangelical church. One Swedish priest, Gunnar Helander, went to South Africa in 1938 and became deeply committed to fighting apartheid. On his return to Sweden, he became one of the most important opinion leaders against apartheid.

Swedish companies were early investors in South Africa, especially in the mining and energy sectors. Companies like Nobel, Atlas Copco, SKF and Sandvik were seen as exploitative. This provoked many people in Sweden, where liberals and social democrats had large and strong organisations.

Another factor was a deliberate strategy by Swedish political leaders to show that anti-colonial positions and actions against apartheid could also come from a Western country. In the UN, Sweden was the first country in the West to support developing countries' right to independence. At the time the perception was that the ANC and other liberation movements got support mainly from countries in the Eastern Bloc. Now we know that some of these Western countries also had various deals with the apartheid government, including trade in arms.

A further factor was the ANC's deliberate and successful strategy to build relations and put pressure on the political leadership in Sweden through local and national popular organisations. 'To knock on the door of the average Swede', as former ANC chief representative Billy Modise expressed it. Over two decades Sobizana Mngqikana, Lindiwe Mabuza and Billy Modise, as ANC chief representatives, travelled round Sweden on hundreds of speaking engagements. They facilitated tours of cultural workers, union and youth representatives from South Africa, who visited Sweden on the invitation of the Isolate South Africa Committee, the Africa Groups of Sweden and various institutions and civil society organisations.

IT STARTED WITH A HOT ROLL...

Well maybe that is an exaggeration. In 1962 the Social Democratic party invited a South African to speak at the party's 1 May celebrations. When the guest came a day early the party chairman and prime minister, Tage

Erlander, asked his political advisor if he would take care of the guest. The advisor was Olof Palme, and the guest was Oliver Tambo. He was offered a roll in the simple townhouse of Olof and Lisbeth Palme in the suburb of Vällingby outside Stockholm. Thus began a long friendship with a significant political impact over decades.

The Sharpeville shootings in March 1960 led young liberals like Per Wästberg and Per Gahrton to demand a boycott of South Africa. In 1960 Sweden was the first country to initiate a consumer boycott of South Africa. Soon about 200 local campaign groups joined the Swedish South Africa Committee. Most subsided after a few years and only a few activist groups remained in university towns.

In 1964 parliament began to give aid to refugee work and legal projects in southern Africa. An important factor was that the governing board of the new fund included representatives from anti-apartheid organisations, from various political parties and also from business and trade unions. This political model continued when the government under Palme in 1972 decided to support the civilian work of the liberation movements (Sällström). At the beginning just 150 000 Swedish crowns (SEK) were donated.[61]

But the idea of supporting the ANC came not only from the Social Democratic party. Motions had been tabled in parliament by Gunnar Helen, the Liberal Party's leader, and by Torbjörn Fälldin of the Centre Party. When the non-socialist coalition took power in 1976, support to the liberation movements increased.

Sweden contributed between 60 and 65 per cent of the budget of the International Defence and Aid Fund (IDAF) for southern Africa, an anti-apartheid organisation. Between 1964 and 1991 the organisation sent £100 million to South Africa for the defence of thousands of political activists and to provide aid for the prisoners' families.

The Swedish Ecumenical Council, an umbrella organisation of churches of all denominations, administered about 500 scholarships.

Between 1986 and 1996 the blue- and white-collar federations LO and TCO and their Secretariat for International Trade Union Development

61 Tor Sellström, *Sweden and National Liberation in Southern Africa, Volume I: Formation of a Popular Opinion (1950–1970)*, Nordiska Afrikainstitutet, Uppsala, 1999. http://www. diva-portal.org/smash/get/diva2:272713/FULLTEXT01.pdf. Retrieved 20 September 2021.

Cooperation channelled almost 200 million SEK to unions in South Africa, mainly to COSATU and individual unions within COSATU. LO also gave direct support to the ANC from the late 1970s.

In the 1980s Birgitta Karlström Dorph was assigned to the Swedish legation in Pretoria and played an important role in identifying and building supportive relations with anti-apartheid organisations. She was called 'Palme's secret agent' in South Africa.[62]

NEW FORMS OF ANTI-APARTHEID WORK

In the early 1970s much popular focus was on the war in Vietnam and the military coup in Chile. The Africa Groups of Sweden had five local groups that organised work in support of liberation movements in several countries in southern Africa. At its height there were about 40 local groups in various parts of the country. The organisation positioned itself on the left and had limited impact initially.

Leaders in the Africa group realised this and initiated talks between Christian and political youth organisations.

The umbrella organisation Isolate South Africa Committee (ISAK) was formed in 1979 and existed for 16 years. I was employed by ISAK in 1980 and was a board member from 1981 to 1994. ISAK was my political home. Between 1984 and 1994 I became a regular traveller to South Africa, collecting information for anti-apartheid work and also working with the ANC underground.

This included visiting resettlement camps for people being forcibly removed with representatives from the South African Council of Churches; meeting civics in different part of the country; meeting lawyers working against the violence in Natal; attending funerals and mass meetings; spending time with and interviewing youth activists in COSAS and SAYCO who were hunted by the police; making friends for life. Anti-apartheid was no longer theory. During a stop in Harare on my way to Sweden, I had a surprise visit from John Nkadimeng and Thozamile Botha, both in the ANC NEC at the time. They wanted a briefing on my meetings with union leaders. My friend Florence de Villiers at the Domestic Workers Union in

---

62   Tor Sellström, *Volume II: Solidarity and Assistance (1970–1994)*, Nordiska Afrikainstitutet, Uppsala, 2002. http://www.diva-portal.org/smash/get/diva2:241772/FULLTEXT01.pdf. Retrieved 20 September 2021.

Cape Town had organised several meetings for me and told them of my plans. She was part of the ANC underground network.

At most the Swedish Isolate South Africa Committee, ISAK, had 78 national member organisations. They included all the Christian and political youth organisations (except the moderate party youth), student and peace movements, women and sports organisations and several unions. All in all, there were 1.5 million members in the organisations that belonged to ISAK, at a time when Sweden had a total population of around 7–8 million people.

I think our strength was in the local work. During the annual campaign week of 1987, 340 different organisations and 160 local umbrella committees reported planned anti-apartheid activities. Some local umbrella committees only consisted of two or three organisations; others were a coalition of 10–15. A distinct feature was that most of the activists in these groups were women. In the local groups political differences were set aside. Liberals and Christian democrats worked hand in hand with Socialists. The core of local committee activists often came from the Africa Groups and the churches. Song groups were often the centre of many activities.[63]

ANC GALA 1985 & SWEDISH PEOPLE'S PARLIAMENT AGAINST APARTHEID 1986

During the summer of 1985 I got a call from Lindiwe Mabuza at the ANC office. She told me that some of the most well-known Swedish artists including Mikael Wiehe and Tomas Ledin were planning a fundraising gala for the ANC. Lindiwe asked me to write a presentation in Swedish about the ANC. One planned concert became two due to public interest, on 29 and 30 November. At the gala the Swedish prime minister Olof Palme made a surprise appearance and donated 5 million Swedish crowns. Broadcast on Swedish national television, the concert raised 12 million Swedish crowns for the ANC.

The Swedish People's Parliament against Apartheid was opened on Friday, 21 February 1986. More than a thousand delegates representing civil society in Sweden and many Swedish and international guests

---

63   About ISAK (in Swedish). https://nai.uu.se/download/18.39fca04516faedec8b2447
        ed/1580744492676/978-91-975634-0-4.pdf.

gathered in Folkets Hus in central Stockholm.

In front of the stage was a huge map of Africa in the ANC's colours – gold, green and black. Interest in the People's Parliament was greater than we on the organisational side had dared to hope for. The size of the event grew during the preparation process, and we were eventually forced to say no to hundreds of delegates. Over 1000 participants represented 154 national organisations and close to 500 local and regional associations. Through their commitment, about 200 volunteers made the event possible. The People's Parliament was the most comprehensive solidarity gathering ever in Sweden. At the opening, we listened to speeches by several of the specially invited guests. Prime Minister Olof Palme was first. Initially he directed himself to his friend Oliver Tambo sitting in front of him, but his final words resonated strongly with the audience:

> This system can live on because it gets support from outside. If the support is pulled away and turned into resistance, apartheid cannot endure. If the world decides to abolish apartheid, apartheid will disappear.[64]

This address would be Palme's last public speech before his assassination just a week later.

ISAK campaigned for a ban on trade and for Swedish companies to withdraw from South Africa. In 1979 the Liberal Party minority government of Ola Ullsted introduced a bill preventing Swedish companies from making new investments in South African subsidiaries.

My reflections after many years campaigning and conversations with leading Social Democrats, including Palme, is that the Social Democrats did not want to challenge Swedish business through sanctions. Some of the unions also strongly opposed sanctions. They preferred to increase support to the ANC and the democratic movement.

The turning point was the formation of and position on sanctions of COSATU in 1985, and the state of emergency in 1985 and 1986. Desmond Tutu called the then Prime Minister Ingvar Carlsson a 'coward' for not imposing sanctions. Winnie Mandela challenged Sweden in an interview I conducted and said in *Aftonbladet*; 'Take your bloody money out of here'.

---

64   Olof Palme's speech at the People's Parliament. http://www.olofpalme.org/wp-content/dokument/860221b_folkriksdag.pdf. Retrieved 28 September 2021.

The introduction of a ban on import of agricultural products in 1986 was soon outdated in favour of a broad ban on trade, which came into force in 1987.

In the history books, politicians in Stockholm do not always recognise the pressure they were under to change their positions. Yet Nelson Mandela recognised this in his 1999 parliamentary speech as he acknowledged the link between popular pressure from NGOs and government decisions.

The international community did not liberate South Africa. That was done by the people in South Africa with huge sacrifices. But the international community supported that struggle, so possibly apartheid ended earlier.

After the 1994 election, ISAK chose to close down. The thousands of people who participated in various forms of solidarity work could feel that they had contributed something positive.

As a liberation movement, the ANC had achieved its main goal: to create a democratic South Africa. The ANC government has implemented major reforms. We, who have a great love for South Africa, are concerned about the continuing poverty, state capture and about the promises of justice after the work of the Truth and Reconciliation Commission that have not been followed up by the government. I think of Nokuthula Orela Simelane and the Cradock Four. Our solidarity and support must continue – but in other forms.

Magnus Walan, former board member and activist in the Swedish Anti-Apartheid Movement, is senior policy advisor at Diakonia, a Swedish church-based development, gender and human rights organisation.

44

Jan Vanheukelom – Viva ANC vs Hoera vir die Boer Hoera!

FLANDERS ONCE FEATURED one of the world's most archaic pro-apartheid lobbies based on *Boerensympathie*: the support from Flemish cultural elites who felt discriminated against in the new bilingual Belgium kingdom and were inspired by the militancy of Afrikaner nationalism. During apartheid's heyday, most of the economic and political levers of power in Belgium were firmly in the hands of a dominant Francophone bourgeoisie. Post Second World War economic transformation, the balance of economic power began to shift towards Flanders. Further shifts in the political and social balance of power in the 1970s and 1980s resulted in splits of the Belgian political parties, trade unions and socio-cultural organisations into separate Dutch-speaking and Francophone units. This was the start of an ongoing process of the creation of a Belgian federal state in 1993.

The intensification of anti-apartheid struggle in South Africa alarmed Flemish nationalist proponents of apartheid. A few days after Steve Biko's murder in October 1977, 200 conservative Flemings formed a new pro-apartheid lobby, Protea. It involved prominent people, including the Belgian public broadcaster in key political, military, social, cultural, religious, economic and financial circles. The former Christian Democrat minister of finance and CEO of the Christian Kredietbank, André Vlerick, headed this noisy and rather influential Flemish lobby group, based on a dangerous and toxic mix of *Boerensympathie,* racial prejudice, anti-communism and financial clout.

In the face of this the Leuven-based Action Committee on Southern Africa (AKZA) adapted its anti-apartheid strategy to constitute a broad-based coalition in Flanders to hit where it hurt.

Three organisations[65] were dedicated to fighting apartheid in Belgium – all supportive of the ANC and its armed struggle, and all three campaigning for the total isolation of apartheid South Africa.

AKZA, grown out of university-based international solidarity movements, started conversations with the largest social movements in Flanders: non-governmental development organisations, trade unions, religious congregations, special interest groups, youth wings of political parties, etc., to find common ground for a broad-based coalition in support of effective sanctions.

This was time-consuming. I remember how we sat down with some of the major social and cultural organisations – some with membership in the millions – to sort out their concerns related to the nature of the struggle, the menu of sanctions to prioritise, the types of pressure points and the concrete actions to take in order to sensitise their own constituencies and a broader public. We compromised over detail but persisted on principle. Thus, we were able to constitute one of the broadest coalitions in Belgium and in Flanders on issues related to international solidarity: the Flemish Anti-Apartheid Coalition, or VAAK.

In 1986, VAAK launched its first collective call for action targeted at those Belgian banks that beefed up the apartheid economy and its parastatals. The Christian-oriented Kredietbank was heavily implicated.

We documented the Kredietbank's involvement in financing South Africa's arms industry, other parastatals and at least one independent homeland. Much later, in 2018, a South African think tank, Open Secrets, and Hennie van Vuuren revealed how André Vlerick had held direct talks with President P.W. Botha. They documented how one of the bank's daughter companies – Kredietbank Luxemburg – had fortified the apartheid military security state apparatus by illegally facilitating more

---

65   Boycot Outspan Actie, BOA (Antwerp); the Action Committee on Southern Africa, AKZA (Leuven); the Comité Contre le Colonialisme et l'Apartheid, CCCA (Brussels).

than two-thirds of all weapons' transactions, despite the mandatory arms embargo by the UN Security Council.

The action model included, among other things, sensitisation, divestment, talks with CEOs, protests at shareholder meetings, etc. VAAK launched a second campaign, a consumer boycott of South African agricultural products. The coalition was broadened with the main consumer organisations and with a network of local anti-apartheid cells built up over the years. These cells consisted of dedicated activists prepared to engage in sensitisation and short-term, direct actions.

On the party-political front, AKZA and the Commité Contre le Colonialisme et l'Apartheid mobilised support of parliamentarians across the political spectrum to join the Association of West European Parliamentarians for Action Against Apartheid, AWEPAA. Both fed the political debates in the Belgian and Flemish parliaments by providing AWEPAA members with ammunition to counter the pro-apartheid lobby (one in four parliamentarians belonged to one or other such lobby) and to set an alternative agenda.

By the time of South Africa's first democratic elections in 1994, Belgian and Flemish policies towards South Africa had changed considerably. The Belgian government supported efforts to level the playing field in the run up to these elections. At the Flemish level, last ditch efforts by conservative Flemish nationalists to rescue Afrikaans (for fear that it would disappear) and Afrikaner privileges were neutralised. Instead, the Flemish parliament and government backed the new, inclusive language policy of the ANC. Both Belgian and Flemish governments started aid programmes for South Africa's Reconstruction and Development Programme.

This political mind shift was illustrated when the TRC started its multilingual hearings in 1996. Perpetrators and victims of apartheid were enabled to testify in their mother tongue. South Africans could pride themselves on this huge homegrown undertaking.

JAN VANHEUKELOM lives in Leuven. Jan was director of the Belgian bilateral development programme with post-apartheid South Africa and later joined ECDPM, the Maastricht-based think tank, to develop tools for improving knowledge about political economy actors that drive change.

45

Koen Vanbrabandt – Belgian Shop Stewards Without Borders

THE KEY ROLE OF SOUTH AFRICAN trade unions in the struggle against apartheid – by bringing the workers together in mass organisations and leading the class struggle – has been an example for trade unions worldwide.

The early 1980s was a real transformation period with various discussions about strategies and tactics. But the impact of the booming trade unions (reaching more than two million from 1980 to 1990), the foundation of COSATU in 1985 and the weapon of massive strikes and stay-aways cannot be underestimated.

Trade unionists worldwide till today should be encouraged by the role that South African trade unions played in the people's struggle, combining 'traditional' trade union work of defending workers' rights in the workplaces with political involvement and community work. Political claims included the demand for the liberation of political prisoners, the withdrawal of the army from the townships and abolishing the rising rents and transport fares.

The goals of a trade union – a combination of building unions with the struggle for decent wages and working conditions in the workplace, plus a broader view towards a better society – inspired us to build a network of shop stewards without borders, including their involvement in international solidarity with workers in other parts of the world.

The Belgian trade union confederation ABVV-FGTB supported the anti-apartheid struggle: on an international level with the International Confederation of Free Trade Unions (Support Economic Sanctions Against South Africa – Sanctions Won't Hurt Black Workers More Than Apartheid) and in Belgium with platforms including civil society organisations such as VAAK (Vlaamse Anti-Apartheidskoordinatie) and AKZA (Aktiekomitee Zuidelijk Afrika). There were campaigns such as 'Don't Buy Cape Fruit' (against Outspan and others) and 'Krugerrand Blood Money'.

Economic ties with the apartheid regimes from countries (including Belgium), banks and multinationals were a reality. They were triggered to do business with South Africa because of the low wages and suppression of trade union activities. By their presence in South Africa to maintain that regime, there is still a lot of work to be done in respect of human rights and workers' rights. This should be high on the agenda of trade unions. Millions of workers worldwide still find themselves in precarious working situations, with no access to a decent wage or social protection. Precarious work for many is also still a reality, including in South Africa.

As trade unionists we oppose extreme-right and racist organisations and ideology. Discriminating on the basis of race can never be tolerated. The extreme right is on the rise again in Europe and other parts of the world. Trade unionists need to take up their role in this struggle and defend democratic and social rights, and freedom of trade union association.

Although history never repeats itself exactly the same way, institutionalised and systematic discrimination, and dominance, is once again taking place, because of a regime that places one racial group against another with the clear intent to maintain this regime. This is the definition of apartheid under international law, and this is also happening against the Palestinians in the Occupied Territories and in Israel. A formal annexation would lead to the confirmation of an existing reality on the ground: a Palestinian Bantustan-state of isolated enclaves controlled by an apartheid state.

This issue was already the scope of the third session of the Russell Tribunal on Palestine in 2011 held in Cape Town and with an ABVV-FGTB delegation present: 'Are Israeli practices against the Palestinian People a breach of the prohibition on apartheid under International Law? We call upon trade unions and social activists worldwide to react against this injustice as we spoke out and reacted against apartheid in South Africa.'

Since 2006 we have built political solidarity and a vast cooperation programme with South African unions on specific issues: raising awareness on HIV/AIDS, membership campaigns, working on occupational health issues and worker health programmes, supporting domestic workers, etc. This will continue in the next years with an emphasis on decent work and social protection for South African workers, and a specific focus on female workers.

Ours is not just a formal relationship. Over the years we have built genuine fraternal ties with South African unionists and activists. Since 2004 South Africans have been invited to congresses held by ABVV-FGTB or its affiliate De Algemene Centrale-ABVV. Several so-called 'immersion visits' in the spirit of international solidarity, de-colonisation and equality have been organised, in which shop stewards participated. In December 2019 we visited South Africa with shop stewards for a week of discussions with comrades and visited Robben Island and the Apartheid Museum.

We want to understand the history of South Africa and the impact that apartheid has on workers, even today. With co-workers we discuss the current situation and the issues regarding the role of the trade union movement today and the inequality that still casts its shadow over South Africa. There are so many lessons we can learn from the struggles against apartheid, for decent work and social protection, against racism and discrimination, against inequality. The battle is not over: not in South Africa, not in the world. An injury to one is an injury to all. Together we stand strong. Long live international solidarity.

Koen Vanbraband is coordinator of the Belgian socialist trade union ABVV-FGTB's solidarity projects and chairperson of ETUN (European Trade Union Network for Justice) in Palestine.

46

Marc Bontemps – Oxfam and the Anti-Apartheid Movement

I REMEMBER THAT SATURDAY, 25 April 1987. With a handful of activists of the local Oxfam shop we walked into two or three supermarkets to put little 'Boycott Outspan' stickers on South African oranges and Cape apples, talk to customers and distribute 'Don't take fruits of apartheid' flyers. The action was based on similar boycotts in Holland.

Well in advance we had contacted small shopkeepers and managers of big outlets; trade unions had informed their members, cashiers and rack fillers. The flyer included a voucher that customers could give to the cashier. It asked the management to stop selling 'fruits of apartheid'.

The results were beyond expectation. We got sympathy from lots of clients, staff, shopkeepers and branch managers. The day illustrated the change of mindset that had taken place in public opinion. Finally we could reap the results of years of bottom-up work with hundreds of volunteers, the evenings and nights of campaigning all over the country, of showing films of apartheid and bringing testimonials of activists.

I remember the night rides to the smallest towns with posters, brochures and material for slideshows at the back of the little car, and next to me Maurice Mthombeni the first political refugee from the region. He was not allowed to speak about politics, so he 'only' explained what he had experienced. And so did Frank, and Jan and Toos, Pierre and Ralph, and Paulette and so many more activists from different solidarity groups Boycott Outspan Actie (BOA), Aktie Comité Zuidelijk Afrika (AKZA), VAAK, FOS, Solidarité Socialist, unions, the Oxfams and so many pioneers in our little frontlines.

Meetings attracted sometimes ten, sometimes a hundred people from social movements and grassroot organisations at local or regional level, evening after evening, weekend after weekend. It was our way of challenging the dominant Protea lobby of politicians and businessmen.[66]

Let us remember the mindset of the 1980s. The Cold War between 'East and West' was pervasive; the installation of cruise missiles mobilised massive crowds.

In Belgium the Oxfams were very active in the peace movement and built bridges between historic and emerging social movements. The Anti-Apartheid Movement came into this slipstream. But the challenge was not easy: as pacifists (pleading for unarmed resistance) keeping distances from the communist bloc, we had to act carefully as ANC (and MK) were positioned in 'the other camp'.

On our side we had strong moral, humanistic and emotional arguments. Economic pragmatism and status quo was claimed by pro-apartheiders. How to tackle them? Campaigns towards consumers were a way to overcome the dichotomy of supporting a struggle that included military actions when Oxfam was a pro-peace organisation.

Oxfam was already involved in Fair Trade. Boycott of the Kruger Rand had been pushed by Catholic opinion leaders. With South African fruit (economically speaking three times more important than gold) we could address our message towards a wider public.

The political sphere remained a challenge. In these areas Oxfam Belgium was at the forefront in the wider Oxfam family. In Brussels we paid for an office for ANC. Here took place one of the assassination attempts against Ambassador Godfrey Motsepe. His protection was not taken seriously by the authorities. We made sure he could at least sleep safely. Thanks to a campaign 'A brick for ANC' a proper ANC House was bought. ANC London paid for half of it.

The work of the ANC representation was not taken seriously by Brussels

---

66   Business lobby to keep trade going with South Africa.

diplomatic environments, so we guided them through our institutions and helped them find their way towards decision-makers, especially at the European level.

Oxfam's work behind the scenes was as important as what appeared in the headlines. Secretary-General Pierre Galand lobbied EU entities for financial aid to COSATU as well as to Kagiso Trust (that supported development institutions opposing apartheid). We can be proud that the Trust is still active.

Since the beginning of the 1980s an ongoing activity of the different anti-apartheid entities was raising funds for projects in refugee camps, for projects inside South Africa, sponsoring and accompanying tours of anti-apartheid militants.

All this energy proved successful: little by little the anti-apartheid movement gained momentum, and then, suddenly, the Protea lobby ended like collapsed pudding. They shut up and went into public hiding. Ashamed? Pragmatic as always in these circles? Hoping for better days and deals to come, later?

From our side we could be proud, we had been proved to be right. We won the battle for public opinion with a fraction of the PR and finances that the apartheid lobby had been able to gather simply because of the human capital we mobilised. Mandela's revolution started conquering our hearts. The development of southern Africa as a whole found a place in political and economic agendas.

You know my preferred Oxfam-slogan? – 'Solidarity is the tenderness of people.'

MARC BONTEMPS is now involved with Fair Trade as the secretary general of Oxfam-Wereldwinkels, a network of 200 local groups in Flanders, Belgium, partnered with the global Oxfam family.

47

Chiara Torcianti – Red City, Black Resistance: Reggio Emilia and the ANC

During the 1960s, the Italian municipality of Reggio Emilia, led by the Italian Communist Party (PCI) from 1948 became known at national level for its progressive policies and internationalist outlook.

Undoubtedly, its politics emerged as a legacy of both antifascist struggle and socialist tradition, historical events that profoundly shaped this modern democratic city. Among its public servants, the former partisan Giuseppe Soncini, communist leader and journalist, was the first intercontinental solidarity promoter and communicator, able to manage a parallel diplomacy with southern Africa while nurturing personal and institutional relations with the main southern African liberation movements such as ANC, ZANU, ZAPU and SWAPO.

In the mid-1960s Reggio's mayor Renzo Bonazzi began a correspondence with Marcelino Dos Santos, a member of FRELIMO leadership. Then on 16 July 1970, a twinning agreement between the Italian town hospital and a medical facility, run by FRELIMO at Cabo Delgado in northern Mozambique, was signed.

So, it was not by chance that, after Mozambique won its independence, Samora Machel encouraged contacts between Oliver Tambo (ANC president) and Soncini. The Solidarity Pact between the ANC and the municipality of Reggio was the first historical outcome of this meeting, signed on 26 June (then known as South African Freedom Day) 1977. This laid the foundation for popular mobilisation against apartheid and colonialism, promoted by local authorities and carried out on the ground by civil society committees able to involve the whole of Italy's democratic forces.

In November 1978, proclaimed by the UN as the International Anti-Apartheid Year, Reggio hosted a two-day 'National Solidarity Conference for the independence and sovereignty of the peoples of southern Africa'. Several African delegates attended this meeting, including Oliver Tambo and Sam Nujoma for SWAPO. Also crucial was the participation of representatives from Italian political parties, trade unions and non-profit organisations.

Indeed, this first conference, as well as the second one held in Rome in 1982, aimed at strengthening solidarity actions against the apartheid system and colonialism in southern Africa.

A concrete outcome was the establishment of a national committee, instituted by the conference and based in Reggio, which embraced Soncini's proposal to send an Italian Solidarity Ship that delivered food, medical facilities and agricultural implements for the peoples of South Africa, Zimbabwe and Namibia.

Thanks to the commitment of Italian civil society, as well as the unexpected involvement of the central government, two ships – *Amanda* and *Rea Silvia* – were sent in 1980 and 1984, as demonstrations of direct solidarity with refugees, displaced persons and exiles in Angola, Tanzania, Zambia and Mozambique.

Furthermore, in March 1978, following the UN global appeal to oppose the racist regime in South Africa, Reggio Emilia began to publish and distribute the Italian version of *Sechaba*. Thousands of copies were sent across Italy to the headquarters of cooperatives, civil society groups, NGOs and trade unions, raising awareness about apartheid and connecting anti-apartheid activities around the country. Antony Mongalo, the first ANC chief representative in Italy, provided the original English texts from the GDR. One of the most dedicated translators in the Italian editorial staff was Bruna Soncini. She was a tireless, passionate activist. From the mid-1970s until South Africa's first democratic elections, Reggio worked side-by-side with all the ANC's representatives in Italy.

Nowadays Reggio Emilia and democratic South Africa, namely the province of Gauteng, carry on this legacy by cooperating in the fields of culture, public history and sport.

CHIARA TORCIANTI is an archivist and history researcher as well as a cultural operator. She works for the Historical Institute of Reggio Emilia (Istoreco), the Archival municipal centre as well as for the Archivio Reggio Africa (Area – Reggio Africa Archives).

48
Jacqueline Dérens – The French Connection

FRANCE AS A COLONIAL POWER was more interested in its own colonies than in southern Africa. The French people did not know much about apartheid till the 1976 Soweto uprising.

The paradox is that post Second World War there were strong links between the French government and the apartheid regime based on their common aversion for communism and Great Britain. Apart from those ideological reasons, the relation was much more concrete: France could buy Namibian uranium for its nuclear programme and South Africa, arms and weapons. Between 1963 and 1975 France became the main arms supplier to South Africa and its principal ally in countering the 1963 voluntary UN arms embargo.

The South African interest in French armaments and war techniques originated from the French colonial war in Algeria. In 1958, South African officers were invited to Algeria to study French anti-guerrilla tactics and torture and followed training courses at the French Supreme Command. According to John Schlapobersky's testimony, his torturer said to him when he was arrested:

Mr Schlapobersky, this isn't Algeria with its inexhaustible supply of terrorists from the Casbah. The French had no chance of controlling the Arabs there. But they taught us enough about how to control our own population here.[67]

The war in Algeria was the trigger for my interest in Africa and, later on, South Africa. My whole generation was deeply disturbed and involved in this conflict. The young men had to go or to be draft dodgers, and the young women could weep or demonstrate against the sending of troops to Algeria. This war split France into two opposite camps, and you could not pretend to be neutral; you had to choose.

In 1975, I joined AFASPA (Association Française d'Amitié et de Solidarité avec les Peuples d'Afrique), an anti-colonialist movement with strong links to the French Communist Party. My training and job as an English teacher entitled me to be in charge of the English-speaking African countries and particularly South Africa. I was soon to demonstrate against a regime which killed children. I distributed leaflets in support of the pupils who refused to give up English and learn Afrikaans, the language of their oppressors. At Gare Saint Lazare, the spot chosen for our leaflet distribution, we were lavishly insulted by the commuters and called N-lovers. It was an incentive to go on with the struggle.

However, the political climate in France and the split in the French left, between the Communist Party and the Socialist Party, did not help and the task was often beyond our will and strength. Nevertheless we managed to build up a strong movement against the double talk of our government. Our campaigns for global sanctions did gain some momentum and we publicly denounced the violation of the arms embargo and the nuclear collaboration between the two countries.

We were also confronted by a very powerful pro-apartheid lobby. The bosses of big corporations, arms dealers and oil companies were the best friends of the apartheid regime and had direct contacts with the French government, which was not keen on sanctions, to say the least. As early as 1962, some right-wing parliamentarians created a Groupe d'Amitié France Afrique du Sud to facilitate the political, economic and cultural relations between the two countries. P.W. Botha, Chief Gatsha Buthelezi and Jonas

---

67   John R. Shlapobersky, *When They Came for Me: The hidden diary of an apartheid prisoner*, Berghahn Books, 2021.

Savimbi were among the guests welcomed in France by this friendship group. The South African Embassy in Paris actively encouraged those hidden but nonetheless friendly meetings.

In 1986, a group of friends from AFASPA decided to create a new organisation to support ANC and SWAPO. Our objective was to mobilise as many people as possible against the apartheid regime whatever their political opinions or religions. Marcel Trigon, then communist mayor of Arcueil, a town in the south suburb of Paris, was elected chairman and I was elected general secretary of Rencontre Nationale contre l'Apartheid. The nomination of Dulcie September as the ANC representative in France, Luxembourg and Switzerland was a real boost to our activities. I had met Dulcie for the first time at UNESCO in 1979 at the Conference for Children International Year and her passionate description of black children dying of malnutrition, deprived of access to medicine, and condemned to poor schooling was very impressive.

RNCA's main activities were focused on the implementation of sanctions. In pamphlets, petitions and public debates, we exposed the ambiguous position of the socialist government. We organised campaigns to free political prisoners and save the lives of those condemned to death and denounced the state of emergency. We managed to attract artists to design posters for us. Ernest Pignon-Ernest and Bruce Clarke were very active, and they succeeded in convincing renowned artists to contribute to the anti-apartheid campaigns.

In 1986, a huge demonstration brought together anti-apartheid activists, trade unionists and political activists and had a real impact: the French government decided to decrease the massive import of South African coal. Gradually the true face of the violence of the regime appeared clearly to the public. Young people wore T-shirts with the slogan Free Mandela and organised demonstrations of their own; petitions were signed; debates and conferences enabled freedom fighters, trade-unionists, leaders from ANC to come and explain what was going on in South Africa and Namibia. Dulcie September was always ready to respond to an invitation and she travelled through France to raise attention to the suffering and fighting South Africa.

Dulcie September's murder on 29 March 1988 came as a shock when it was announced on the radio and television. Parisians flocked to 28 Rue des Petites Ecuries where she had been shot dead at her office door. There was anger and tears in front of such a cowardly act – five bullets in the head of a defenceless woman. Her funeral was attended by a crowd of about 20 000 people.

Her murder was and has been on my mind since. I simply can't forget it. A few days before she was killed, we were talking about the last logistic details for a demonstration in front of the South African Embassy in Paris to save the Sharpeville Six. Dulcie had just received a warning from the French Home Affairs Ministry not to be present at the demonstration, the same ministry that had refused her protection after a mugging in the Metro and various other threats. So her speech was to be read by Marcel Trigon. The weather can be whimsical in March and on the day of the demonstration it was freezing cold. The speech was long, so I cut some of it before giving it to Marcel Trigon. Dulcie was fuming because I dared cut an ANC speech. This was on a Friday, and the following Tuesday she was shot dead. A few days later I was to accompany the ANC delegation to the morgue to identify her body.

The French police did not go too far in its investigations. In July 1992, four years after the murder, Judge Borkel closed the case because the murderers could not be identified for lack of evidence. For Dulcie September's family and friends this conclusion is a gross denial of justice. In 1988, apartheid had a policy of 'total onslaught' on its enemies and ANC representatives were apartheid enemies, therefore this crime should qualify as an apartheid crime.

More than 30 years after this cruel murder, family, friends and investigative journalists are leaving no stone unturned to find out the truth and want answers to those questions. Who killed Dulcie? Why Dulcie, representative of the ANC in France? Why was justice denied? Who wants to keep secret links between France and South Africa hidden? Apartheid is no more but we cannot allow the crime to be erased.

JACQUELINE DÉRENS as former general secretary of Rencontre Nationale contre l'Apartheid (RNCA) and later chair of Rencontre Nationale avec le Peuple d'Afrique du Sud (RENAPAS) now dedicates her time to writing and discovering more about Dulcie's murder.

49
Alphaeus Hunton – African American Icon Defends Solidarity with Africa

WILLIAM ALPHAEUS HUNTON JR, who led the Council on African Affairs and edited its publications from 1943 to 1955, was born in 1903 in Atlanta, Georgia. His parents, William Alphaeus Hunton Sr. and Addie Hunton, were national and international leaders of the YMCA and YWCA respectively.

The younger Alphaeus Hunton graduated from Howard University, received a master's degree from Harvard University, and taught English at Howard from 1926 to 1943. He was active in the National Negro Congress and moved to New York in 1943 to work for the Council on African Affairs.

As editor of the council's magazine *New Africa*, Hunton received a letter from a reader questioning the group's emphasis on Africa. According to James H. Meriwether (2002, 271), the letter was written in July 1950. The letter and Hunton's reply are included in a book by Hunton's widow.[68]

---

68   Reprinted from Dorothy Hunton, 'Alphaeus Hunton: The Unsung Valiant' in Minter, William, et al. (Richmond Hill, NY: D. K. Hunton, 1986), pages: 60–62. This article was reproduced with kind permission from Minter, William, Hovey, Gail and Cobb, Charles Jr. (editors), E.S. Reddy: Behind the Scenes at the United Nations in 'No Easy Victories: African Liberation and American Activists Over a Half Century, 1950–2000'. Published

'Dear Sir, I have come upon a copy of your paper *New Africa*. I have read and re-read with fervent interest the articles contained therein. First, allow me to ask a question. Why in the world would one worry about the racial conditions in Africa when we as a minority group catch hell in this country? Chances are that I'll never make it to Africa, therefore, I'm not the least bit interested in what goes on over there, but very concerned about conditions here at home.

'I would appreciate an answer to this question and also any literature you have concerning the problems of our illustrious race, and additional information from your organisation.'

Alphaeus replied:

'You ask why one should worry about racial conditions in Africa, when as a minority group we catch hell in the USA? It is a question that arises frequently, although usually asked by liberal minded white people instead of Negroes.

'The answer is two-fold. First, we have to be concerned with the oppression of our Negro brothers in Africa for the very same reason that we here in New York or in any other state in the Union have to be concerned with the plight of our brothers in Tennessee, Mississippi or Alabama.

'If you say that what goes on in the United States is one thing, quite different from what goes on in the West Indies, Africa or anywhere else affecting black people, the answer is, then you are wrong. Racial oppression and exploitation have a universal pattern, and whether they occur in South Africa, Mississippi or New Jersey, they must be exposed and fought as part of a worldwide system of oppression, the fountainhead of which is today among the reactionary and fascist-minded ruling circles of white America. Jim-Crowism, colonialism and imperialism are not separate enemies, but a single enemy with different faces and different forms. If you are genuinely opposed to Jim-Crowism in America, you must be genuinely opposed to the colonial, imperialist enslavement of our brothers in other lands.

'Our great leaders from Frederick Douglass to Paul Robeson have emphasised and re-emphasised this lesson in both word and deed. It was Douglass's support of the Irish people's freedom struggle in his day that made it possible for Britain to rally the British workers to fight [with] the

---

by Africa World Press, 2007. E.S. Reddy spoke with Lisa Brock in New York City on 20 July 2004. The book is available at http://www.noeasyvictories.org/select/02_reddy.php. Retrieved on 2 August 2021.

North in the Civil War. The workers of England took their stand on the side of Lincoln and emancipation. This leads to the second important part of the answer.

'It is not a matter of helping the African people achieve freedom simply out of a spirit of humanitarian concern for their welfare. It is a matter of helping the African people, because in doing so we further the possibility of their being able to help us in our struggles in the U.S. Can you not envision what a powerful influence a free West Indies or a free west Africa would be upon American Democracy? ...'

ALPHAEUS HUNTON worked closely with Paul Robeson, W.E.B. Du Bois and other African American intellectuals during the 1940s into the 1950s. Their Council on African Affairs mobilised behind the Defiance Campaign in 1952. Hunton was arrested in the McCarthy era for refusing to testify to the House Un-American Activities Committee. After 1958, he went to Ghana, then to Guinea (Conakry,) finally settling in Zambia, where he died and is buried.

50

Zeb Larson – USA Protest Began with the 'Germ' of a Movement

YOUNG ACTIVISTS TODAY IN the United States frequently look back on the anti-apartheid movement as a source of inspiration for their own organising. Bill McKibben's 350.org explicitly invokes South African divestment as the model for their work to force investors to abandon fossil fuels.

The attention paid to the anti-apartheid movement is in no small part because opposition to apartheid began with such a small constituency of supporters. During one of the first major campaigns to terminate bank loans to South Africa by protesting Chase Bank in New York City, union leader A. Philip Randolph explicitly called attention to their small size, saying 'there is, at best, only the germ of an Anti-Apartheid Movement in this country'.[69]

Within 20 years of writing those words, that germ of a movement had become large enough to override a presidential veto on sanctions against South Africa. Passage of the Comprehensive Anti-Apartheid Act in 1986 imposed sanctions on the apartheid government, however imperfect, and further isolated an already isolated regime. In a country where the president has a powerful prerogative over foreign policy, this was a

---

69   Letter to Bishop Wetmore (Undated). Library of Congress, A. Philip Randolph Papers, Box 16, Committee of Conscience Against Apartheid.

stunning rebuke. It accelerated business withdrawal from South Africa as well and was accompanied by a host of city and state laws that punished companies for doing business in South Africa.

Opposition to apartheid became a popular cause in the US for a host of reasons. Apartheid was painfully similar to the system of Jim Crow segregation in the American South. The violence of the system of apartheid was fundamentally odious and became difficult to defend even for that system's quiet defenders. Zealously anti-communist, heavily militarised and nuclear-equipped, South Africa also worried many people who feared that it would precipitate a new global conflict in one of its neighbours. All of these factors and others helped to forge solidarity activism.

What unified many of them, however, was a growing belief that US capitalism was a central pillar of apartheid in South Africa. American businesses subsidised and stabilised apartheid through their presence, and for Americans who were otherwise generally far removed from events in South Africa, ending the US business presence became their best means of contributing to the liberation movement. Passing sanctions only became possible when a sufficient number of people had been convinced that the US business presence played no constructive role in South Africa and did a great deal of harm.

The first major campaign against the US business presence in South Africa happened in New York in 1965. Chase Bank and a consortium of other financial institutions issued a revolving loan to the South African government that had been vital in stabilising consumer confidence in the wake of the Sharpeville massacre. Coordinated by the Students for a Democratic Society, the American Committee on Africa (at the time the only national group devoted to activism in and around African liberation), Clergy and Laity Concerned, and a few other groups began pickets and sit-ins; the protests were to be understood 'as symbolic of protest against American involvement in the South African economy'.[70] Significantly, the organisers began coordinated depositor withdrawals from the bank, with

---

70   See Minter, Hovey and Cobb, *No Easy Victories*, p. 24; Press Release, 'Students Meet on Chase Manhattan-First National City Boycott, 10 August 1966,' Part 1: ACOA Executive Committee Minutes and National Office Memoranda, 1952-1975,' Folder 'South Africa-ACOA Programs – Activities-Bank Campaign-Press Releases, 1966'; Proposal for a Campaign on First National City and Chase Manhattan Banks in New York, Undated (earlier than April 1966). http://kora.matrix.msu.edu/files/50/304/32-130-1327-84-GMH%20ACOAproposal.pdf. Retrieved 17 February 2018.

high-profile groups like the Methodist Church and Cornell University taking their money elsewhere. Ultimately, the South African government cancelled the loan, and activists took it as a sign that corporations would yield to bad publicity.

Anti-apartheid activism slowed down for a few years following the Chase campaign, in no small part because opposition to the Vietnam War dominated activist circles. But in the early 1970s, criticism of corporate activity in southern Africa exploded all over again. The single most famous and visible example of this was the fight to end Polaroid's presence in South Africa. Polaroid was an unusual choice in many ways because it did not have a large business presence in South Africa. However, Polaroid was also a player in the hated passbook system: by producing the photographic equipment and know-how, Polaroid became complicit in the system of apartheid.

Ken Hunter and Caroline Williams, two Polaroid employees, founded the Polaroid Revolutionary Workers Movement in 1970 to protest Polaroid's support of the apartheid government. Polaroid, stung in many ways by the unexpected criticism, found itself on the defensive. With some encouragement from the US government, Polaroid decided to support a so-called 'enlightened' business code for working in South Africa.[71] It pledged to stop selling to the government and to work with their subsidiary to cultivate better workplace practices. In reality, this campaign failed: a report by the South African Institute of Race Relations found that it made little difference in wage levels.[72] But this campaign revealed the extent to which companies were nervous about criticism over South Africa and how much it could affect them. In 1977, when it emerged that Polaroid's goods were being secretly sold to the government, the company formally withdrew from the country.

Polaroid was not the only example of this, however. Shareholder resolutions became a tool to embarrass companies and to force public debate over business activity. Churches often led in this activity, as they were institutional investors but also frequently in sympathy with the fight against apartheid. The Episcopal Church launched one such resolution in

---

71   Polaroid Meeting, 14 January 1971, National Archives, RG 59, Records Relating to South African Economic Affairs, 1965–1972, Box 4, Polaroid 1972.

72   Independent Report on Polaroid, 1972, Howard University, Charles Diggs House Sub-Committee on Africa Papers, Box 127, Polaroid Corp.

1970 against General Motors, urging the company to abandon its South African operations. Other churches followed suit: the United Church of Christ annually forced votes on the behaviour of the Newmont Mining Company and Mobil Oil.[73] By themselves, these actions did not compel companies to withdraw wholesale from South Africa, but they elevated public awareness of the links between US businesses and apartheid.

Finally, activists at the local level began to embrace divestment as a tool to change corporate behaviour and increase public awareness of apartheid. Divestment was aimed at institutions like churches, universities and unions that had investments with companies working in South Africa. Small schools in the United States began agitating for divestment in the 1960s: Antioch College in Ohio had a divestment group in 1966. By the mid-1970s, progress around university divestment became more visible: the Madison Area Committee for Southern Africa (MACSA) in Madison, Wisconsin or the Southern Africa Liberation Committee (SALC) in East Lansing, Michigan were just two examples of larger, university-level divestment groups. In 1977, Hampshire College in Massachusetts became the first institution to divest all its money from companies working in South Africa. It was followed shortly by Michigan State University and the University of Wisconsin, among other schools.

This same dynamic played out in cities and states. While groups like MACSA and SALC also encouraged divestment in the towns that they worked in, places like Chicago, Philadelphia and Boston had thriving divestment movements as well. The primary fight was to divest city pension funds from companies working in South Africa; a second fight was over selective purchasing, meaning that cities could not acquire goods or services from certain companies. The first such selective purchasing law was passed in Gary, Indiana, targeting just a few companies: IBM, ITT and Motorola. But it was quickly followed by Madison and East Lansing's divestment in 1976–1977.

Philadelphia became the first major city to pass divestment legislation in 1982, and once finished with cities, activists generally moved to states. By 1986, the number of divestments increased to 17 states, 60 cities and nine counties, not including universities or other institutions. These efforts created political coalitions of union workers, churches, student

---

73   'How Stock Fights Affect Your Faith,' *Detroit Free Press*, 21 March 1972.

groups, leftists and African American institutions, the last of which was an especially important factor in liberation activism. Some groups remained active after divestment and raised funds for the liberation movements, while others became dormant, but, critically, they remained aware of apartheid and the US role in helping to sustain apartheid.

Divestment in many ways highlights one of the unique features of the US anti-apartheid movement: its decentralisation. US cities and states have far more latitude over the control of their finances, and unlike Britain's Anti-Apartheid Movement, the larger national groups like the American Committee on Africa or TransAfrica that worked on apartheid did not exercise very much control over local and regional groups. Instead, both ACOA's and the national approach in the 1970s was to act as a clearinghouse of information. Public awareness of Africa in the 1970s was extremely poor (not unlike today), and South Africa received very little attention from the mainstream media. Consequently, ACOA devoted itself to research and support for groups pursuing divestment through the 1970s and 1980s.

These were not the only campaigns of this type, however. Bank loans to South Africa were another point of action, harkening back to the Chase campaign, and South Africa's dependence on foreign capital made it uniquely vulnerable. In 1977, ACOA and a host of other partner organisations such as the American Friends Service Committee created the Committee to Oppose Bank Loans to South Africa. Local committees sprung up in cities throughout the US, and used pickets, sit-ins and attacks in the media to compel lending institutions to stop offering loans to South Africa. Compared to the 'germ' that A. Philip Randolph had referred to in 1966, the number of COBLSA committees highlighted how diffused an issue apartheid had become in the US. The campaign mostly wound down by 1983, but it contributed to the growing perception of South Africa as a credit risk.[74]

Hand-in-glove with this was a campaign against sales of the Krugerrand. Krugerrands were an easy symbol for Americans of the abuses of apartheid, and unlike many other South African goods such as ores and minerals, the Krugerrand was much easier to boycott. Both COBLSA and other groups

74 Draft Copy Philadelphia Bank Ties to SA, Madison State Historical Society, Beate Klein Becker Papers, Box 2, S.A. Loan; Robert Massie, *Loosing the Bonds*, Doubleday, 1997, p. 591.

helped to organise boycotts of institutions that sold the coin.

The national push for sanctions against South Africa gained momentum. From the early 1960s onwards, activists had hoped for sanctions legislation, but its prospects were continually blocked by a lack of interest among many members of Congress and outright hostility by the executive branch. That changed in this period as legislators became more aware of apartheid, and certain leaders such as Ted Kennedy in the Senate and Ron Dellums in the House of Representatives began to gather more attention in their demands for sanctions. The election of Ronald Reagan in 1980 made little difference, as the previous president, Jimmy Carter, had only taken relatively weak action against South Africa. South Africa came up several times in bills in the early 1980s as activists encouraged sympathetic legislators to force debate on issues, such as a 1982 IMF loan to South Africa.

The issue exploded in November 1984. Randall Robinson, the leader of TransAfrica, a lobbying group concerned with Africa and the Caribbean, launched a sit-in at the South African embassy in Washington DC on 21 November. Coming the day before the Thanksgiving holiday in the US, it gained a great deal of media attention, and TransAfrica began organising sit-ins and protests of other South African consulates throughout the United States. ACOA, other groups and local city and state divestment groups now began lobbying legislators in earnest for the passage of a sanctions bill targeting South Africa. Many Republicans, especially those in the Senate, began to fall in and call for some kind of action against South Africa if only to lessen the demands coming from their constituents.

The intransigence of the Reagan administration ended up working against them: Senate Republicans like Richard Lugar who did not necessarily support sanctions found themselves trapped and opted for sanctions. A sanctions bill failed in 1985 because of last-minute executive action that was largely cosmetic, but activists kept up the pressure by pointing out the shortcomings of the executive action. 1986 saw the passage of the Comprehensive Anti-Apartheid Act (CAAA). Despite its name, it did have loopholes, but it placed severe limits on the trade that could be done with South Africa and further contributed to the country's isolation. Activists continued to pursue divestment and other tactics to keep up the pressure, but the CAAA remained a singular achievement:

a popular president was forced to reverse course on foreign policy by members of his own party.

ZEB LARSON is a graduate of Ohio State University with a PhD in History. His research deals with the anti-apartheid movement in the United States.

51

Mosie Moola – Anecdotes from India

THE ROLE PLAYED BY India during the decades of struggle against apartheid is well documented.

I had countless heart-warming experiences and examples of internationalist solidarity during the 14 years I spent in India, having been deployed there as chief representative of the African National Congress mission.

When my wife Zubie and I arrived in Bombay in 1971, my work was to organise and build upon India's support for our liberation movement, both at an official level but also to try and make the struggle against apartheid known to many ordinary Indians.

Soon upon our arrival in the early 1970s, I made contact with a few young and upcoming progressive artists, playwrights and actors as Bombay was the hub of India's expansive film industry. One of the first projects we embarked upon was to persuade a young playwright, Imtiaz Khan, himself the son of a prominent family of actors and producers in the Indian film industry, to write a play against apartheid.

Imtiaz wrote an anti-apartheid play *And the Night Shall See the Dawn*. He enlisted his fellow young actors and friends.

Two of the actors in the play, Shabana Azmi and Amjad Khan, were spotted by directors in the film industry and in later years went on to become two of India's most successful actors and personalities, with

Shabana Azmi eventually being elected as a member of parliament and Amjad Khan becoming one of India's biggest movie stars.

Shabana was the daughter of progressive communist poet Kaifi Azmi. Through these and other cultural collaborations, the ANC managed to bring on board many Indian artists to vocally support the anti-apartheid struggle.

An interesting anecdote I recall was when the larger-than-life Amjad Khan became a household name across India as an actor. He always greeted me with a raised fist, bellowing 'Amandla!', once in the middle of a scene being shot, to the annoyance of the film director who had to scream, 'cut' while Amjad and I exchanged hugs and a few words.

This was just one of many such occasions when the knowledge of our cause in the fight against apartheid spread among the larger Indian population.

There is a fairly well-known saying in India told to me on countless occasions, which was, 'We gave South Africa Gandhi, and you gave us the Mahatma.'

Indians knew of South Africa because of Gandhi's early time spent in South Africa as a newly minted barrister and as someone who developed his concept of 'Satyagraha', the nonviolent struggle against colonial oppression.

So India was rife for us to make the struggle against apartheid known to as many Indians as we could reach.

What I recall vividly are the meetings in far-flung regions of India, where small groups of trade unionists, civil society activists, workers' cooperatives, religious people and others invited the ANC representative to speak to villagers and farmers in groups of a dozen or so. The goodwill of these most economically vulnerable people taking the time and making the considerable effort to express their solidarity with us was always intensely moving.

A grassroots comrade who had organised a small anti-apartheid meeting on one of the small islands in the southern Indian state of Kerala shared the following anecdote. The comrade said that as they were on the boat, being rowed by a man who was singing a song in Malayalam, the language spoken in Kerala, he heard what sounded like 'Mandela' in the boatman's song. He asked the boatman who this 'Mandela' was. What followed was a stern rebuke from the boatman telling the small party of activists that 'You folks who are educated and come from the city don't know who Mandela is!'

Many times even the poorest of the poor donated a single rupee in a show of solidarity with the struggle against apartheid.

When my wife and I moved to New Delhi to assume my role as ANC chief representative, we were always amazed by the support displayed to us by school children, universities, tiny book clubs and others.

Two schools in New Delhi in particular incorporated anti-apartheid activities as part of their extra-curricular drama, school choir, essay writing and quizzes on apartheid, as well as art competitions to conscientise the students about the liberation struggle.

Springdale's School and Bluebells School formed 'Africa Clubs' where students learnt South African freedom songs in Zulu and Xhosa. They sang these songs at functions the schools held to commemorate the 16 June Soweto uprising and on 21 March, Sharpeville Day.

What was astounding was that the vast majority of such meetings and anti-apartheid activities were the result of people choosing to throw their complete support and solidarity behind our cause.

In the mid-1980s, some of India's musical luminaries held concerts in support of the ANC and the struggle against apartheid. These were giants of classical Indian music and internationally recognised maestros of the sitar, the tabla and other Indian instruments.

To sum up the groundswell of solidarity and support extended to the ANC, I wish to share the following anecdote. During the late 1980s 'Freedom at 70' campaign for the unconditional release of Mandela and other political prisoners, Amnesty International held a concert at the Jawaharlal Nehru Stadium in New Delhi. International stars like Tracy Chapman, Sting, Youssou N'dour and Bruce Springsteen performed to tens of thousands of people. In the build-up to the concert – partly sponsored by the sporting goods company Reebok – I received many calls from concerned Indians wanting to know whether the 'bok' in Reebok meant that the company sponsoring this huge event had any links, however tenuous, to South Africa. This of course because of the 'bok' suffix, which many Indians knew was the name of the South African rugby team the 'Springboks'!

MOSIE MOOLLA was ANC chief representative in India from 1972–1978 and 1982–1989. He served the South African government as ambassador to Pakistan and Iran, holds the Order of Luthuli (silver) and lives in retirement in Johannesburg, with his son Afzal, a prolific poet of note.

52

Vladimir Shubin – The Soviet Union and Liberation Struggle in South Africa

DURING MANY YEARS OF the liberation struggle in southern Africa the Soviet assistance, especially its *armed* form, remained a top secret. Only in 1970, almost ten years after the assistance began, the head of the Soviet delegation to an international solidarity conference in Rome Professor Vasily Solodovnikov,[75] then director of the Africa Institute and vice-president of the Soviet Afro-Asian Solidarity Committee (and later Soviet Ambassador to Zambia) stated its nature for the first time. In an interview given for *Pravda* on 7 July 1970, he said that Moscow was supplying the liberation movements with 'arms, means of transport and communications, clothes and other goods needed for successful struggle' and that 'military and civilian specialists [were] being trained in the USSR'.

However, the assistance began much earlier. Moscow archives show that the question of military cooperation between the USSR and the South African liberation movement was raised for the first time when Moses Kotane, South African Communist Party general secretary and a

---

75 Solodovnikov was the first Russian citizen who received the Order of Companions of O.R. Tambo.

prominent ANC leader, visited Moscow in late 1961 with Yusuf Dadoo. Informing their Soviet interlocutors about the situation in South Africa, they expressed the opinion that

> [U]nder the conditions of the reign of terror by the fascist government which has at its disposal a huge military and police machinery, the peaceful ways of reaching the tasks of liberation and revolutionary movements at present are excluded.[76]

The Communist Party of the Soviet Union (CPSU) supported this position. The archive documents show that the decision to use 'violence' was taken by South Africans; and that while the Soviet leadership respected that, it emphasised the priority of political work.

Direct contacts between Moscow and the ANC were re-established when Oliver Tambo, then deputy president and head of the external mission, visited the Soviet Union for the first time in April 1963 accompanied by Moses Kotane. No substantial material support then came from the West and the capacity of the African countries was rather limited. During his Africa trip in early 1962 Nelson Mandela received about £25 000 in cash or in pledges. 'Money collecting is a job which requires a lot of time. You must be prepared to wait. A visit to socialist countries has become imperative,' he wrote in his report, later captured by police in Rivonia.

On 5 April 1963, at the meeting with Boris Ponomarev, Tambo informed the Soviets that the ANC urgently needed £250 000 for its activities. Indeed, $300 000, more than 40 per cent of the ANC's needs, was provided later in the year. Regular financial assistance to the ANC continued for almost three decades, though the annual figures differed.

Tambo also raised the need for military training when he was in Moscow in 1963. The need for highly specific guerrilla training was evident. In June 1963 two Umkhonto we Sizwe (MK) groups, totalling about 40 personnel, were sent to the Soviet Union. Among them was a young university graduate, Martin Thembesile Hani, whose nom de guerre was Chris Nkosana, the future commissar and chief of staff of MK and later SACP general secretary. He spent almost a year in 1963–1964 'in the environs of Moscow', studying in a highly specialised establishment known

---

76   Centre for Storage of Contemporary Documentation, Minutes of the Secretariat, no 1, item 3g, 2 November 1961.

among the liberation movements as the 'Northern Training Centre'. Hani said later: 'How can the working class forget the Soviet Union? I went to Moscow when I was 21 for military training. I was accepted there and treated wonderfully.'

Hani returned to the USSR for further studies in the early 1970s and that course helped him during his clandestine stay in South Africa and his activities in Lesotho. He recalled later:

> We had undergone a course in the Soviet Union on the principles of forming an underground movement ... then the building of guerrilla detachments. The Soviets put a lot of emphasis on the building of these underground structures, comprising at the beginning very few people.[77]

Large-scale training of special courses for ANC in various military specialties were organised in late 1963 at Odessa on the shores of the Black Sea. Odessa was famous for its resistance to the German and Romanian invasion, and from 1941–1944 the catacombs were used as hideouts by guerrillas. The first MK group was headed by Joe Modise, the future South African minister of defence who was known in those days as Thabo More; Moses Mabhida was its commissar. All in all, 328 Umkhonto fighters were trained there from 1963 to 1965 in two groups. It was not easy to organise their studies; the MK groups were rather diverse in age and education level. The report from Odessa in the Russian archive shows that the age of 163 cadets in the second group ranged from 14–57, only six had finished higher school, while 30 were illiterate.

The Soviet political leadership closely observed the training of the ANC cadres in Odessa. A special group, led by Petr Manchkha, head of the African section of the CPSU International department, was sent from Moscow in June 1964. The group was satisfied with the progress of studies, singling out their strict discipline and high morale, and at the same time emphasised the need for broader guerrilla training.

With the launching of the armed struggle in several countries in southern Africa, the need for a specific training establishment suitable for large contingents of trainees from liberation movements became acute. It was created in Perevalnoye in the Crimea, near the city of Simferopol.

---

77   *Echo*, 18 February 1990, cited in Vladamir Shubin, *ANC: A view from Moscow*, Jacana, 1999, p.161.

There, good use was made of the Second World War experience of the Crimean guerrillas, who had operated in mountains, forest and bush – in other words, in terrain rather similar to southern Africa. The centre in Perevalnoye was also used as a site for 'practice' by the freedom fighters who studied in Moscow. Mosima (Tokyo) Sexwale, a former MK fighter, political prisoner, post-April 1994 premier of Gauteng province and later a minister, who underwent training in the 'Northern centre' in 1975–76, recalls how 'Colonel [later Major-General] Fyodor' [Fedorenko] commander of the 'Northern' centre, who had headed a guerilla brigade, showed them war-time trenches and hide-outs when he came to see the ANC group there.

The training of the MK personnel in the USSR continued for almost three decades, and became increasingly sophisticated. Let us hear 'from the horse's mouth', this time from General Siphiwe Nyanda, the first African chief of the South African National Defence Force (SANDF). He came to the USSR in 1985, with a group of MK commanders who included Charles Nqakula, later South African minister of defence, and Nosiviwe Maphisa-Nqakula, another former minister of defence and now speaker of the National Assembly:

> In the USSR, we were staying in an apartment on Gorki Street, Moscow, where the lectures were conducted. For the practical exercises, we went to a place outside Moscow... The course covered the following subjects among others, (1) Communications, (2) Underground work including: surveillance; secret writing, secret meetings; photography; (3) Military Work including ambush; attack; artillery effectiveness and small arms. All were useful.[78]

In 1979, at the request of Oliver Tambo, the Soviet sent instructors to the ANC camps in Angola. The person who became widely known in the ANC as 'Comrade Ivan' – Navy Captain Vyacheslav Shiryaev[79] – headed the first group. He was succeeded by 'Comrade George' (late Colonel German Pimenov), 'Comrade Michael' (Colonel Mikhail Konovalenko) and 'Comrade Victor' (Colonel Victor Belush). More than 200 Soviet specialists were stationed with MK in Angola in the period 1979–1991.

---

78   Siphiwe Nyanda to Vladimir Shubin, 10 February, 2002.

79   Shiryaev was also awarded the Order of Companions of O.R. Tambo.

Without doubt the direct involvement of Soviet officers in training MK personnel helped raise the level of combat readiness of ANC armed units and, in particular, of the organisers of the armed underground.

The attitude of the Soviet leadership to support the liberation struggle in South Africa was clearly expressed by Prime Minister Alexey Kosygin in June 1969 when he met the SACP delegation, led by J.B. Marks. The delegation reported:

> [Alexey Kosygin] ... informed our delegation that the Soviet people are very interested in South Africa. He also said that they recognise that the South African struggle is probably the most difficult one in the world. He assured us of their total support for our struggle and invited us to ask for any support we may require whenever we need this.[80]

Such a need appeared the next month. At the ANC conference in Kabwe in 1985, Oliver Tambo said: 'In 1969 as a result of complications that our movement faced in this region, we had to evacuate [most of] our army to the Soviet Union at very short notice.'[81] Unfortunately, not a single African country was ready to replace Tanzania as a home for the MK fighters when the camp in Kongwa was closed.

From 1963 to 1990 the ANC was supplied several thousand Kalashnikovs, 3362 SKS self-loading carbines, 6000 pistols, 275 RPG grenade launchers, 90 Grad-P portable rocket launchers, over 40 Strela 2 M anti-aircraft rockets launchers, 30 Malyutka anti-tank rocket launchers, over 60 mortars and other equipment.

Moscow in many ways supported numerous attempts by the ANC leadership to bring MK fighters back to South Africa. Groups of them, often Soviet-trained, unsuccessfully tried to penetrate home via Mozambique in 1967 and via Zimbabwe in 1967–1968. Then in the early 1970s Moscow assisted the ANC in 'Operation J', an attempt to land a group of fighters on the coast of Transkei. The USSR not only provided means for the purchase of the ship but trained an advance party in Moscow and then the main

---

80   Mayibuye Centre Historical Papers, ANC Collection (London), 'Report of the work of the delegation of the SACP to the International Conference of Communist and Workers Parties, Moscow, 1969', p. 2.

81   Mayibuye Centre Historical Papers, ANC Lusaka Collection, 'African National Congress National Consultative Conference, President's statement', p. 19.

one in Baku at the naval base. Unfortunately, the operation failed, due to technical problems.

From 1987 training of air force and navy officers began, and future chiefs of these services in the SANDF of a democratic South Africa were Soviet trained. Apart from military institutions, about 200 South Africans graduated from the civilian universities in the USSR, mostly with master's degrees, and about 200 more studied for a shorter time at the Institute of Social Sciences, Higher Trade Union and Higher Komsomol (YCL) School.

The most striking example of co-operation and mutual trust was Soviet involvement in Operation Vula, aimed at the creation of the armed underground network inside South Africa which began in 1987–1988 and extended into the post-February 1990 period. Let us hear once more from General Nyanda:

> The Moscow visit of 1988 was the final leg of my preparation to infiltrate the RSA. It afforded me the opportunity to brush up on my disguises and gain more confidence in these... From an operational point of view, the Moscow leg was probably the most important for my cover story. Without exception, those who were not privy to the information believed I was in the Soviet Union for [military] studies. The enemy therefore never expected me to be right on his doorstep![82]

These facts unequivocally rebuff faulty judgements of Moscow's relations with ANC in that period. Late British academic (and a former editor of *African Confidential*) Stephen Ellis and his South African co-author, a renegade from the ANC and SACP who shamelessly used the pen-name *'Sechaba'* ('People'), claimed in their book *Comrades against Apartheid* that at the Gorbachev-Reagan summit in Reykjavik in October 1986 'redefining zones of influence' took place and the Soviet Union 'committed itself to withdraw its forces or to refrain from seeking the overthrow of the existing order [in South Africa], leaving the field to the USA and its allies on the ground'.[83] They alleged that South Africa was included in Reykjavik 'in the category of countries where the USSR would henceforth refrain from aggression (sic)'. Yet, according to the published minutes of Gorbachev-Reagan discussions, neither of them even mentioned South Africa.

---

82   Siphiwe Nyanda to Vladimir Shubin, 10 February 2002.

83   Stephen Ellis and Tshepo Sechaba, *Comrades against Apartheid*, James Currey, 1992.

The approach to the political settlement was discussed in detail at the confidential tripartite consultations involving the USSR, the ANC and Cuba in Moscow in September 1987; and a common position on all major issues was confirmed.

Apart from direct assistance to the ANC's armed struggle, described above, Moscow contributed to the eradication of the apartheid regime by its support of independent African states, especially Angola that suffered from Pretoria's aggression. For example, the Angolan brigades during the battle at Cuito Cuanavale in 1987–1988 usually had about six to eight Soviet 'assessors' on a permanent basis or seconded from higher echelons of command.

A final note. Moscow's support to liberation movement in South Africa was vital not just because it was massive, there were at least three other important factors: First, Moscow often provided assistance at the crucial moments of the liberation struggle at times or in the areas and when and where others were unable or unwilling to help. Second, the Soviet Union's contribution was not limited to training and material assistance, but also encouraged non-racialism in southern Africa, when 'whites', in particular the Soviet instructors in Africa and the staff of the military training centres in the USSR, established fraternal relations with 'blacks'.

Finally, Soviet involvement, especially in the training of MK cadres, helped the ANC from slipping into the use of terrorist methods. Avoiding that was a 'trademark' of all the movements supported by Moscow.

The tragic developments in the Soviet Union in 1991 that finally brought about its end had a negative effect on the ANC as well. Gorbachev and then Yeltsin began to establish ties with the outgoing racist regime at the expense of the incoming one; De Klerk was received in the Kremlin in June 1992 ahead of Nelson Mandela.

However, the situation did change to the good later, as demonstrated by the adoption in 2013 of the joint declaration on the establishment of a comprehensive strategic partnership between the Russian Federation and the Republic of South Africa. Highly significant among the fields marked for enhanced cooperation is the item: 'Activities to preserve the historical memory of cooperation in the struggle against apartheid and education of young generations of both countries in the non-racial spirit.'

VLADIMIR SHUBIN is Principal Research Fellow, Institute for African Studies, Russian Academy of Sciences, and Research Fellow, Centre for Military Studies, Stellenbosch University (South Africa). Among his many publications are *The Hot 'Cold War': Soviet Union in Southern Africa* (2008) and *ANC: A View from Moscow* (1999). For many years he was secretary of the Afro-Asian Solidarity Committee and head of the Africa Section of the CPSU International Department. He was awarded the South African Order of Companions of O.R. Tambo (silver) and resides in Moscow.

The chapter is part of research undertaken for 'International solidarity and struggles against apartheid. Historical memories in Russia and South Africa', funded by the Russian Foundation of Basic Research and the South African National Research Foundation.

53

Héctor Igarza Cabrera – Cuba Paid its Debt to History

Cuban combatants are willing to sacrifice their lives for the liberation of our countries, and in exchange for that aid to our freedom and the progress of our population; all they will take from us are the combatants who fell fighting for freedom. – Amilcar Cabral

To understand Cuba's affinity with Africa one needs to go back in colonial history to the slave trade, for Cuba is a product of those times.

More than 12 million Africans were captured and in chains, sold as merchandise in the public squares of the Americas, including in Spanish-colonised Cuba, to perform forced labour. This is not counting the thousands who died in shipwrecks, or of disease, in subhuman conditions and overcrowded transportation, whose bodies were thrown into the sea.

From those slaves taken to work on plantations in America, Cuba inherits its culture, its identity and its African blood. Those slaves contributed first to the Cuban struggle against Spanish colonialism, and later against US imperialism. For this reason the children of Cuba, in human solidarity, travelled to cooperate with the African peoples of the

Congo, Algeria, Guinea-Bissau, Ethiopia, Angola, Namibia, South Africa and others. Cuba did not travel to Africa in search of mineral wealth and other natural resources. Cuba went to pay off its debt to history.

After the defeat of fascism during the Second World War, many countries in Africa achieved independence without the need for armed struggles against their former colonisers. Those colonial powers, however, took advantage of historical links to maintain influence and used methods, including the assassination of independence leaders, such as Patrice Lumumba in the Congo, coups and corruption to continue dominating through neo-colonialist methods.

Through armed struggle in Angola, Mozambique, Guinea-Bissau and Cape Verde, the Portuguese colonial power fell and their independence – including that of Sao Tomé and Príncipe – was possible. In time Zimbabwe, Namibia and South Africa would follow, with the full support of Cuba.

In December 1975 Cuba provided military assistance requested by the Popular Movement for Liberation of Angola (MPLA) to safeguard the sovereignty of that country. Cuban internationalists managed to paralyse the invasions from Zaire in the north and South Africa in the south, both aggressors supported by the United States. Angola's independence was proclaimed.

Angola faced another crisis in 1987 when racist South African troops invaded again. On the Angolan government's urgent request, some 55 000 Cuban soldiers arrived in Angola, landed in the southwest towards Namibia, while other units advanced 800 kilometres to the east. At Cuito Cuanavale, in March 1988, they gave the coup de grace to the South African army, which withdraw definitively from Angola, tail between legs.

Commander Fidel Castro explaining the victory stated that, 'in this way, while in Cuito Cuanavale the South African troops were bled, 40 000 Cuban soldiers and 30 000 Angolans in the southwest, supported by approximately 600 tanks, hundreds of artillery pieces, 1000 anti-aircraft guns, and the daring MIG-23 units that seized air dominance, were advancing towards the Namibian border, ready to literally sweep away the South African forces that were garrisoned in that main site'.[84]

South Africa was forced to the negotiating table, which culminated in

---

84   Speech delivered by President of the Republic of Cuba Fidel Castro Ruz, at the commemorative ceremony for the 30th anniversary of the Cuban Military Mission in Angola and the 49th anniversary of the Granma landing, FAR Day, 2 December 2005.

the Peace Accords signed by South Africa, Angola and Cuba at the UN headquarters in December 1988. They were called quadripartite because the US was present and chaired the sessions. Cuba participated on the Angolan side and the South Africans on the opposite. Fidel recalled on the 30th anniversary of the start of the war in Angola, 'the internationalist mission was fully accomplished. Our combatants began the return to the homeland with their heads held high, bringing with them only the friendship of the Angolan people, the weapons with which they fought with modesty and courage thousands of kilometres from their homeland, the satisfaction of their duty accomplished and the glorious remains of our fallen brothers',[85] thus confirming the words of Amilcar Cabral.

The feat in Angola and the fight for the independence of Namibia and against fascist apartheid was carried out by more than 300 000 internationalist combatants and about 50 000 civilian collaborators who completely voluntarily carried out the mission in Angola. It was also a significant contribution to the liberation of Zimbabwe in 1980.

CUBA AND SOUTH AFRICA, FIDEL AND MANDELA

At the first Summit of Heads of State and Government of the Non-Aligned Summit in Belgrade in September 1961, Cuban President Osvaldo Dorticós Torrado denounced apartheid. During the UN Conference on Trade and Development in Geneva in 1961, Che Guevara, the minister of industry of Cuba, accused South Africa of violating the Charter of the United Nations by its inhuman and fascist policy of apartheid. He called for South Africa's expulsion from the UN. Speaking at the 19th General Assembly of the UN in New York in December 1964, Guevara pointed to the UN's failure to act against apartheid.

In 1960, Cuba began to receive students from the Republic of Guinea, Congo Brazzaville and Mali. In 1963, Cuba sent a team of doctors, dentists and nurses to newly liberated Algeria. Cuba participated in all important anti-apartheid conferences around the world until it was possible to produce an international movement for sanctions against South Africa. Che Guevara's trip around Africa in 1963 was a significant turning point in strengthening Cuba's relationship with liberation movements of the continent.

---

85   Speech delivered by President of the Republic of Cuba Fidel Castro Ruz, 2 December 2005.

Mandela and Fidel admired each other long before they met in 1991 in Havana, shortly after the South African leader was released. Mandela saw in 1959 how young Cubans defeated the Batista dictatorship, while he revolted against the racist Pretoria regime. At the Rivonia Trial in 1964, where he was sentenced to long years in prison, of which he served 27, Mandela became a symbol of the resistance. Mandela arrived in Cuba on 25 July 1991, and Fidel received him on the steps of the plane. For three days, Mandela received unbounded affection wherever he met the Cuban population. Upon receiving the José Martí medal, the highest distinction offered by the government of Cuba, Mandela said: 'We never doubt Cuba. We endured almost 30 years in jail because we knew we had many friends throughout most of the world and Fidel was one of the strongest.'

During his visit, Mandela thanked Castro's government for supplying arms to the ANC in the early 1960s and said the writings of Che Guevara had inspired him during his 27-year imprisonment. He said the Cuban army's resistance of invading South African forces in Angola during the 1970s and '80s had strengthened the anti-apartheid cause and led to his freedom.

During the 1960s, contacts with the ANC representatives took place mainly in the capitals of already independent African countries in which Cuba had already opened embassies, such as Tanzania, Ghana, Ethiopia, Egypt and others. Relations between Cuba, the ANC and the South African Communist Party (SACP) began in the 1970s and were consolidated, especially when delegations of both organisations met during the First Congress of the Communist Party of Cuba held in 1975, the same month that Cuban troops began to approach Angola in response to the call of the leader of MPLA, Agostinho Neto.

On the level of military cooperation, Joe Slovo and Joe Modise were the individuals responsible at the highest levels for coordinating all military cooperation between Cuba and the South African liberation movements.

Relations on the level of military training began in the 1970s with the increased Cuban involvement in Angola. Much of Cuba's contact with the anti-apartheid alliance was in southern Africa, between the Cuban leadership and the ANC and SACP leaderships in Lusaka, Dar Es Salaam, Conakry, Maputo, Harare and other cities in the region. From 1976 to 1988 almost all MK training took place in Angola by Cubans and Soviets, mainly in the Novo Katengue camp.

Cuba assisted in the training of the combatants on a large scale from the mid-1980s. Following the June 1976 student uprisings, dozens of young South Africans came to study in Cuban universities for the post-apartheid era. The Isle of Youth was home to thousands of students from Africa and Asia, including South African and Namibian students. Some graduates of these schools were later accredited as diplomats in Cuba and other countries.

Earlier, in March 1976, the first defeat of the South African troops in Angola at the hands of the Cuban soldiers was consolidated. That and the strengthening of the MPLA's power in Angola made relations between Cuba and South African revolutionaries closer. SWAPO fighters from Namibia also benefited, as did Zimbabwean fighters who arrived in Angola in large numbers for training from Cuban and Soviet instructors.

In 1978 Cuba provided offices, residences, cars and other resources for the coordination of aid and the training of its troops, both in Cuba and abroad, to the ANC and SWAPO especially in Angola.

During the 1980s, Cuba began to train ANC security personnel in courses on urban struggle, communications, counter-intelligence and the study of apartheid security services. Learning about the means and methods of the special services of South Africa was also advantageous to Cuba – it was advised materially and technically by their counterparts from the United States and Israel. Other European powers had voted in the UN for the end of apartheid but discreetly collaborated with the military-industrial scaffolding.

During the struggle, Cuba supplied arms and ammunition, uniforms and other types of equipment for the armed struggle.

Leadership of the ANC and the SACP travelled regularly to Cuba for purposes of coordination and to expand political-military collaboration. The international department of the Central Committee of the Communist Party of Cuba appointed Rafael Lorenzo, a permanent official at the Cuban embassy in Lusaka, in the 1980s, to take care of this task. At the Cuban Embassy in Angola, the mission fell first to Neuris Vernier and then to Angel Dalmau. The latter was responsible for relations between the ANC and SWAPO and Cuba and the leaders of both movements. Dalmau, on the Cuban side, was a decisive link in the preparations and holding of the VII Congress of the SACP including Secretary General Joe Slovo to organise the Congress that was held in hiding in a small Cuban village in the province of Matanzas called Yumurí. The Congress was successfully held from 7–12 April 1989, one year after Cuito Cuanavale.

Dalmau was the first Cuban ambassador to a free Namibia and the first ambassador to a post-apartheid South Africa.

FIDEL AND HENRY KISSINGER

Fidel Castro was a man of high principle based on firm internationalism, as shown by this anecdote about his relations with Henry Kissinger, US Secretary of State. In 1975 Kissinger had a secret note delivered to Fidel by an emissary. It invited Fidel to secret negotiations for the normalisation of relations between the two countries. For Kissinger, this was routine business in his successful career as a negotiator, since he had scored that victory in relations with China. For Cuba it possibly meant relative rather than absolute peace, since Kissinger was a trickster. But for Fidel the negotiations rested on important foreign policy principles.

The negotiations were cancelled when Kissinger learnt of two Cuban initiatives: the strong international campaign for the independence of Puerto Rico, the US neo-colonial appendage and, more daring still, the plan to send thousands of Cuban combatants to Angola in 1975. Fidel preferred to confront the US in Cuba and in Africa before reaching a pyrrhic agreement with Kissinger, who, for his part, led a covert action to prevent the MPLA from obtaining victory in the November 1975 elections in Angola by encouraging South Africa and Zaire to invade.

Washington financed the National Front for the Liberation of Angola (FNLA), headed by Holden Roberto, based in Mobutu's Zaire, and the National Union for the Total Independence of Angola (UNITA), led by Jonas Savimbi supported by the apartheid regime. The minister of the Cuban armed forces, Raúl Castro, travelled to Moscow to request material and arms for the troops that Cuba had despatched to Angola, against the sentiment of the Soviets, involved in an alleged peaceful coexistence with the United States.

Fidel put his internationalist duties first – faithful to African traditions, heritage, culture and blood – rather than falling into the trap of Kissinger and the United States. For Fidel, being an internationalist was paying a debt to humanity.

At his inauguration as South Africa's first black president, Nelson Mandela, while shaking hands with heads of state, held Fidel Castro in a bear hug and whispered, audibly, 'You made this possible.'

HÉCTOR IGARZA CABRERA is a Cuban journalist and diplomat. He has served diplomatic missions in Gabon, Mozambique, Zimbabwe and Liberia, and was ambassador in the Democratic Republic of Congo and France. He is currently the director of North Africa and the Middle East at the Ministry of Foreign Affairs of Cuba.

54

Ronnie Kasrils – Turning Point at Cuito Cuanavale

DURING OCTOBER 1987 A ferocious battle commenced in a remote part of south-east Angola which Nelson Mandela regarded as 'a turning point for the liberation of our continent and my people'. He was referring to a prolonged siege by the South African Defence Force (SADF) and its UNITA surrogates of a dusty settlement between the Cuito and Cuanavale rivers. Fidel Castro, whose Cuban forces were instrumental in the six-month defence of the outpost, has stated: 'The history of Africa will come to be written as before and after Cuito Cuanavale.'

Conversely the generals and most scribes of the former SADF maintain that victory was theirs. Then SADF commander General Jan Geldenhuis claimed that the Cubans avoided outright defeat by 'kicking the ball into touch'. Loyal army reservists, such as Koos van der Merwe and Pete Groenewald (later opposition MPs in the post-apartheid democratic parliament) claimed they had won the war since the SADF only lost 45 troops in the siege. Before weighing up these counter claims let us provide the background to the battle and then consider its outcome.

The prelude started in July 1987 when Angolan government forces (FAPLA) advanced on Jonas Savimbi's UNITA stronghold at Mavinga – 300 kilometres from his Jamba sanctuary on the Caprivi Strip.

At first the offensive progressed well, with FAPLA inflicting heavy casualties on UNITA. Then early in October, FAPLA's advancing 47th Brigade, at the Lomba River, 40 kilometres south-east of Cuito Cuanavale, was all but destroyed by SADF forces hastening to UNITA's rescue. Catastrophe followed with other brigades wilting under bombardment. FAPLA stragglers retreated to Cuito Cuanavale. The outpost could have been overrun then and there. The interior of the country would have been opened up to domination by UNITA with Angola being split in half – something Pretoria and Savimbi had been aiming at for years. But the SADF, far too cautious, failed to seize the initiative. This allowed an initial contingent of 120 Cuban troops to race to the town from Menongue, 150 kilometres to the north-west, and help organise the defence. Nevertheless, Pretoria predicted Cuito Cuanavale's imminent fall.

For five months the SADF threw everything they had at the beleaguered outpost. They relentlessly pounded the defensive ring with their 155mm G-5 guns and staged attack after attack led by the 61st mechanised battalion, 32 Buffalo battalion, and later 4th SA Infantry group. The defenders doggedly held out, reinforced by 1500 elite troops arriving from Cuba in December.

By 23 March 1988, the last major attack on Cuito Cuanavale was 'brought to a grinding and definite halt,' in the words of none other than 32 Battalion commander, Colonel Jan Breytenbach. Often in contestation with the SADF generals, he writes: 'the UNITA soldiers did a lot of dying that day' and 'the full weight of FAPLA's defensive fire was brought down on the heads of Regiment President Steyn and the already bleeding UNITA.'[86] The SADF deployed upwards of 5000 men plus several thousand UNITA troops but the Cubans and six thousand FAPLA defenders repulsed them.

Pro-SADF accounts focus on the engagements leading up to Cuito Cuanavale and the siege itself, cunning battlefield manoeuvres and achievements, tactical efficiency and resourcefulness, but cannot conceal the fact that they failed to conquer the town. They play down the later decisive military developments in the south-west on the Namibian border that commenced in April 1988. Colonel Breytenbach observed: 'With a lack of foresight the South Africans had allowed the bulk of their available

---

86   Jan Breytenbach, *The Buffalo Soldiers: The story of South Africa's 32-Batallion 1975–1993.* Galago, 2004.

combat power to be tied down on the Cuito Cuanavale front.' In his view this should have been regarded as a secondary front. This was in stark contrast to General Geldenhuys claiming that the new front opened up by the Cubans in the west was akin to Castro 'kicking the ball into touch'. In fact, Castro used his own sporting analogy – that of boxing: Cuito Cuanavale in the east was the left fist blocking the blow, whilst in the west the powerful right fist struck.

Undoubtedly wars are not won by defensive engagements. The significance of Cuito Cuanavale is that the defenders not only saved the day but bought the time to enable the Cuban-Angolan side to turn the tables and by April 1988 launch a stunning offensive in the west that changed the course of southern African history. The ball was not in touch but very much in play with the SADF desperately defending its own goal line.

This offensive comprised 70 000 strong Cuban, FAPLA and SWAPO troop deployment along a front stretching 800 kilometres from Namibe in the west along the railway line through Lubango onto Menongue and Cuito Cuanavale in the east. The SADF forces at Cuito Cuanavale were haplessly marooned.

A master stroke was the rapid construction of airstrips at Cahama and Xangongo near the border, which brought the strategic Ruacana and Calueque hydroelectric dam systems, on the Cunene River, within striking distance. Soviet Mig-23s had demonstrated their superiority over South Africa's aged Mirage fighters (a consequence of the arms embargo) and now that they commanded the skies the network of SADF bases in northern Namibia were at their mercy.

The end for the SADF was signalled on 27 June 1988. A squadron of Migs bombed the Ruacana and Calueque installations, cutting the water supply to Ovamboland and its military bases and killing 11 young South African conscripts. A Mig-23 executed a neat victory roll over Ruacana. The war was effectively over.

The Cubans could have marched into Namibia but exercised restraint, with all parties, including the USA and Soviet Union, looking for compromise and a way forward in negotiations. Fidel Castro was not looking for a bloody encounter which would have cost many lives on both sides. Neither were apartheid's generals and political leaders. They could afford casualties even less than the Cubans and Angolans, considering the popular mass struggle reinforced by growing armed activity within South Africa itself, and the disaffection amongst white conscripts, many refusing to serve and facing imprisonment instead.

The central negotiation issue was UN Security Council Resolution 435, concerning South Africa's withdrawal from Namibia, and the departure of Cuban troops from Angola. The last SADF soldier left Angola by August 1988, and Namibia became independent in March 1990.

The acid test relating to who was victorious at Cuito Cuanavale is reflected in the outcome. The SADF, which had carried out continuous incursions into Angola since that country's independence in 1975, was compelled to withdraw totally; the independence of Namibia was achieved; the prospect for South African freedom was nigh. Whilst negotiations agreed on Cuban troop withdrawal from Angola, and relocation of ANC military camps to Uganda, this was no setback compared to the enormity of the historic gains.

The demise of the SADF's generals is reflected in failure at and after Cuito Cuanavale. Their political influence and the grip on power of P.W. Botha was weakened, paving the way for the rise of F.W. de Klerk and the end of military dominance in the country. Any chance of the hawks leading a coup to avert ANC rule was nullified. Little wonder then that both Nelson Mandela and Fidel Castro termed the Battle of Cuito Cuanavale a turning point for Africa's freedom.

FURTHER READING

Jan Breytenbach, *The Buffalo Soldiers: The story of South Africa's 32-Batallion 1975–1993.* Galago, 2004.

Piero Gleijesis, 'Cuito Cuanavale revisited'. *Mail & Guardian,* 9 July 2007. https://mg.co.za/article/2007-07-09-cuito-cuanavale-revisited/. Retrieved 31 July 2021.

Ronnie Kasrils, *Armed & Dangerous,* Jacana Media, 2013, pp. 214–217.

55

Hans-Georg Schleicher – GDR Training of 1000 MK Cadres

A MASS RALLY IN BERLIN, just days before the start of the Rivonia Trial in South Africa, showed East German solidarity with the struggle against apartheid.

The National Front of East German parties and organisations called for massive protests against the persecution of apartheid opponents under the appeal, 'Freedom for the South African people!' One of the speakers at the Berlin rally was Harold Wolpe, who had just escaped from prison in South Africa and was canvassing support for the London-based world campaign for the release of South African political prisoners.

The GDR had launched a special solidarity campaign to assist democratic forces in South Africa in their struggle against the racist regime. Parties and organisations mobilised members, with the trade union confederation FDGB playing a major part in organising rallies in cities and towns. South African trade unionists Arnold and Jeannette Selby – who were among the first South Africans to be granted political asylum in the GDR – spoke at some of these events.

The East German youth organisation FDJ was active at universities, schools and academic institutions. The Democratic Women's League (DFD) called on its regional executives to use branch meetings to adopt protest resolutions. Prominent East German artists and writers joined the campaign.

A Congress delegation including Moses Kotane, Duma Nokwe, John B. Marks and Yusuf Dadoo visited the GDR during a Month of Solidarity in December 1963. They addressed meetings in Dresden and Leipzig and held interviews in the media. There was a great deal of media coverage which also looked at the close ties between West Germany, apartheid South Africa and colonial Portugal. The imprisoned Nelson Mandela received tens of thousands of birthday cards from East German children.

ROOTS OF GDR SOLIDARITY

The GDR became one of the socialist states most actively involved in international solidarity with the struggle against apartheid. Support for the liberation struggle was a basic foreign policy principle and even enshrined in the GDR constitution. This solidarity was based on historic anti-colonial traditions of the German labour movement and the anti-fascist resistance struggle, which had a strong impact on GDR solidarity with the struggle against colonialism and racism. A monument in Berlin is a reminder of the German anti-fascists fighting in the international brigades in the Spanish civil war of the 1930s.

The global geo-political situation also had an impact. The GDR considered support for the liberation struggle in southern Africa as a joint cooperative effort with the liberation movements in their anti-imperialist struggle and claimed an active role in the 'world revolutionary process' based on common values.

The GDR was a frontline state in the Cold War. The East-West conflict found a particular form in the confrontation of the two German states. This was a major factor in the GDR's foreign policy, affecting its solidarity, and included a credible dissociation from the insinuated collaboration of the Federal Republic of Germany with the apartheid regime. Exposing West German economic interests in South Africa and existing Western connections with racist minority regimes in southern Africa was an additional element of GDR support for the liberation movements.

From the 1950s and early 1960s African liberation movements received political and material support from the GDR and were offered training facilities.

The GDR's commitment included strengthening political and

ideological cooperation and the offer of scholarships to party schools. The ruling Socialist Unity Party (SED) had direct party-to-party relations with liberation movements like FRELIMO, MPLA, ANC, ZAPU and SWAPO. In the 1980s Pallo Jordan recalled a sense that some of the GDR leadership thought that the ANC was a bit overcautious conducting the armed struggle. But according to Jordan these were differences about tactics rather than principles.

A trademark of GDR solidarity was swift aid in emergency situations and the streamlining of resources. ANC Secretary General Alfred Nzo once commented that the ANC's first port of call was GDR, because it would respond almost immediately to appeals for emergency aid including airlifting supplies. The amount of assistance provided to the ANC by the GDR Solidarity Committee alone from 1961 to 1989 came to more than 60 million GDR marks. This excluded military training and related supplies.

Major areas of assistance were scholarships and training (about 210 scholarships for academic and vocational training), the production and distribution of propaganda material (*Sechaba*, *African Communist* and many other books and pamphlets were printed in and often distributed from the GDR). Humanitarian and educational support was continually expanded, GDR teachers and other experts worked in ANC camps.

From 1973 the GDR supplied solidarity goods directly to the ANC and through the OAU Liberation Committee for distribution to liberation movements. The country offered extensive diplomatic support in the UN and other international forums. The GDR was a member of the UN Special Committee against Apartheid, which arranged for one of its high-level meetings to be held in Berlin.

Semi-diplomatic missions of liberation movements were based in and financed by the GDR. The ANC was represented in Berlin by such a diplomatic mission, officially opened by Oliver Tambo in 1978. The ANC received financial contributions for diplomatic and conference expenses.

The GDR pursued an offensive foreign policy in Africa, establishing extensive diplomatic structures and networks to support liberation. As Max Sisulu put it, the GDR was 'in charge of Africa'.

Military and underground training

In the early 1960s the ANC, like other African liberation movements, asked the GDR to provide weaponry and military training to support their

armed struggle. Originally the GDR confined herself to the supply of paramilitary goods. Military training for individuals was an exception.

As early as 1961–1962 some South Africans were trained in the GDR
for undercover operations and sabotage. Later on small groups and
individuals, among them veterans of Wankie, received refresher courses in
the GDR before their infiltration into the operational area, among them
Chris Hani and James April. The focus of that training was underground
work, and the coordination of political and military actions. Training was
tailored to the needs of the struggle.

From 1967 the GDR started supplying weapons to African liberation
movements. Military training was expanded. The GDR became one of the
major supporters for the armed liberation struggle in southern Africa. The
understanding was that armed struggle had to be subordinated to the
political struggle. Support was increased substantially in critical situations
like 1974–1976 when massive supplies were delivered to the MPLA in
Angola, and also in the final stage of the Zimbabwean struggle with a
major GDR airlift operation for ZAPU to Lusaka.

After the 1976 Soweto uprising the ANC made an urgent request for
more assistance in military training. Thousands of young South Africans
joined the ANC and MK in exile. Providing shelter and training for them
was a challenge. The ANC turned to the GDR, among others, for help.
GDR assistance to the ANC more than doubled.

From 1976 on, about 80 MK cadres were flown to the GDR for special
military training each year for 12 years. The training base was a secret
camp in a forest near Teterow in northern GDR. Military drill, general
security concerns, intelligence and counterintelligence, information and
propaganda activities were the centrepiece of the courses, which lasted six
months for each batch of 40 trainees. They were trained in a wide range of
combat operations, such as ambush, raids, construction of underground
bunkers and tunnels.

MK commanders considered the GDR training as very creative and
practical, focusing on survival and absolute secrecy. There was a special
focus on underground work, military intelligence, reconnaissance and
communication.

In addition to Teterow, there was specialised training for individuals
and small groups in intelligence and security work. Some came from

South Africa for short or longer courses, making their friends and relatives believe they were in Great Britain. Medical treatment and rehabilitation for hundreds of wounded and disabled freedom fighters took place in a special ward of a major Berlin hospital. About 130 South Africans received medical treatment in the GDR.

I remember a special flight of the GDR airline Interflug, where the whole plane was turned into an ambulance transporting severely wounded freedom fighters from Luanda to Berlin. Often the medical treatment was followed by rehabilitation courses, including vocational training.

PREPARING FOR A NEW SOUTH AFRICA

In the 1980s the GDR foreign policy focused on security and disarmament. GDR was carefully balancing commitment to international solidarity for the armed struggle with a foreign policy of peaceful coexistence. This was not at odds with unrestricted support for ANC and SWAPO. Solidarity for the struggle against apartheid was never affected – the GDR even offered new areas of support like the training of diplomats for the ANC.

Some partners had considered the seemingly efficient GDR a model. However, the GDR was cautious about offering its own socialist model as a blueprint. It was happy to lend assistance and provide education and training. The GDR deliberately avoided any paternalistic attitude.

In 1989–1990 the collapse of the GDR understandably came as a shock for many of its partners. The journal *Sechaba* remembered the GDR with a frontpage picture of the opening of the ANC Mission in Berlin years before and titled its editorial on the GDR 'A friend to *Sechaba*'.

The GDR's solidarity left traces. There is still an existing emotional predisposition in favour of the GDR within the older generation of freedom fighters in southern Africa. This results from the intensity and seriousness of GDR cooperation, swift reaction to requests for help, as well as backup measures – the food supplies and medical care provided by the GDR and the personal relations typical of solidarity work.

HANS-GEORG SCHLEICHER lives in Berlin. He served until 1990 as a diplomat of the German Democratic Republic (GDR) in various African countries and the United Nations in New York. He was involved in and is published widely on the African liberation struggles.

56

Declan Kearney – Ireland's Firm Internationalism

I FIRST BECAME AWARE of Ronnie Kasrils when the BBC broadcast an interview in the immediate aftermath of the Bisho massacre in September 1992. His political leadership shone through. We in Ireland were watching very closely what was happening in South Africa, always hungry for information.

The rapidly changing context of the liberation struggle was increasingly bringing leaders such as Ronnie, Joe Slovo, Chris Hani and others to international prominence. Those who had been central to the leadership of MK, and the armed and underground struggles, were now emerging as public leaders.

I continued to observe the ANC's transition to government from afar; reading Ronnie's book *Armed and Dangerous* in 2004.[87]

As the centenary of Sinn Féin's foundation approached in 2005, I was Sinn Féin's regional party chairperson in the north of Ireland. I took a chance and invited Ronnie to Ireland to represent the ANC in a programme of commemorative events. We were delighted when President Thabo Mbeki approved Ronnie's visit to represent both the ANC and the

---

87   Ronnie Kasrils, *Armed and Dangerous*, Jonathan Ball, 2004..

South African government. Another phase of closer relations between Sinn Féin and the ANC commenced, and an enduring friendship between Ronnie and me began.

The fraternal links between the national liberation struggles in South Africa and Ireland are long established. Internationalism is integral to Irish republicanism. We learnt from struggles elsewhere, while many other liberation movements, including the ANC and MK, studied the history of the IRA's campaign.

Irish people clearly identified the similarities between the conditions of apartheid in South Africa, and the unionist, one party, sectarian state created in the north of Ireland after Ireland's partition in 1921. In 1963 John Vorster, then South Africa's justice minister, spoke with envy of the Special Powers Act being enforced here.

There has always been a special connection between Ireland and the struggles of our friends in South Africa, Palestine, Cuba and the Basque Country.

The armed struggle of MK, and dedication and sacrifice of its political soldiers, inspired freedom-loving peoples across the globe from the 1960s until democracy was finally secured.

The resolve of the Robben Island POW's in particular was a source of inspiration for political prisoners everywhere. Walter Sisulu spoke in 1995 of the esteem in which the 1981 Irish republican hunger strikers were held by ANC prisoners. Afterwards, in 2001, Gerry Adams and Ahmed Kathrada unveiled a memorial plaque to the hunger strikers on Robben Island.

In the apartheid years the refrain 'Free Nelson Mandela' became an international call to action. Irish people rallied in support of the global anti-apartheid campaign. Gerry Adams and others had previously picketed the Springboks game at Lansdowne Park in 1970. Young workers mounted a totemic strike at Dunnes Stores, Dublin from 1984 to 1987, after they refused to handle South African products. Their strike eventually led to the Irish government banning the importation of South African fruit and vegetables.

At Queen's University, Belfast, I and other student activists successfully campaigned to rename the Students Union entertainment space from McMordie Hall (after a unionist politician) to Mandela Hall in 1986.

Former South African minister and chairperson of the Irish Anti-Apartheid Movement, Kader Asmal, wrote in *Politics in My Blood* that the IRA provided military training to MK in the 1970s.[88] Stephen Ellis referenced the MK and IRA connection in *Comrades Against Apartheid* in 1992[89] and in *External Mission: The ANC in Exile, 1960–1990* in 2013.[90] Joe Slovo visited Ireland during MK's armed struggle, and further strengthened the links between Irish and South African freedom fighters. Belfast-based, South African academic Adrian Guelke has also referred to historic links between MK and the IRA. He was the victim of an assassination attempt by a unionist death squad in 1991, which was acting under direction from the South African Defence Forces's (SADF) intelligence branch.

In the mid/late 1980s Britain's intelligence services began to reorganise and rearm the state controlled, unionist death squads, as a key plank of their war effort in Ireland. Agents were sent to South Africa to engage directly with Armscor and SADF representatives and arrange for the importation of high-grade military assault weapons, RPG launchers, grenades and explosives. The procurement of these munitions resulted in an intensified assassination campaign against Sinn Féin politicians, activists and family members aimed at trying to break the republican resistance. Nearly seven times more people were killed by the death squads in the three years after these arms were imported than in the three years before that.

The links between Sinn Féin and the ANC became very important as the Irish peace process started to emerge in the early 1990s.

In 1995 Gerry Adams led a party delegation to South Africa which met Madiba. Joe Slovo had died six months previously, and Gerry visited his grave where he spoke of Comrade Joe's life and example, and then laid a wreath on behalf of the republican struggle. Later, in 1998, President Mandela authorised a series of highly significant ANC visits to Ireland.

Thenjiwe Mtintso gave a very influential speech at the Party Ard Fheis (Congress) and paved the way for a later delegation, including Cyril Ramaphosa and Mathews Phosa. These comrades visited IRA POW's in

88   Kader Asmal and Adrian Hadland, with Moira Levy, *Politics in my Blood*, Jacana Media, 2011.

89   Stephen Ellis and Tshepo Sechaba, *Comrades against Apartheid*, James Currey, 1992.

90   Stephen Ellis, *External Mission: The ANC in Exile, 1960–1990*. Hurst & Company, 2013.

the prisons and met political activists all over Ireland. This was a defining period immediately before the Good Friday Agreement peace settlement in 1998. Subsequently, in 2000, Cyril Ramphosa returned again to act as an independent arms inspector, and to verify the IRA's commitment to putting its weapons beyond use.

Ronnie Kasrils returned to Ireland with another ANC delegation in 2006, again with the approval of President Mbeki. At that time the republican leadership was assessing how we could open a new site of struggle through critical engagement with the policing and criminal justice system in Ireland. Like others before, Ronnie and his delegation engaged extensively with our activist base. We discussed the primacy of strategy; the ANC's four 'Pillars of Struggle'; the Vietnamese 'Fighting Factors'; and Sinn Féin's 'National Strategic Objectives'. This process foreshadowed another major strategic initiative by the Sinn Féin leadership in 2007. Ronnie has continued to visit Ireland ever since, where he personifies all that is best in the history of MK and the South African liberation struggle. When Madiba died in 2013 it was deeply symbolic that both Gerry Adams and Richard Mc Auley were asked to represent Sinn Féin in the international guard of honour.

Since the election of President Cyril Ramaphosa to state president, he has authorised a process of intensive engagement between the ANC and Sinn Féin to develop new programmes of bilateral cooperation, with a particular focus on Irish unity.

In July 2021, our two party presidents, Cyril Ramaphosa and Mary Lou Mc Donald, and other leadership figures met together online. It was especially apt that both Comrade Cyril and the now former Sinn Féin President Gerry Adams participated.

President Ramaphosa reiterated the ANC's unswerving support for a united Ireland. He spoke evocatively about the unbroken bonds of solidarity between the ANC and Sinn Féin.

While the national and democratic phases of struggle remain unfinished in both South Africa and Ireland, the primacy of politics which strategically guided the military campaigns of MK and the IRA have changed the circumstances for both our countries, and opened up new pathways towards peaceful and democratic change.

Umkhonto we Sizwe has a proud legacy among international freedom struggles. This will ultimately be fulfilled when South Africa's national democratic revolution, and the vision of the Freedom Charter are realised for all South African citizens.

Amandla.

A Luta Continua.

Tiocfaidh Ár Lá (Our Day will Come).

DECLAN KEARNEY has been active in Irish republican politics since 1980. He is the national chairperson of Sinn Féin, elected to the assembly in the north of Ireland and now also serves as a minister in the executive office of the northern power-sharing administration.

57

Don't Handle Them – The Boycott of Grapefruit at Dunnes Stores, Ireland

ONE FINE DAY IN JULY 1984 a Dunnes Stores[91] checkout girl Mary Manning at the Henry Street, Dublin branch plonked down two grapefruit and stated, 'I won't handle them'.

The citrus was the produce of apartheid South Africa, and Mary's union IDATU (Irish Distributive and Administrative Trade Union) had joined a boycott of the fruit. Shop steward Karen Gearon downed tools in solidarity, and soon so did other union members.

Mary and ten co-workers who joined the strike were suspended. These were Manning and Gearon, Liz Deasy, Michelle Gavin, Vonnie Munroe, Alma Russell, Tommy Davis, Sandra Griffin, Theresa Mooney, Cathryn O'Reilly and Brendan Barron.[92] As the chorus in the Christy Moore song explains it, 'Dunnes Store, the branch in Henry Street, is where the trouble all began. That led to the strike, the famous strike, of ten young women and one young man.'[93]

---

91   A general dealer selling everything from clothes to plants, fruit and vegetables.

92   Patricia King, 'Remembering the Dunnes Stores Strike 35 years ago', Irish Congress of Trade Unions, 5 November 2019. https://www.ictu.ie/press/2019/11/05/remembering-the-dunnes-stores-strike-35-years-ago/. Retrieved 26 July 2021.

93   Christy Moore, Dunnes Stores, Released 2004. https://www.youtube.com/watch?v=TER_

Archbishop Desmond Tutu met the striking Dunnes workers and invited them to South Africa. Not all of them were able to take up the invitation but seven travelled to South Africa to meet the Arch in 1985. They were denied entry – and promptly sent back, much to the disgust of the Irish media. What? Sent back after being invited by a prominent Anglican cleric, winner of the Nobel Peace Prize.

The strike went on for three years. Communities got involved, organisations took to the streets. The Irish government stirred in the face of the public outcry and was the first Western government to ban all South African imports in April 1987 and cut economic ties with the regime. Mission accomplished.

But it didn't end there. When Nelson Mandela visited Dublin in 1990, he met the Dunnes strikers.

He told them that their actions had kept him going while he was in prison. In 2013, Mary was invited to the funeral of Nelson Mandela.[94]

Then here's to the girls of Dublin City who stretched their hands across the sea,
Their action surely is a lesson in workers' solidarity.
And here's to the folk who heeded the boycott, who won't buy Cape and spurn Outspan
And also the lad who joined the lasses – ten young women and one young man.[95]

OM

M3KNVCE. Retrieved 26 July 2021.

94   Patricia King, 'Remembering the Dunnes Stores Strike 35 years ago', Irish Congress of Trade Unions, 5 November 2019. https://www.ictu.ie/press/2019/11/05/remembering-the-dunnes-stores-strike-35-years-ago/. Retrieved 26 July 2021; Padráig Durnin, 'Anti-apartheid in Ireland: The Dunnes' Stores Strike, 1984–1987'. https://www.historyworkshop.org.uk/anti-apartheid-in-ireland-the-dunnes-stores-strike-1984-87/. Retrieved 26 July 2021.

95   Ewan MacColl (1986). 'Ten Young Women And One Young Man'. https://ewanmaccoll.bandcamp.com/track/ten-young-women-and-one-young-man. Retrieved 26 July 2021.

58

Urko Aiartza – 'Solidarity is the Tenderness Among Peoples'

WITH THIS PHRASE, BASQUE volunteer Pakito Arriaran ended the last letter he sent to his parents (before dying in the mountains of Salvador) fighting with the Farabundo Martí Liberation Front (FMLN) in September 1984. He was one of dozens of ETA Basque volunteers who fought in Nicaragua, Salvador and Guatemala in the 1980s. Numerous Basque internationalists fell in Latin America participating in the struggle as volunteers.

Internationalism and solidarity with anti-colonial struggles was at the heart of the Basque nationalist movement. Basque nationalism, like Irish Republicanism, always had a strong relationship with anti-colonial struggles – for both suffering from centuries of oppression and assimilation attempts.

Sabino Arana, founder of the Basque Nationalist Party, was sent to jail for his solidarity with the Cuban independence at the end of the 19th century. In his writings he denounced European appropriation of African land. During the Anglo-Boer War, he defended the Africans against British and Boer colonisers: 'The British conquest of Transvaal is unjust, as was unjust the encroachment of the land by the Boers.' He denounced 'the inhuman cruelty with which whites treat everywhere and, every time, other races'.

The Basque nationalist movement at the beginning of the 20th century was Catholic and conservative in many aspects and, at the same time, it was extremely progressive in terms of solidarity with anti-colonial struggles. The nationalist movement supported Cuba, Philippines, the Riffian uprising of Abd el Krim, the Sandino revolt in Nicaragua, the Egyptian and Libyan revolts, Abyssinia, the Indian National Congress struggle and, of course, the Irish cause for freedom.

Regarding Africa, the position was very clear: 'Africa for Africans'. They even proposed to Irish and Catalan Republicans the creation of a 'League of oppressed peoples', including Moroccans, Indians and Egyptians.

We emphasise the experience of international solidarity during the Spanish Civil War. French, German, Italian, British, American, some South Africans and others formed the International Brigade, in defence of the Spanish Republic against the fascist coup led by General Franco. British labour unions received thousands of Basque children fleeing from the indiscriminate bombardments of the fascist forces supported by Mussolini and Hitler.

After the Second World War, a new generation of Basque youth began organising resistance against Franco's regime. They were influenced by the past but also the struggles of Cuba, Vietnam and Algeria. Internationalism and solidarity with anti-colonial struggles were at the heart of the movement's philosophy.

ETA (Basque Country and Freedom) was formed in 1959 from a previously clandestine group of students. Their objective was the freedom of the Basque Country and, similar to the generation of Mandela, Sisulu and Tambo, their understanding was that there was no other option than to respond with violence to the totalitarian regime oppressing their peoples. ETA's first armed action occurred the year MK started its operations.

The destinies of the South African liberation movement and the Basque Liberation movement crossed for the first time in a country that both movements admired so much: Algeria.

After ETA's first armed operation, the Spanish regime's response was brutal with hundreds of detainees arrested and tortured. A new generation of exiles sought refuge in France and Belgium, where communists assisted them to travel to Algeria. There they met liberation movements from all over the world.

The Basque delegation established comradely relationships with the African National Congress and its representatives there, together with the MPLA and FRELIMO.

Relationships among movements went from sharing experiences, knowledge and contacts to public support. For reasons related to geography, culture and language, the Basque movement strengthened ties with Latin American liberation movements, as well as Western Saharawis and Palestinians.

But apart from friendly and comradely relations, there were also practical initiatives with African movements like one in which Basques, Angolans and South Africans worked together with the Red Crescent and Red Cross to try to obtain prisoner of war status for liberation movement fighters at the UN.

There were attempts to show international solidarity inside the Basque Country, confronting the fascist regime. On 13 July 1968, on the anniversary of the International Declaration of Human Rights, an ETA commando stormed the San Sebastian International Film Festival where an American film was being shown. They distributed leaflets and Vietnamese flags among the audience. In the leaflet ETA denounced colonialism, imperialism and apartheid, and expressed solidarity with the struggles of Vietnam, Angola, Mozambique and South Africa among others, calling for international revolutionary solidarity. ETA leader Xabier Ganuza was arrested in this operation and sent to prison.

When Franco died, the regime promoted a transition towards a new Constitution in Spain. In a referendum, the Spanish Constitution did not have the support of the majority of the Basque Country as this new dispensation did not recognise their right to self-determination. For this reason, armed conflict continued.

The formation of civil society movements, parties, unions, etc., and international solidarity inside the Basque Country flourished with the formation of the Coordination of the Solidarity Committees, strengthening solidarity with the diverse liberation struggles in the world. This movement later on crystallised in a group called Askapena (liberation) which was banned at the beginning of the 21st century together with many other Basque organisations.

Dulcie September, the ANC representative in Paris, was invited to participate in the 50th anniversary of the bombing of Gernika in 1988. Her last words there were, 'The South African military power will not stop us, the western countries' collaboration will not stop us. Our liberation will come soon.' A year later she was assassinated in Paris, certainly by apartheid agents. It was the same period when Basque refugees were being killed by Spanish death squads recruited by fascist mercenaries. Dulcie left a big impression in Gernika where a place in her memory can be found.

An ANC tour helped to strengthen solidarity with the South African anti-apartheid movement. Conferences, posters and protest songs to free Mandela were widespread. Mandela and other Robben Island prisoners, like the Irish hunger strikers, were an example of dignity and struggle for the hundreds of Basque prisoners in Spanish jails.

It was not one-way solidarity. South Africans, like Lynne Cooper, who fled South Africa after Steve Biko's killing, settled in the Basque Country on the French side of the border. She married a Basque rugby player who had visited South Africa on a French rugby tour, (Zelaia) and her home in France became a refuge for those escaping Spanish repression. She was a clear example of 'two nations, same struggle'.

After South Africa's freedom, both liberation movements kept interacting; as many solidarity struggles were common to us. Be it during the annual Sinn Féin conferences in Ireland, in the Polisario Front camps, at Cuban or Palestine solidarity events.

At the beginning of the 21st century, when the Basque liberation movement started looking for a peaceful and negotiated solution to the conflict, our ties strengthened as we sought to learn from the South African experience.

Mandela's words in 1999 during the Spanish king's visit to South Africa were encouraging. 'We sincerely hope that all those involved in the Basque peace process will find encouragement in our humble experience that even long-standing and seemingly insurmountable differences can be resolved through negotiation,' he said. The Basque liberation movement intensified our relationship with ANC/SACP members and the South African government, receiving support, encouragement and experience. Basque delegations visited South Africa and met with Thenjiwe Mtintso, Kgalema Motlanthe, Cyril Ramaphosa, Aziz Pahad, Ebrahim Ebrahim, Jeremy Cronin, etc. Comrades like Robert McBride, Mac Maharaj, Solly

Mapaila and Obed Bapela visited Basque Country and encouraged the Basque movements to move towards a peaceful solution.

Sometimes things were not easy, and comrades like Yunus Carrim were not allowed to enter Spain for a visit during the Spanish right-wing government. Organisations like the Nelson Mandela Foundation and the Tutu Foundation supported peace efforts, and some South African played relevant roles in ending violence. South African human rights lawyer Brian Currin was pivotal in the process, supporting and facilitating the Basque Liberation Movement efforts through the International Contact Group. Ronnie Kasrils became a member of the International Verification Commission to verify ETA's ceasefire and its decommissioning. It was not easy. Spanish right-wing government always tried to find obstacles for those efforts. Brian Currin suffered enormous pressures, and Ronnie Kasrils went on a covert operation to meet underground ETA members for a first decommissioning step. When they made this event public, Ronnie and other Commission members were stopped at the Bilbao Airport by Spanish Army police and sent to testify in front of the anti-terrorist court in Madrid. They said they could not identify the underground ETA members they had met or the secret place they had been taken to.

This is the short history of two movements fighting for the same values: freedom, social justice, self-determination and peace among peoples. I am sure our destinies will continue to cross for many years in the solidarity struggles with Western Sahara, Palestine and all the oppressed people of the world. Because as Dulcie September said: A luta continua!

Urko Aiartza Azurtza is a member of the Gipuzkoa Bar and a lawyer for human rights groups at national and international courts and institutions. He has represented the Basque liberation movement in South Africa and as senator in Madrid. Urko is the director of the Olaso Dorrea Foundation and its TM eLab, a laboratory of ideas in the Basque Country.

59

Ramzy Baroud – Palestinian & South African Solidarity

Dᴜʀɪɴɢ ᴏɴᴇ ᴏғ ᴍʏ South African speaking tours years ago, I was approached by two South African men. They seemed particularly grateful, for reasons that initially eluded me. 'We want to thank the Palestinians for their support of our struggle against apartheid,' one said, with much sincerity and palpable emotions. It was a brief but profound conversation. Suddenly, such terms as solidarity and intersectionality acquired whole new meanings.

Initially, I thought the gratitude was with reference to the popular support exhibited by the Palestinian people for South Africans during the painful and often violent anti-apartheid struggle. But it was not. The two middle-aged African men were thanking me for the support and military training they received from their peers in the Palestine Liberation Organisation (PLO) during their own involvement in the ANC's armed resistance against apartheid.

I was already familiar with this war, which was fought alongside the massive popular resistance staged by ordinary South Africans at every level. I also knew that much rewriting of the discourse pertaining to the anti-apartheid liberation movement had taken place following the release from prison of Nelson Mandela in February 1990, in an attempt to marginalise many actors who played key roles in supporting South Africans who, eventually, overturned apartheid. When it became clear that the apartheid regime was no longer sustainable, official Western narratives began to shift, abruptly discarding their former allies in Pretoria. However, the likes of Cuba, Algeria, Libya, the PLO and other governments and entities that operate outside mainstream Western political paradigms were cast aside from the post-apartheid discourse, so as not to offend Western sensibilities.

I knew much of this, but I did not know to what extent that support proved significant to the liberation of South Africa. The fact that the two men still owned their PLO-supplied military fatigues with Palestinian flag insignias told of a story that the media wanted to hide. However, despite pressures from various Western governments, Mandela and his comrades remained profoundly grateful to those who supported them when London, Washington, Tel Aviv and others did their utmost to prop up the morally corrupt and politically outdated racist apartheid regime. In an interview in June 1990, merely three months after his release, Mandela responded to the director of the US Armed Control and Disarmament Agency during the Ronald Reagan Administration, Kenneth Adelman. The latter had questioned Mandela's warm embrace of PLO leader at the time, Yasser Arafat, along with Cuba's Fidel Castro and Libya's Muammar Gadhafi.[96]

'Yasser Arafat, Colonel Gadhafi, Fidel Castro support our struggle to the hilt,' Mandela was quoted saying at the time, adding, 'There is no reason whatsoever why we should have any hesitation about their commitment to human rights in South Africa. They are placing resources at our disposal to win the struggle.'

The latter part of that statement is worth a pause: 'They are placing resources at our disposal to win the struggle.' The word 'resources' spoke of actual, tangible support, and the use of the present continuous, 'they are placing' indicated that the support carried on until, at least, the moment that Mandela uttered these words. The two men were grateful for that ongoing support and, despite my strong criticisms of the Palestinian leadership then, and especially now, I felt truly proud.

I grew up in a refugee camp in the Gaza Strip, to refugee parents from a small Palestinian village called Beit Daras which, like nearly 500 others,

---

96   Richard Pyle, 'Mandela explains support for PLO, Gadhafi, Castro with AM-Mandela', AP, 22 June 1990. https://apnews.com/article/9412d3c54ecaff161e89f57f0225bde3.

were ethnically cleansed and later destroyed by Zionist militias.[97] These Zionist militants formed what later became the Israeli army, and Palestine, depopulated and conquered by force, unjustly became Israel. My earliest memories were rife with politics, revolutions, Israeli soldiers, Palestinian freedom fighters and a constant stream of violence. The walls of my refugee camp, Nuseirat, were the canvases through which the rebellion was daily communicated: 'Join the Friday Strike against Zionist Oppression', 'Long Live Our Noble Martyrs', 'No to Treason and Surrender' and a thousand other variations of these statements and also other political slogans that were not of direct reference to Gaza, Palestine and the Palestinian people. Congratulatory words to the 'Comrades of the Cuban Revolution', 'Down with American Imperialism in South America' and so on. Through the 1980s, graffiti portraying Mandela, calling for an end to apartheid and reminding us, refugees, that our struggle and that of black South Africans was one and the same.

Such phrases as the 'Mandela of Palestine', for example, entered the Palestinian revolutionary discourses with reference to Palestinian prisoners who spent many years in Israeli prisons. Similarly, 'Guevara of Gaza', or 'Guevara of Palestine' were also familiar depictions, delineating Palestinian affinity with the anti-imperialist struggle in South America. In short, we, the refugees of Palestine, had fully claimed Mandela and the South African people's struggle for justice as our own, long before that struggle was exploited by Western nations in a desperate attempt to whitewash their colonial sins in Africa and throughout the global South. Not only did Israel remain committed to the Pretoria apartheid until its final days, but it also violently cracked down on Palestinians who expressed solidarity with South Africa's anti-apartheid movement.[98] Like Washington, Tel Aviv, too, considered Mandela a 'terrorist'.[99] Similarly, all Palestinian prisoners in Israel, every single one of them, was also, in Israel's twisted colonial logic, a 'terrorist'.

---

97   Ilan Pappé, *The Ethnic Cleansing of Palestine*, Oneworld, Oxford, 2006.

98   Avi Shilon, 'Why Israel supported South Africa's apartheid regime', *Haaretz*, 11 December 2013, https://www.haaretz.com/opinion/.premium-why-israel-supported-apartheid-regime-1.5298552. Retrieved 28 August 2021.

99   Olivia B. Waxman, 'The U.S. government had Nelson Mandela on terrorist watch lists Until 2008. Here's why'. *Time*, 18 July 2018. https://time.com/5338569/nelson-mandela-terror-list/. Retrieved 28 August 2021.

When I visited South Africa for the first time, I did not feel like an outsider, offering platitudes about solidarity. It truly felt that I was returning to my own liberated homeland. These were not simply my own feelings, conjured up through specific experiences as a Palestinian refugee from Gaza. South Africans, too, felt, and continue to feel, that way about Palestinians. It should come as no surprise that the pro-Palestine movement in South Africa is one of the strongest and most vibrant anywhere in the world. And that support is neither condescending, patronising or conditional, but one based on real emotional rapport of shared experiences, a people's struggle against the menaces of racism, colonialism and apartheid.

In Palestine, we continue to see South Africa as a model, not only in terms of the power, courage and sacrifices of the South African people, but also as a model of global solidarity against colonial oppression, racism and injustice in all of its forms. I am proud to say that, just as Palestinians – though fighting our own difficult fight against Zionist colonialism and Israeli apartheid – played a part in the liberation of South Africa, perhaps in the same way a future generation of South Africans will, also proudly, make that claim once beloved Palestine is liberated.

RAMZY BAROUD is a journalist and the editor of *The Palestine Chronicle*. Dr Baroud is a non-resident senior research fellow at the Center for Islam and Global Affairs (CIGA) and also at the Afro-Middle East Center (AMEC).

60

Kofi Hope – The Canadian Anti-Apartheid Movement

On 30 May 1986 the largest anti-apartheid demonstration in Canadian history was held in Toronto, Ontario. Ten thousand people marched through the heart of the city, the crowd swelling to 15 000 in front of the provincial legislature to hear Desmond Tutu speak.

This would be a watershed moment for the Canadian anti-apartheid movement, the culmination of decades of work to bring the struggle from a fringe issue to part of the national conversation. It was the result of a decade and half of sustained consciousness-raising and advocacy by the national network.

While there were a handful of groups exclusively dedicated to the cause like TCLSAC, Toronto Committee for the Liberation of Southern African Countries, and IDAFSA, the International Defence and Aid Fund for Southern Africa (Canada), just as critical were larger established Canadian third-sector organisations. Churches, non-profits and trade unions served as bases of support for activists to develop the movement, providing national profile, funding and key infrastructure as the movement grew.

The movement began in earnest in Canada in the 1970s. While the earliest documented activities took place in the 1960s, during that decade South Africa was just one element of larger work around support for liberation movements across southern Africa. Much of the work was limited to policy advocacy from a core group of academics and institutional actors. Further many of the activists who would become leaders in the movement were still living in southern Africa, as church-based missionaries or student volunteers.

By the 1970s things shifted, the ANC opened an office in Toronto which was able to become a full-time operation by 1978. In 1975 the Taskforce for Church and Corporate Responsibility (TCCR) launched a crucial coalition for activism around divestment. Rallies, speakers' series and direct actions like stuffing bank deposit boxes with 'No Loans to South Africa' cheques proliferated. Canadians Concerned with Southern Africa (CCSA) was formed in 1975, an important solidarity organisation within the movement that attempted to become the single national formation for the movement, but never fully achieved that goal. By the late 1970s around 200 000 Canadian dollars a year was being raised from the public for liberation support.

In June 1980 IDAFSA (Canada) was established, a national branch of UK-based Defence and Aid. Over the next five years it went from a few hundreds of supporters to 10 000 by 1986. By the mid-1980s a full social movement around anti-apartheid existed in Canada.

After the mid-1980s the movement became increasingly institutionalised, with millions of dollars now available from government and the public and established non-governmental organisations taking on the role of administrating the funds. While the Canadian government made major strides in the 1980s around its position on apartheid, it very much remained as scholar Linda Freeman described 'the ambiguous champion'. Canadian government pressure on South Africa was inconsistent, filled with half-measures, and required constant advocacy and pressure from civil society.

A core part of the movement's work was providing on-the-ground support (non-military financial and in-kind donations). CUSO (Canadian University Services Overseas) for many years was the leading organisation in coordinating this work, operating a liberation support office in Lusaka, Zambia, from the mid-1970s, which worked directly with the local ANC office and helped organise liberation support from groups across the Western world.

I estimate in the 1980s there was a core of 500 individual activists at the heart of the movement, with about 150–200 core organisations engaged and hundreds of other groups temporarily mobilised to contribute. By 1994, tens of thousands of Canadians had supported the movement through attending events or financial contributions.

The Canadian Anti-Apartheid Movement was a set of overlapping networks. There was an NGO network with major national organisations at the core like CUSO, OXFAM, YWCA and IDAFSA (Canada). Then there were church-based networks, with the United Church of Canada, Anglican Church and Canadian Catholic Organisation for Peace and Development at the core. Trade union networks were defined by a cleavage between activists aligned with the Canadian Labour Congress supporting some of the new labour formations in South Africa and those supporting the SACTU Solidarity Committee, which maintained exclusive support for the ANC-aligned South African Congress of Trade Unions.

Despite being one of Canada's most expansive transnational solidarity movements, the anti-apartheid movement remains relatively unknown in the broader historical memory of the country. Many parts of this history remain understudied, such as the role of Canadians who worked directly in clandestine operations with the ANC. Another area for future study is the role of black-led formations in the movement. While black South African 'exiles' living in Canada were very much involved in the movement, black Canadians had a more complex relationship.

Following the advent of non-racist immigration policy in Canada in the 1960s, Canada saw a significant growth in its black population, primarily coming from the Caribbean and concentrated in Toronto and Montreal. Activists within these communities tended to mobilise within Pan-Africanist or black nationalist traditions and their groups were generally isolated from the larger predominately white movement. In 1985 the Anti-Apartheid Coalition of Toronto was created, with two black activists within the movement chosen as co-chairs, to attempt to bridge these gaps. A more detailed accounting of this history will be important work for future scholars.

Canada made noted and significant contributions to the global movement to end apartheid. The movement also contributed to helping shape the inclusive and multi-cultural Canadian society that exists today, with legacies seen in Canada's contemporary international development sector and anti-racist movements.

KOFI HOPE is a Rhodes Scholar and has a doctorate in Politics from Oxford University. He is the co-founder and CEO of Monumental, a Toronto-based social enterprise. He is an active voice within the Canadian media about issues of equity and social justice and has led multiple organisations focused on supporting black youth in Toronto.

61
Dominic Bellissimo – Canadian Workers' 'Modest' Contribution

ONE COULD BE FORGIVEN for thinking that greying Tories were the vanguard of Canada's anti-apartheid efforts after witnessing the official delegation to Mandela's memorial years ago. It is a cruel irony of history that the likes of Conservatives Brian Mulroney, Joe Clarke and other politicians are lionised while those who were in the trenches against apartheid are written out of history.

Those ordinary Canadians who fought against apartheid have tragically been overlooked, and those who decried Mandela as a 'communist terrorist' elevated as humanitarian heroes in his passing.

While the Canadian movement lagged behind those in Europe and the US, where there had been anti-apartheid groups since the Defiance Campaigns in South Africa in the 1950s, Canadians played a significant role in the struggle within the labour movement and other sections of civil society for decades.

The 1970s saw the solidarity movement expand dramatically, from a few student-based divestment groups to major campaigns against Canadian banks and corporations. I will focus on union involvement in the 1980s and early 1990s since Kofi Hope, in his article, has looked at the tapestry of organisations falling under the anti-apartheid movement that swelled into a broad-based coalition of NGOs, churches and activist groups from coast to coast, pressuring the Canadian Federal government to implement sanctions and divestment.

Enver Domingo, George Ponnen[100] and Jeanette Snyder worked tirelessly for SACTU in both Canada and the US. By 1980, Brenda Wall and Ken Luckhardt were the force behind the SACTU Solidarity Committee challenging the anti-communist line of the Canadian Labour Congress.

The solidarity shown by the labour movement during this period lagged behind the mass democratic movements in the community for several reasons.

Partly Cold War and anti-communist rhetoric sought to marginalise the liberation and South African labour movement as 'Communist-led and directed' by the Soviet Union or other Socialist countries. While the World Federation of Trade Unions (WFTU) took a clear class-based position against apartheid, the Canadian labour movement remained affiliated to the International Confederation of Free Trade Unions (ICFTU), which took a more cautious class collaboration approach in its policies. Although 'anti-apartheid' in its policy, there was little more than a resolution on paper to support it.

The Canadian Labour Congress International department was reluctant to commit to a position beyond 'support for black trade unionists' but cautioned affiliate unions not to engage in politics. Its outlook has always been social democratic or liberal in its solidarity work. International development and labour sponsored projects got significant attention over working class solidarity.

It is important to distinguish between the leadership of the central Canadian labour bodies and the local union membership who often became energised in the fight against apartheid and were proud to show international solidarity with their fellow sisters and brothers abroad.

Working with progressive union locals and some national union leadership, successful solidarity campaigns gained momentum in the mid-1980s.

Leaders like Bob White of the United Auto Workers, and later the Canadian Auto Workers, met with SACTU leaders and endorsed local unit fundraising. Jean Claude Parrot (of the Canadian Union of Postal

---

100   George Ponnen was a veteran trade unionist from Durban exiled to Canada.

Workers) stood out as a staunch anti-apartheid voice pledging money and labour power in the various divestment and boycott campaigns. The United Food and Commercial Workers supported members' right to refuse to stock South African products; International Longshore and Warehouse Union locals refused to move cargo; the Communication Workers sent taped messages of solidarity to South African workers. International Wood Workers supported sanctions on pulp and paper exports to South Africa. And the solidarity expressions grew throughout the decade. At one point 40 Canadian labour organisations released statements in support of boycott and divestment campaigns.

With the level of solidarity increasing, cracks began to appear between the positions of the labour hierarchy versus what their local membership thought. Regular SACTU tours, and later of COSATU leaders, were arranged and introduced at labour conventions. A SACTU 'strike fund' was established and more than 350 separate union locals contributed money monthly.

Newsletters were mailed by thousands to Canadian union members often with in-kind mailing costs assumed by various union locals. Calls for sanctions, boycott and divestment became the rallying cry for millions of Canadian workers. The broadest unity was achieved when demands focused on the action of dismantling apartheid rather than debating the ideal 'post-apartheid government'. Broad coalitions supported the tours of Archbishop Desmond Tutu and Oliver Tambo to Canada.

For those voices who sympathised with the unpopular South African regime, the dominant mode of attack was not to claim that apartheid was *acceptable*, but that its opponents, including the ANC and SACTU, were dangerous – even posing an existential threat to that country. Significant members of the Canadian ruling class and Conservative politicians often echoed this caution.

However, with the struggle intensifying inside the country and the commitment of thousands of activists, the average Canadian was proud to be seen as anti-apartheid by the early 1990s. The unbanning of organisations and the impending release of Madiba meant that it was now 'safe' for politicians and unions of all stripes to be seen as supporting the former prisoner and future president of South Africa. Political change is a process.

To this day, in a number of union conventions, we hear 'An Injury to One Is an Injury to All'!

DOMINIC BELLISSIMO has worked with the Canadians Concerned about South Africa (CCSA) and the ANC support coalition (AMSCO). Dominic was a member of the Nelson Mandela Children's Fund (Canada) and presently assists the partnership between the South African Democratic Teachers Union (SADTU) and the Ontario Secondary School Teachers' Federation.

62

N. Barney Pityana – Black Consciousness & the World Council of Churches

THE IDEOLOGY OF BLACK CONSCIOUSNESS emerged from the university and college of apartheid black higher education institutions in 1968. It began as a revolt against the paternalism of the liberal national student union NUSAS and a critique of its credentials as an anti-apartheid organisation.

Although NUSAS was theoretically open to membership of all students, the reality was that it was dominated by students, theories and ideas from a handful of the white, English-speaking institutions. It also remained the case that judging by its leadership, its resolutions and the agendas of such institutions the overwhelming ideas were white 'liberal' concerns about academic freedom and in politics 'a liberal world-view'. Meanwhile the vast majority of black students were confined to segregated universities and colleges according to the apartheid diktat. The few black students, remnants of the 'open universities' clamour, were treated at the English universities with thinly veiled tolerance but with no less discrimination excluded from student life, residences and in many instances their academic progress suppressed.

At the national conference of the University Christian Movement held in Stutterheim in July 1968 a black caucus was formed to provide support and solidarity to black students and to engage the agenda of the organisation from the perspective of the black student community across all campuses. A planning meeting was held in December 1968 and an inaugural conference of the South African Students' Organisation took place at the University of the North at Turfloop in July 1969 where Steve Biko was elected president.

The founding National Executive Committee was charged with the task of refining the ideological statements, organising at all black campuses, including teacher training and nursing colleges and theological seminaries; committing to deliberately redefining the meaning of 'blackness' in a manner that stood the apartheid ideology on its head, and establishing the headquarters of the organisation.

The truth, however, was that the organisation began without resources. The initial support was 'bankrolled' by the SRCs of the University of Natal Black section, University of the North and the University of Zululand. As more universities enrolled with SASO a trickle of funds was raised from member subscriptions and from student membership fees. The available funds were bound to be infinitesimal compared to the ambitions of this nascent organisation, SASO.

This was a challenge on at least two fronts. SASO was founded on the principle of black solidarity and black pride. It was unthinkable that we could go cap-in-hand to the places and institutions where we knew that funds were available largely for causes that we despised but which we could divert to a worthy cause. We were very alert to being subjected to political manipulation and conditionalities of funding. For that reason, we were wary of soliciting support from contemporaries like NUSAS although we remained on good relations with the then leadership of NUSAS.

We cultivated support from other organisations that we considered 'white liberal' like the South African Council of Churches, the Christian Institute, the South African Institute of Race Relations and the University Christian Movement (UCM). We could do so, we believed, with a clear conscience because we were aware of the funding support that they received from overseas donors. These became the organisations that assisted us to source international donor funds and made the initial contacts for us with international donor agencies. We believed that we could do so without deviating in any manner from our slogan *Black man, you are on your own!*

The solidarity was however two-fold. We had ideas that an authentic black organisation should be resourced from within the black community. But that sacrificial giving of our time and talents was to begin with us. Accordingly, we devoted our time fully to the work of SASO without any remuneration. We even suspended our studies for this cause. We supported and sustained ourselves by sharing whatever we had, and we managed a very modest lifestyle. Steve Biko, Ranwedzi Nengwekhulu, Strini Moodley and I served as the first full-time officers of SASO without remuneration. As student leaders we exuded confidence about this project, and we travelled the length and breadth of the country to conscientise students and communities about our message and ideology of Black Consciousness. It had to begin with us.

We imagined that black business and professionals could be challenged to sustain a truly black organisation. A key factor in SASO was the duty we had to become integrated in every respect to the black lives and aspirations of the young blacks and the ambitions of the black community. That work yielded fruit in at least one respect. It made SASO known in black communities especially in the urban areas, and it also apprised us of the reality and extent of black fear that we noted in the hesitancy and warnings we received from well-meaning black professionals and the *nouveau riche*.

The second level was international solidarity. This also served the same purpose. It was about raising funds but also spreading the SASO Black Consciousness and black solidarity ideology.

The first such direct foray into the international community was when a delegation of UCM was invited to attend the conference of the UCM-United States in 1968. Basil Moore and Bobby Kgware had their first exposure to Black Theology and Black Power ideas. Basil Moore came back from that conference and penned a very influential paper on Black Theology and Black Power. Contacts were made there with the emerging Black Consciousness thinking and fraternal bonds were formed.

The second came by way of a student exchange programme with Norway. Goolam Abram and Nchaupe Aubrey Mokoape, medical students at the University of Natal, were there to raise awareness and cultivate solidarity support with student formations in the Nordic countries. Unlike other student leaders, we could not travel overseas as we were refused passports.

International financial support came via church leaders who visited from abroad and South Africans who travelled overseas. Almost always they distributed the materials we had produced and thus they became the voice of SASO. Many of them typified the emerging voice of black resistance as a new independent source of hope for the country.

We did not shy away from identifying South Africa-based conglomerates and corporations and asking them to commit to supporting our cause. Some did but many others would not commit. We did so because we truly believed that they were managing the wealth of our nation and, in many cases, we conceded that they were exploiting our people and resources for minimal benefit. Likewise, we were open to discussions with foreign embassies that sought us out. It was from such sources that we collected a lot of literature and resources that were otherwise banned in the country and could not be found at university libraries.

The greatest and most abiding solidarity, however, was in the information and propaganda that we shared with a flurry of international visitors who knocked on our doors. We were very conscious that apartheid was well entrenched in the understanding and consciousness of many countries. With them we frankly discussed our analysis and strategies and said we were confident that a new wave of resistance against apartheid was emerging. We were deliberate and forthcoming in defining SASO and Black Consciousness as the new voice of black resistance.

We believed that BC was not just an anti-apartheid organisation but represented a groundswell that was destined to reclaim the humanity of the black person. BC did not even claim at first to be a liberation movement in competition with others. It was more important to give content to our yearning for freedom. That quest was an assertion of our humanity and dignity for which we owed no one any favours. But more than that, however, we truly believed that something more enduring was afoot, the birth of a new truly African humanity. I believe that with such an ideological approach an ethical provenance was established that could have brought about a much better quality of leadership for South Africa than we experience today.

BARNEY PITYANA IS professor emeritus of law, University of South Africa, retired vice chancellor, University of South Africa, theologian, human rights activist and author. Pityana was the president of SASO (1970–1971) and became the first secretary general of SASO (1971–1973).

63
Michael Lapsley – The ANC's Church Front

I LIKE TO THINK OF myself as a New Zealand-born, southern African internationalist.

My first introduction to apartheid was as a child in Aotearoa/New Zealand. Our priest brought a petition to our local church called 'No Māori's No Tour'. The Springboks had invited the All Blacks to South Africa providing they left the Māori players behind.

Secondly, as an adolescent, I read Trevor Huddleston's *Naught for Your Comfort* about forced removals. From that time, I was clear that the apartheid version of Christianity was the opposite of what I had learnt on my mother's knee.

Personally, I was on another mission, to follow Jesus. At 17, I went to the monastery in Australia, training to be a priest and joining the Anglican religious order, the Society of the Sacred Mission (SSM). SSM sent me as a priest to South Africa in 1973 to become a university student and later a university chaplain.

The day I arrived in South Africa, I stopped being a human being and became a white man. For me joining the liberation struggle was about recovering my own humanity in solidarity with black people struggling for basic human rights.

From early on I was very attracted to the ideas of Black Consciousness and the goals of the ANC. While on home leave in New Zealand in 1975, I read Nelson Mandela's, *No Easy Walk to Freedom.* It helped me to see clearly that the apartheid government was an extremist and terroristic regime.

When I arrived in South Africa in 1973, I was a convinced pacificist. With the killing of schoolchildren in 1976, I became convinced that in our context and with our history, armed struggle had become morally legitimate, necessary and justified.

In July 1976, I was elected as National Chaplain of Anglican Students, when students were being detained, tortured and killed. The church had long been a site of struggle inside and outside South Africa. It is not accidental that the first three presidents of the ANC were ministers of religion.

At the end of September 1976, I was expelled from South Africa. In agreement with my religious order, I went to Lesotho and completed my degree at the National University of Lesotho.

With about 20 per cent of the students coming from South Africa, Namibia and Zimbabwe the politics of national liberation were central on the campus, with strong support for all the southern African liberation movements.

A year or two after arriving in Lesotho, I formally applied to join the ANC. The way I looked at it, the illegitimate government of South Africa had expelled me. The ANC were morally legitimate representatives of the people of South Africa. As an ANC member, I was becoming a citizen of a country for which we were still struggling. My fellow Kiwi, Bishop John Osmers, also applied to join the ANC.

For a time, I was the chairperson of the only above ground unit of the ANC, based at the National University of Lesotho directly accountable to Comrade Chris Hani. As a unit we had to communicate and popularise the vision of the ANC for a free South Africa, win support and recruit for the ANC and its People's Army to help make South Africa ungovernable. We worked with Basotho students as well as the many South African students who could still cross the border. Our clandestine activity included smuggling banned ANC literature and recruiting couriers to deliver messages to key operatives inside South Africa. All our work was coordinated with the underground political and military structures of the movement.

Our public role included organising fundraising dinners to buy sporting equipment for the Solomon Mahlangu Freedom College (SOMAFCO) at Mazimbu in Tanzania.

I applied to teach at SOMAFCO and was accepted. I told my bishop that this was my prayerful decision. My decision was countermanded by President Oliver Tambo who said other people could teach but it was more important for me to remain in Lesotho. I went back to the bishop to tell him that actually God wanted me to remain in Lesotho. The bishop wryly asked if the name of the Holy Spirit was Oliver Tambo.

As well as the public role, I facilitated contacts between church people in South Africa and the ANC in exile. Some of us became part of what was known as the Church Front, later the Religious Front and the Interfaith Chaplaincy. There was a pastoral role of caring for young South African exiles en route either to school or to military training. Most South Africans belong to a faith community. At the same time a perverted form of Christianity was the major ideological weapon used by the apartheid state. Accounts of the liberation struggle that deny or gloss over the major and critical significance of the faith communities are seriously revisionists.

Those of us in the ANC in exile were in dynamic contact with leaders and activists in all the member churches of the South African Council of Churches and the Roman Catholic churches. These included leaders such as Ds Beyers Naude, Dr Allan Boesak, Archbishop Desmond Tutu, Archbishop Dennis Hurley and Frank Chikane.

Whilst so many of the nation's political leaders were either in prison or exile, the liberation-oriented faith leaders became doubly important. Over decades the fight for freedom was fought theologically within and by the structures of faith communities and para church bodies like the Christian Institute and, years later, the Institute for Contextual Theology and the Call of Islam. Many Christian student organisations saw themselves as part of the struggle, such as the NCFS of the Catholic Church, the Anglican Student Federation, YCS and SUCA. Churches were part of worldwide denominational bodies like the Anglican Communion, the Lutheran World Federation and ecumenical bodies like the World Alliance of Reformed Churches and the World Council of Churches. These bodies proclaimed apartheid a sin and a heresy or false doctrine.

A high point in the theological battle against apartheid was the publication of the Kairos Document in 1985 entitled *Challenge to the Church: A Theological Comment on the Political Crisis in South Africa.* State Theology, Church Theology and Prophetic Theology were the three theological strands described with the authors, mainly black, all embracing Prophetic or Liberation Theology.

Liberation Theology, which was increasingly accepted by progressives in churches across the country, was a theology of endurance, resistance and hope. It found echoes in similar thought and practices among Muslims, Hindus and Jews.

In 1969, the World Council of Churches (WCC) set up a Programme to Combat Racism and a Special Fund. The fund made financial contributions to liberation movements to the fury of the apartheid regime and especially conservative white churchgoers. The Archbishop of Cape Town Bill Burnett said that the Church of the Province of Southern Africa (which included Lesotho) did not support the programme or fund. Fr John Osmers and I succeeded in passing a motion in the Lesotho Diocesan Synod in support of both and took a collection for the fund. We then wrote a polite note to the archbishop, asking him to stop saying he spoke for the church in relation to the WCC. I wrote some articles for the ANC's monthly magazine *Sechaba* and the *African Communist,* including an analysis of how the Just War theory related to our liberation struggle.

On 9 December 1982, the SADF massacred 42 people in Maseru. Although I was away from Lesotho on a speaking tour in New Zealand organised by the local anti-apartheid movement, church authorities and the local leadership argued that if I was allowed to remain in Lesotho, the troops would come back and that some of them might die in the crossfire. Members of my order in the Free State also said that my presence in Lesotho endangered their lives. I relocated to the UK.

My order freed me to work full time for the London office of the ANC. I authored an article for a World Council of Churches publication, 'The struggle was also my life'. I travelled the length and breadth of the UK, mobilising the faith community inside and outside South Africa to oppose apartheid and be part of the struggle for freedom.

During that year, the World Service of the BBC interviewed me over a period of four days as to why I, as a priest, had joined the ANC. My message became increasingly simple and direct: apartheid is an option or a choice for death carried out in the name of the Gospel of Life and therefore it was an issue of faith to oppose it.

Before going to Zimbabwe at the end of 1983 I participated in a joint ANC-SWAPO speaking tour of Canada visiting 20 cities in six weeks, strengthening support for our two liberation movements. In Harare, where I was to do a master's degree at the University of Zimbabwe, I was integrated into ANC structures. This included chairing an ANC Education Committee to facilitate the education of exiles from creche to university.

Kingsley Mamabolo, Jabu Moleketi and I edited a popular magazine for the Zimbabwean public called *Struggle Update*. In 1985, I had the honour of being elected a delegate to ANC's Kabwe conference in Zambia.

After completing my master's degree, I became a parish priest in Mbare, an African township in Harare. Living there made it possible to discreetly recruit youth to act as couriers between the internal and external structures of the ANC and MK.

I was able to provide a safe house for MK leaders and operatives, including comrades such as Joe Modise and Thabang Makwetla. As an ANC chaplain, I was on hand for the weddings and funerals of cadres. When it came to the funerals of exiles, I felt it was important to be a voice of hope: *God is with us. Our cause is just. One day we shall triumph.*

After a fall out with the Anglican Bishop of Harare, I was employed by the Lutheran World Federation (LWF) in Zimbabwe. My task was to raise consciousness through popular education specifically among Lutherans across Zimbabwe about apartheid's destabilisation policy. I participated in the ongoing mobilisation of the faith community in South Africa and globally, including discreetly meeting church people from South Africa visiting Zimbabwe.

By the mid-1980s, the apartheid regime had detained more than 10 000 children under the age of 18, 90 per cent of whom had been tortured. To focus worldwide attention a major international conference was convened in Harare from 24 to 27 September 1987 under the heading 'Children, Repression and the Law in Apartheid South Africa'. LWF seconded me full time to assist Horst Kleinschmidt with organising the conference. I was tasked with recruiting many township youth as volunteers. The conference enabled a large South African delegation to meet directly with President Oliver Tambo.

I was privileged to participate in an ecumenical solidarity visit to Nicaragua and Cuba. It was the beginning of my love affair with the Cuban people. I had deep admiration for the achievements of the Cuban revolution. We formed the Friends of Cuba Society with comrades from the South African Communist Party on my return from exile in 1992. I was its chairperson in the Western Cape and became the first national president. It was an opportunity to give back what Cuba had taught the world about international solidarity.

Around 1987, the Zimbabwean authorities told me I was on a South African government hit list. I was provided with armed police guards 24 hours a day. Why would a government wish to kill me? Yes, it is true I was a freedom fighter but the only automatic weapon I have ever used is my tongue.

Shortly after Nelson Mandela's release, the Canadian churches invited me for a national speaking tour. I said, the curtain has just gone up on the last act of the apartheid drama, but we don't know how long it will take and at what cost. Back in Zimbabwe, I was due to relocate and become a parish priest in a township in Bulawayo.

On 28 April, two days before the first formal negotiations between the ANC and the government, I opened an envelope containing religious magazines. When I opened one, it exploded, destroying both my hands, an eye and damaging my ear drums.

I knew immediately that the apartheid regime had got me. I also knew that they had lost, and I had won as I was alive. I felt God's presence with me.

Zimbabwe and Australia provided excellent medical treatment. I became a recipient of international solidarity in the form of messages of prayer, love and support from across the globe. People of the world accompanied me on my journey of healing.

In 1993 in South Africa I became chaplain at the Trauma Centre for Victims of Violence and Torture. As a nation, besides political and economic transformation, we have to deal with our psychological, spiritual and emotional wounds. With other friends, we have created an experiential healing of memories workshop as a parallel process to South Africa's TRC.

In 1998, we started the Institute for Healing of Memories. We are a social healing NGO that works globally.

The Friends of Cuba Society is seeking to do for Cuba what Cuba taught the world. In a similar and modest way, I am trying with others, to accompany people across the world on their journey of healing just as I was accompanied on mine. Today I am the President of the Healing of Memories Global Network working across the world.

ALAN MICHAEL LAPSLEY is a South African Anglican priest. In 1993, he became chaplain of the Trauma Centre for Victims of Violence and Torture and later the Institute for Healing of Memories (IHOM) in Cape Town. He is the founder and president of Friends of Cuba Society (FOCUS) South Africa.

64

Ronnie Kasrils – Epilogue: The Good People

When I was a boy and I would see scary things in the news, my mother would say to me, 'Look for the helpers. You will always find people who are helping.' – Fred Rogers

WAS IT ALL WORTHWHILE? That's the inevitable question those who engaged the apartheid system in an epic political-military struggle are asked several decades into South Africa having won its freedom. Undoubtedly that question runs through the minds of those who sacrificed in so many different ways.

After a promising start under Mandela the country degenerated during the Jacob Zuma years. It was rocked by one scandal after another. Among these, the ripping off of state resources, crony capitalism and the stench of corruption; the obscene costs of Zuma's Nkandla homestead; the Marikana massacre of 2012; the mayhem of anarchy in July 2021, instigated by disaffected elements of the former president. All this within a failing economic system, soaring unemployment, the widening gap between rich and poor, and systemic inequality.

South Africa – once the darling of the international community – had all the appearances of a failing state owing to self-induced calamities by an emergent elite motivated by greed and self-interest, rather than the values of service to the people. Yet, in a world of woe, South Africa is no exception. The country suffers from the malady affecting the rest of the planet. Political power, a vital and incalculable achievement by the forces of liberation, came through a negotiated settlement which averted a bloody civil war – but at a price of arguably unforeseen consequences. The country was ensnared within a neo-liberal, free-market global economy reinforcing existing power relationships and structures of financial and trade dominance. This inevitably perpetuates and maintains the class, race and gender relationships that the ANC, along with other liberation movements, aimed to transform.

Whatever possibilities those striving for real change envisaged evaporated among other factors with the collapse of the Soviet Union. The prospect of escaping the hegemony of Western diktat had seemingly disappeared. The Cold War and a bipolar world were replaced by the writ of a Pax Americana; the Washington Consensus; the convenience of a 'war on terror'; the bogey of Islamophobia; the Middle East in ruins; the tyranny of sanctions and blockades; trampling of international law and an emasculated UN. The once-powerful anti-imperialist, international solidarity movement was a shadow of its former self, with the hope of those who sought to change the world for the better apparently dashed.

Yet, appearances are deceptive. Just as the apartheid system, with its vast resources and disparity of power, compared to the oppressed people of the country, was riven with contradictions and could not survive the rising surge of people's power.

What was decisive was the just cause of the people, unity in action, a resolute people's struggle, international solidarity, turning the tide. So too, with the apparent power of the USA, and its allies. The mass struggles against imperialist domination, the anti-war movement, the phenomenal emergence of the Black Lives Matter protests, never-ending Palestinian resistance, widespread rage against racism and white supremacy, the popular determination to protect the environment – these are illustrative of current grassroots level opposition.

All at the time of the Covid-19 pandemic and the inequity of the vaccine apartheid of the wealthy states.

Those with experience of struggle, who have experience of raising awareness among the mass of the people, of linking theory with practice, of building popular organisations, of the decisive need of forging unity in action, of countering the lies and disinformation of the ruling powers, must ensure that legacy never dies. This is especially so in a world where international solidarity, which is always evident, must be preserved, developed and advanced.

Was it worthwhile?

The cause for pessimism is understandable. South Africa remains the most unequal country in the world despite reforms such as social welfare grants, subsidised water and electricity, free AIDS medicines, government commitment to a national health service, and free tertiary education. Yet unemployment is skyrocketing, service delivery to the poor is failing, poverty is increasing. The demise of the apartheid system was a turning point in history, not an end in itself. It opened the way for the next stage of struggle – one in common with humanity.

The contribution of the Ubuntu Brigade made a difference.

All credit to all who participated in that process. Yes, it was worthwhile.

We must ensure their role is understood in South Africa and globally. The example of international solidarity in action is a powerful inspirational force.

We hope this book assists the reader recognise the value of 'the helpers', the good people.

One knows the good people by the fact
That they get better
When one knows them. The good people
Invite one to improve them, for
How does anyone get wiser? By listening
And by being told something.
Bertolt Brecht, 'Song About the Good People'

Index

Pixley ka Isaka Seme (Lawyer) 23
Plaatje, Sol 23
Pillars of Struggle, Four 17, 42, 140, 310
Pimenov, George German 144, 286
Plimenteira, Max 70
Polaroid 274
Polaroid Revolutionary Workers Movement
(PRWM) 274
Political-Military Council (PMC) 295, 343
Polisario 316–317
Polokelo, Mamatsela 143
Ponnen, George 328
Portuguese Colonialism 4, 16, 26, 65, 206, 235
Programme to Combat Racism 11, 339
Pretoria Central 56, 82, 95
Pretoria Minute 106, 134
Prisoners of War (POWs) 100, 308, 309
Protea 253, 260, 261
Pule, Ernest Lekoto 94

Q

Qaboos bin Said Al Busaidi (Sultan) 85
Qacha's Nek 142
Queen's University 308

R

Raadschelders, Lucia 164
Rabkin, Sue 87
Radebe, Jeff 127
Radio Freedom (RF) 4, 12, 185–187
Radio Havana Cuba 182
Radio Liberation 186
Radio Madagascar 187
Radio Nacional de Angola 186
Radio Nederland Training Centre 187
Ramano, Gilbert 43
Ramaphosa, Cyril (President) 309–310, 317
Ramatlabama 118
Randolph, Philip 272, 276
Ranoto, Madimetsa 41
Rawlinson, Peter (Sir) 241
Reagan, Ronald (President) 206, 209, 211,
229, 230, 277, 288, 320
Red Crescent 316
Red Cross 316
Reconstruction and Development
Programme (RDP) 255
Redhill School 183
Reddy, E.S. 9, 139, 214–215, 219–223, 269
Red International of Labour Unions
(RILU) 8
Reebok 281
Reeves, Ambrose (Bishop) 10, 214
Reggio Emilia 9, 235, 262–264

Regional Political Military Commands
(RPMC) 35, 141
Religious Front 338
Republic of Cuba 58, 292, 293
Resha, Robert 38, 223
Resistência Nacional Moçambicana
(RENAMO) 69, 73, 86, 87, 141, 163,
164, 169
Revolutionary Council (RC) 4
Rhodes, Cecil John 37
Riele, Mariejie 164
Riffian uprising 315
Rivonia 33, 180, 185, 186, 284
Rivonia Raid 3
Rivonia Trial 3, 39, 148, 215, 294, 302
Robben Island 34–36, 144, 240, 258, 308, 317
Roberto, Holden 230, 296
Robeson, Paul 220, 270, 271
Robinson, Randall 277
Rock Against Racism (RAR) 153
Roman Catholic Churches 338
Roosevelt, Franklin D (President) 48
Round, Stuart 105–106
Ruacana 300
Rubusana, W.B. 23
Ruchnoy Protivotankoviy Granatomyot
(RPG) 68, 109, 115, 287, 309
Russell, Alma 312
Russell Tribunal 257

S

Sabotage Campaign 3, 39
Sachs, Albie (Judge) 66, 86, 91, 169
Saharawis 316
Sällström 248, 249
Saloojee, JoJo 24, 131, 178
Saloojee, Riaz (Cal) 88, 102–109, 123
SA National Defence Force (SANDF) 5, 42,
43, 71, 72, 77, 109, 115, 286, 288
SA Naval College 200, 201
SA Navy 8, 196, 200, 201
Sasolburg 88
Savimbi, Jonas 230, 267, 296–299
Scandinavia 24, 226
Schlapobersky, John 265
Schoon, Marius 135
Schreuder, Menno 106, 107
Scott King, Coretta 194
Scott, Michael (Reverend) 9
Seaman's Training college 200
Sechaba 191, 263, 288, 304, 306, 339
Second World War 9, 16, 80, 84, 117, 160,
171, 172, 292, 196, 220, 253, 265, 286,
292, 315